CASAN
AVARITIA

MATT FRACTION
GABRIEL BÁ

colors by Cris Peter
letters by Dustin Harbin

CASANOVA VOL. 3: AVARITIA. Contains material originally published in magazine form as CASANOVA: AVARITIA #1-4. First printing 2012. ISBN# 978-0-7851-4864-7. Published by MARVEL WORLDWIDE, INC., a subsidiary of MARVEL ENTERTAINMENT, LLC. OFFICE OF PUBLICATION: 135 West 50th Street, New York, NY 10020. Copyright © 2011 and 2012 MILKFED CRIMINAL MASTERMINDS, INC. All rights reserved. $14.99 per copy in the U.S. and $16.99 in Canada (GST #R127032852); Canadian Agreement #40668537. "Casanova," the Casanova logo, and all characters featured herein and the distinctive names and likenesses thereof, and all related indicia are trademarks of MILKFED CRIMINAL MASTERMINDS, INC. No similarity between any of the names, characters, persons, and/or institutions in this magazine with those of any living or dead person or institution is intended, and any such similarity that may exist is purely coincidental. ICON and the Icon logo are trademarks of Marvel Characters, Inc. **Printed in the U.S.A. Manufactured between 5/31/12 and 6/26/12 by QUAD/GRAPHICS, DUBUQUE, IA, USA.**

Representation: Law Offices of Harris M. Miller II, P.C.

10 9 8 7 6 5 4 3 2 1

ICON Edition

Editor   Alejandro Arbona

book design

Gabriel Bá

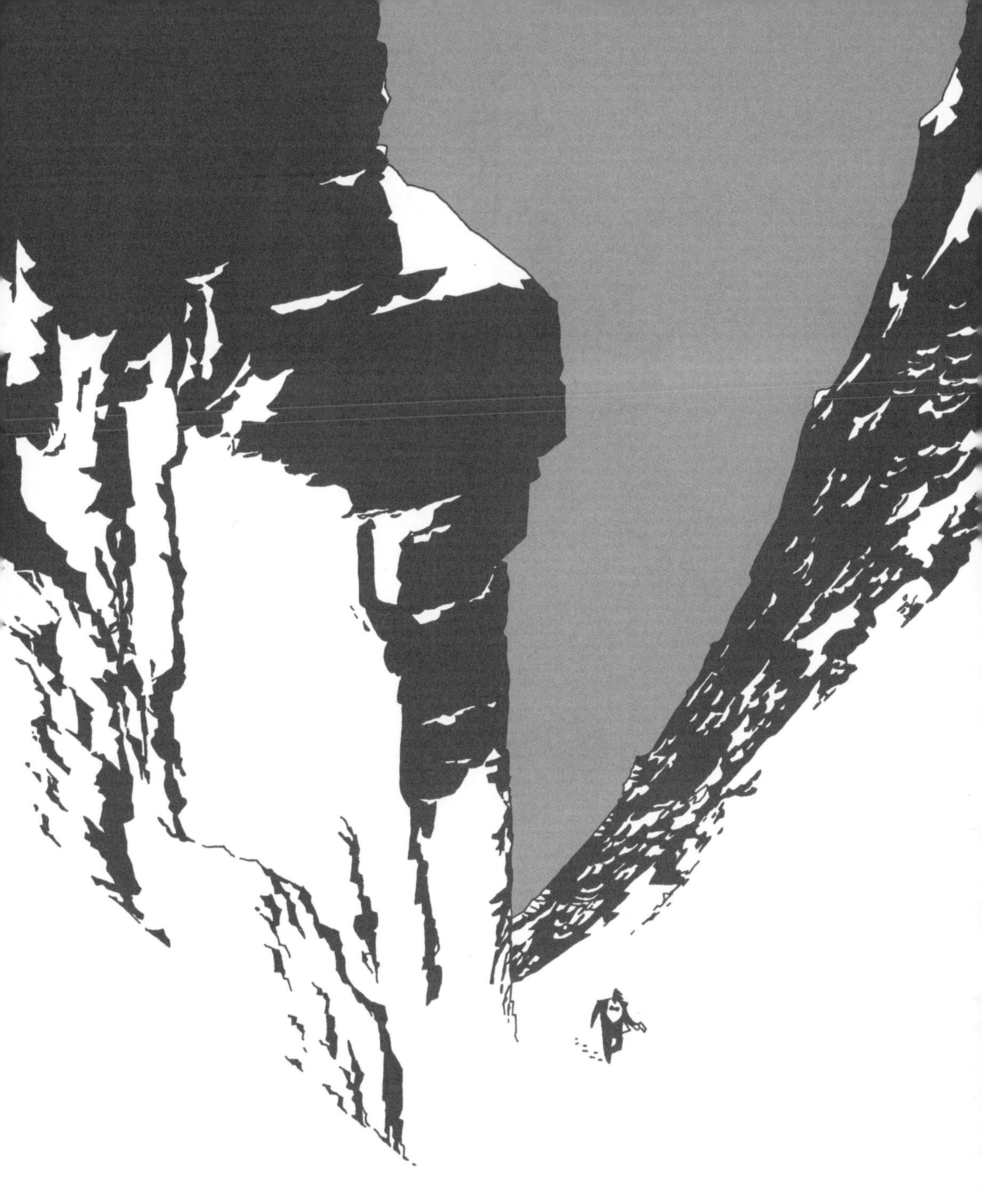

Matt Fraction:
For Bill King and Martha Maricoat Dunigan
who taught me everything

Gabriel Bá:
For Jean Giraud Moebius and Katsuhiro Otomo

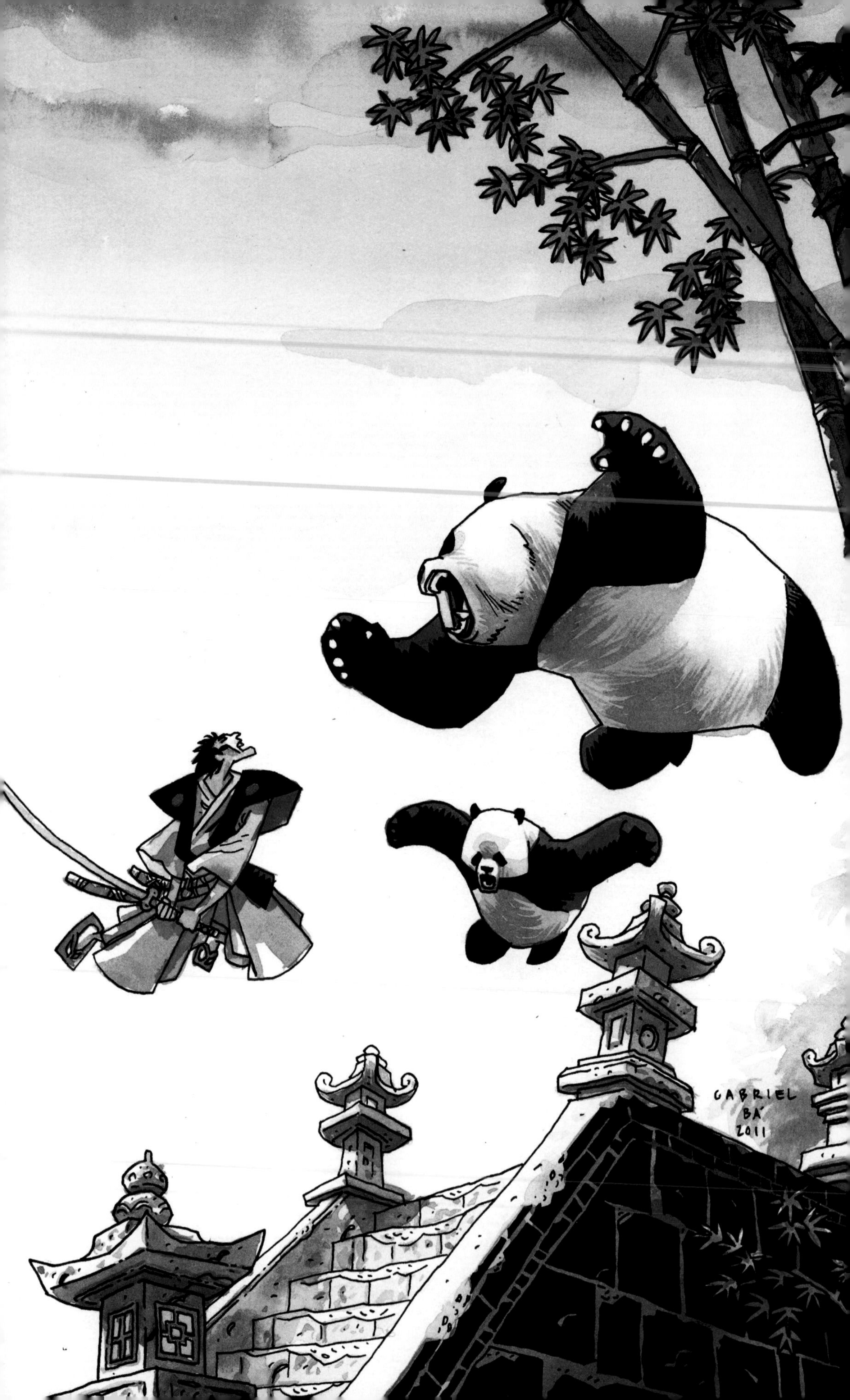
GABRIEL
BÁ
2011

"Time forks perpetually into
countless futures. In one of them
I am your enemy."

Jorge Luis Borges
THE GARDEN OF FORKING PATHS (1958)

"...(A)lways remember what
Jean-Luc Godard said:
'It's not where you take things from
– it's where you take them to.'"

Jim Jarmusch (2004)

"... I (...) intend to sound an urgent
word of warning relative to rather
obvious pre-nova conditions."

William S. Burroughs (1963)

"Everybody has a plan until
they get punched in the mouth."

Mike Tyson (date unknown)

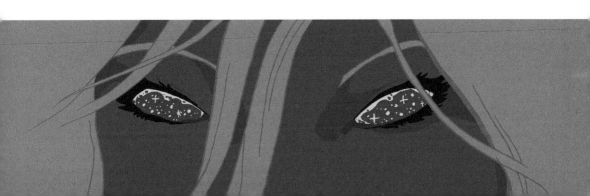

CHAPTER 1
W.A.S.T.E.-FREE WILDERNESS

1. THE WIZARD BUYS A HAT

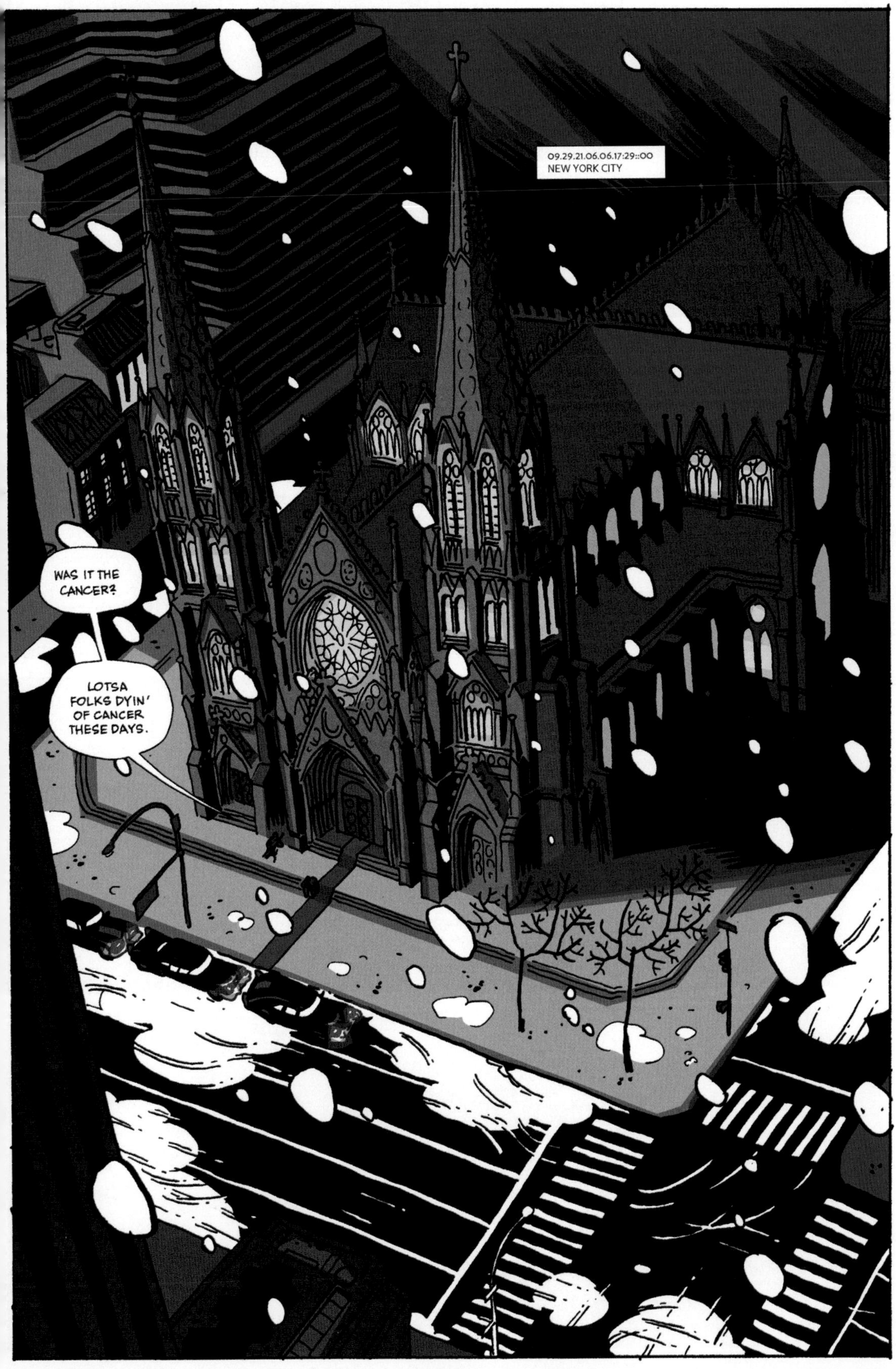
09.29.21.06.06.17:29::00
NEW YORK CITY
WAS IT THE CANCER?
LOTSA FOLKS DYIN' OF CANCER THESE DAYS.

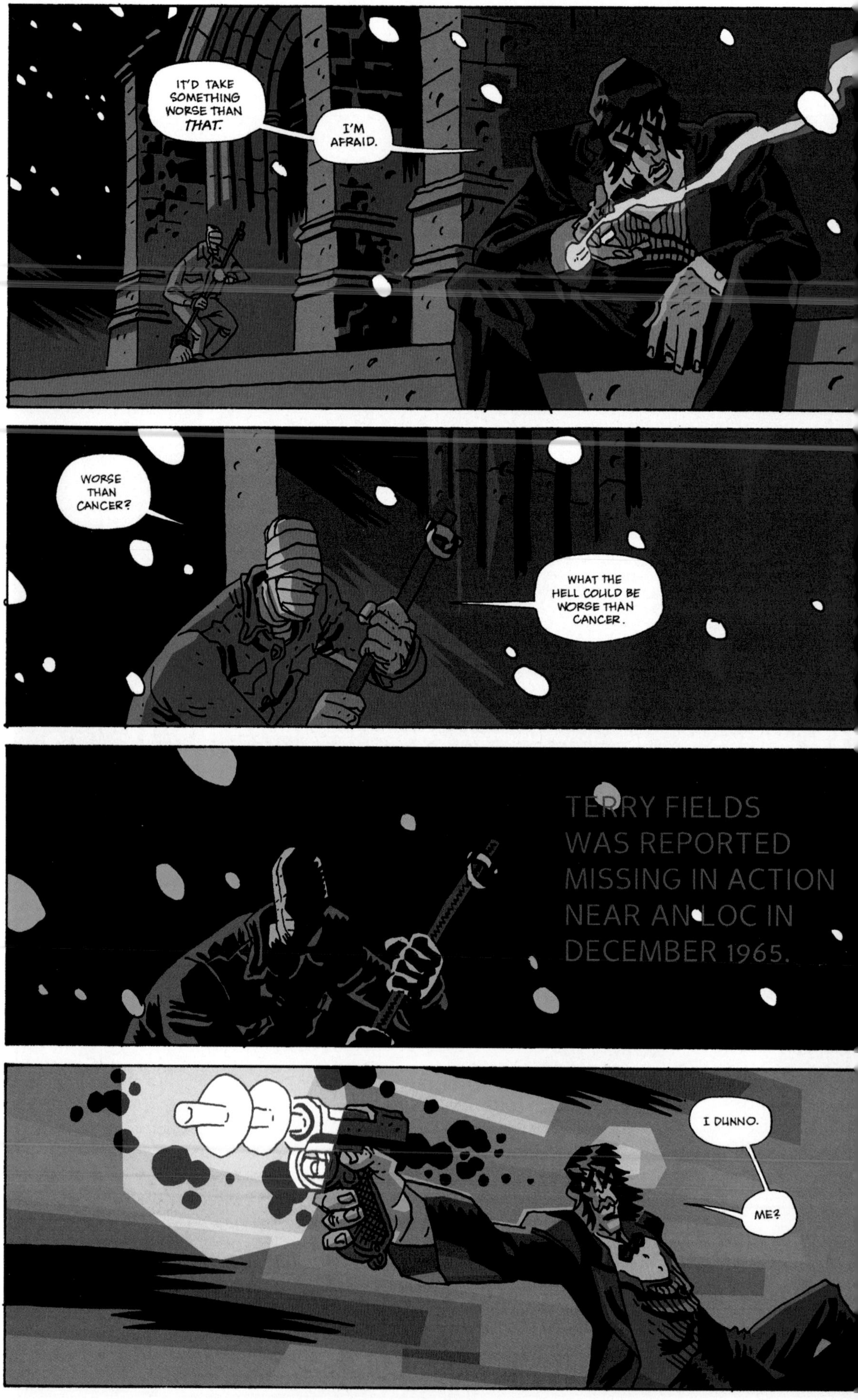
IT'D TAKE SOMETHING WORSE THAN *THAT.*
I'M AFRAID.
WORSE THAN CANCER?
WHAT THE HELL COULD BE WORSE THAN CANCER.
TERRY FIELDS WAS REPORTED MISSING IN ACTION NEAR AN LOC IN DECEMBER 1965.
I DUNNO.
ME?

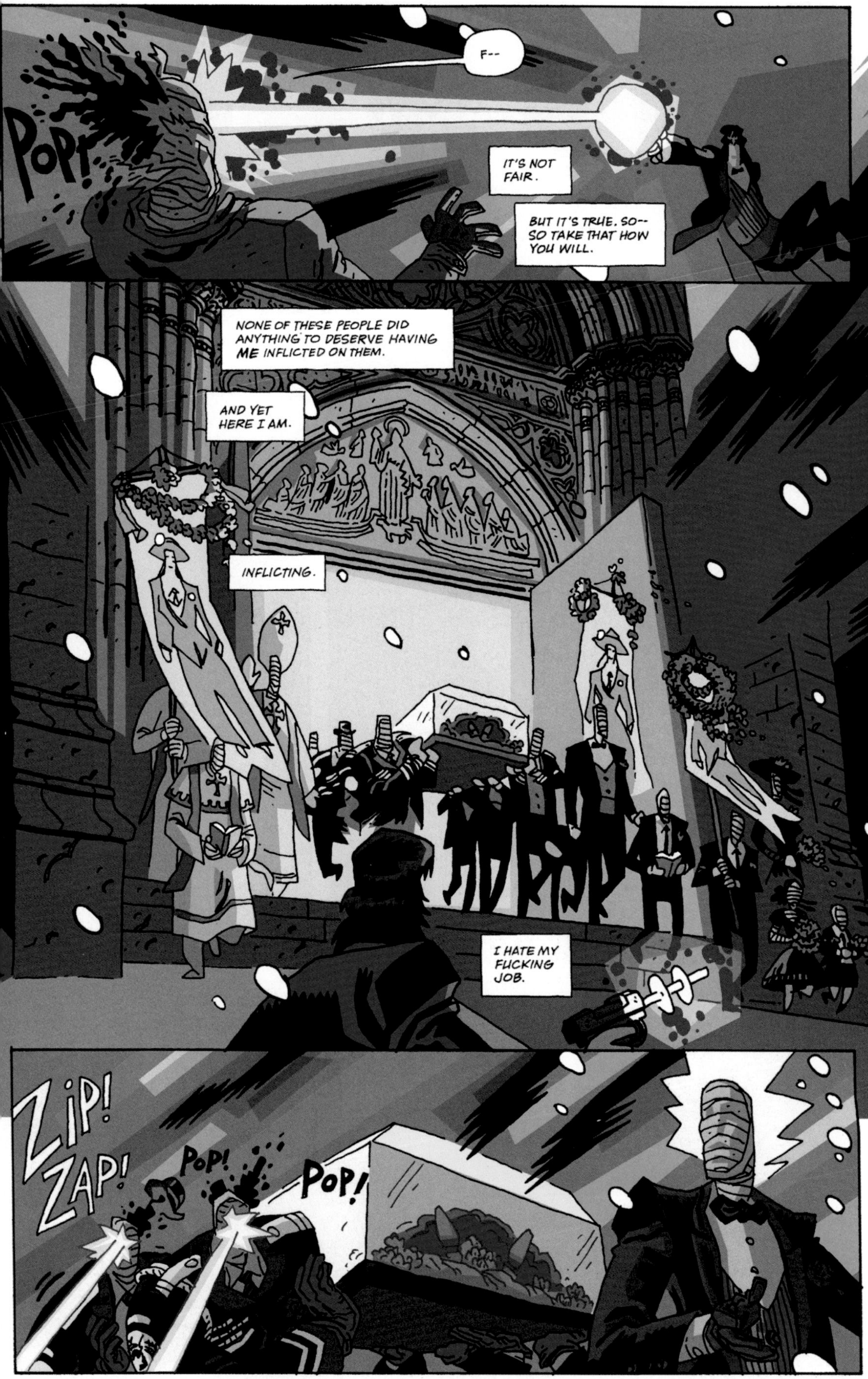
POP!
F--
IT'S NOT FAIR.
BUT IT'S TRUE. SO-- SO TAKE THAT HOW YOU WILL.
NONE OF THESE PEOPLE DID ANYTHING TO DESERVE HAVING ME INFLICTED ON THEM.
AND YET HERE I AM.
INFLICTING.
I HATE MY FUCKING JOB.
ZIP! ZAP!
POP!
POP!

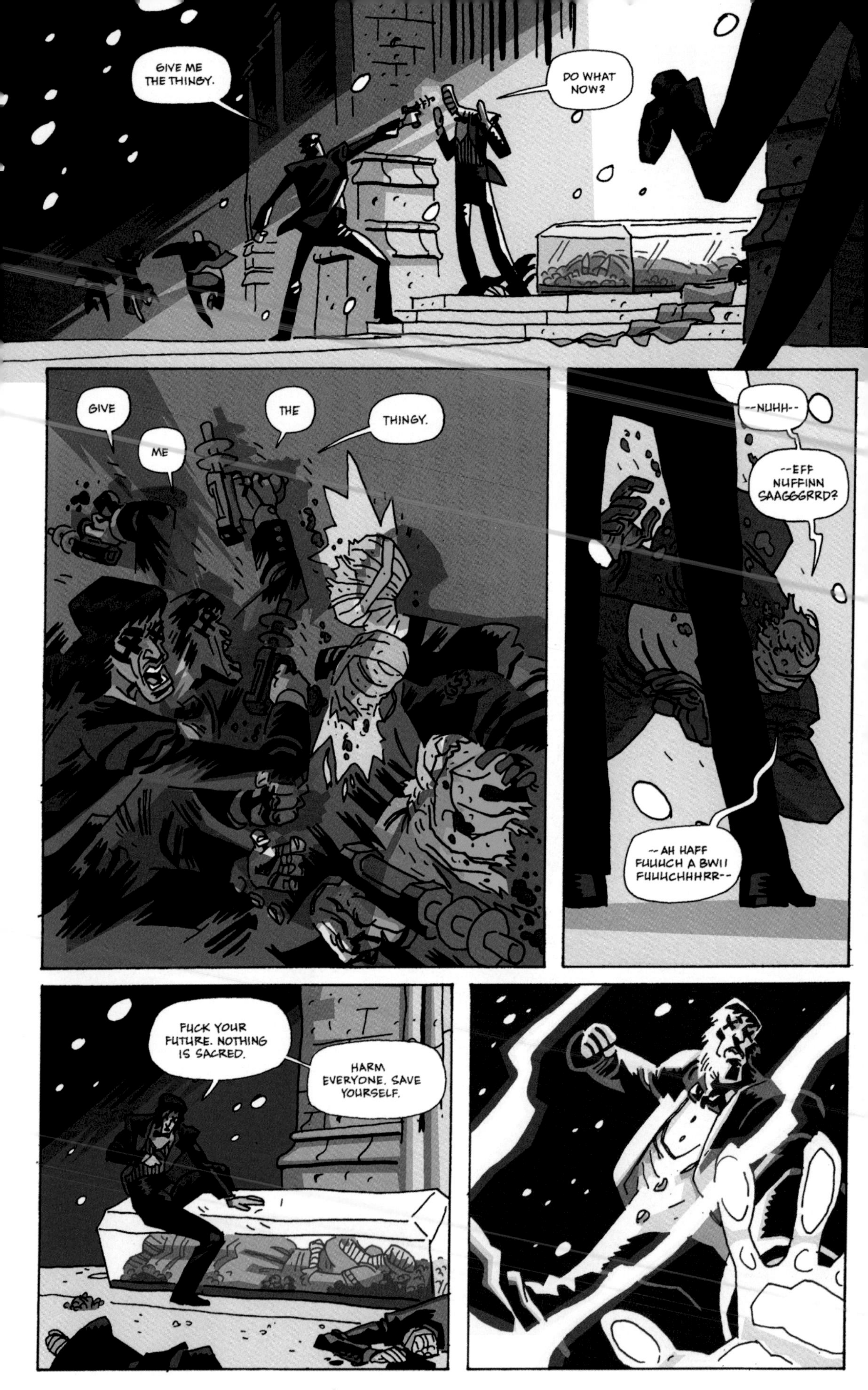
GIVE ME THE THINGY.
DO WHAT NOW?
GIVE
ME
THE
THINGY.
--NUHH--
--EFF NUFFINN SAAGGGRRD?
--AH HAFF FUUUCH A BWII FUUUCHHHRR--
FUCK YOUR FUTURE. NOTHING IS SACRED.
HARM EVERYONE. SAVE YOURSELF.

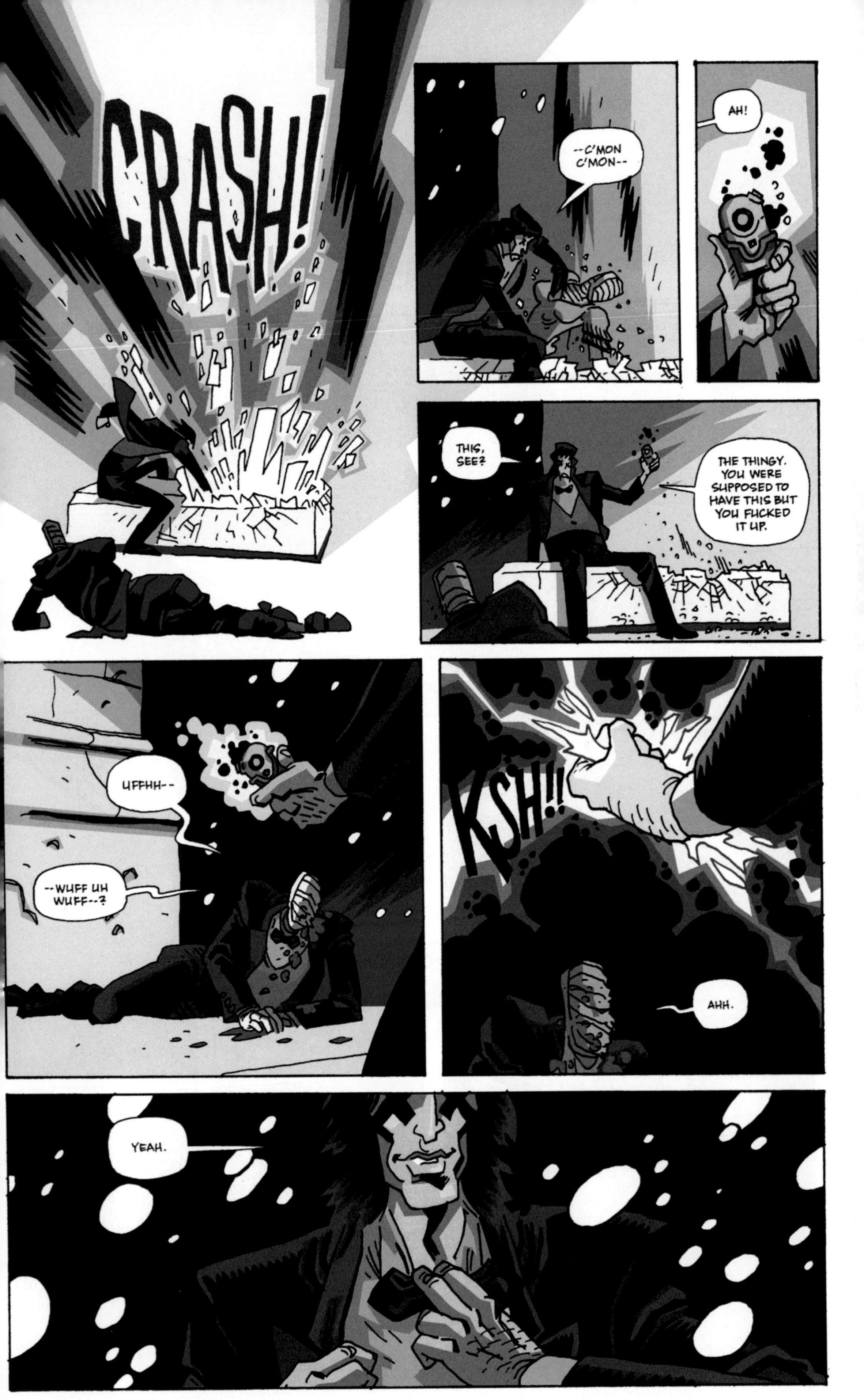
CRASH!
--C'MON C'MON--
AH!
THIS, SEE?
THE THINGY. YOU WERE SUPPOSED TO HAVE THIS BUT YOU FUCKED IT UP.
UFFHH--
--WUFF UH WUFF--?
KSH!!
AHH.
YEAH.

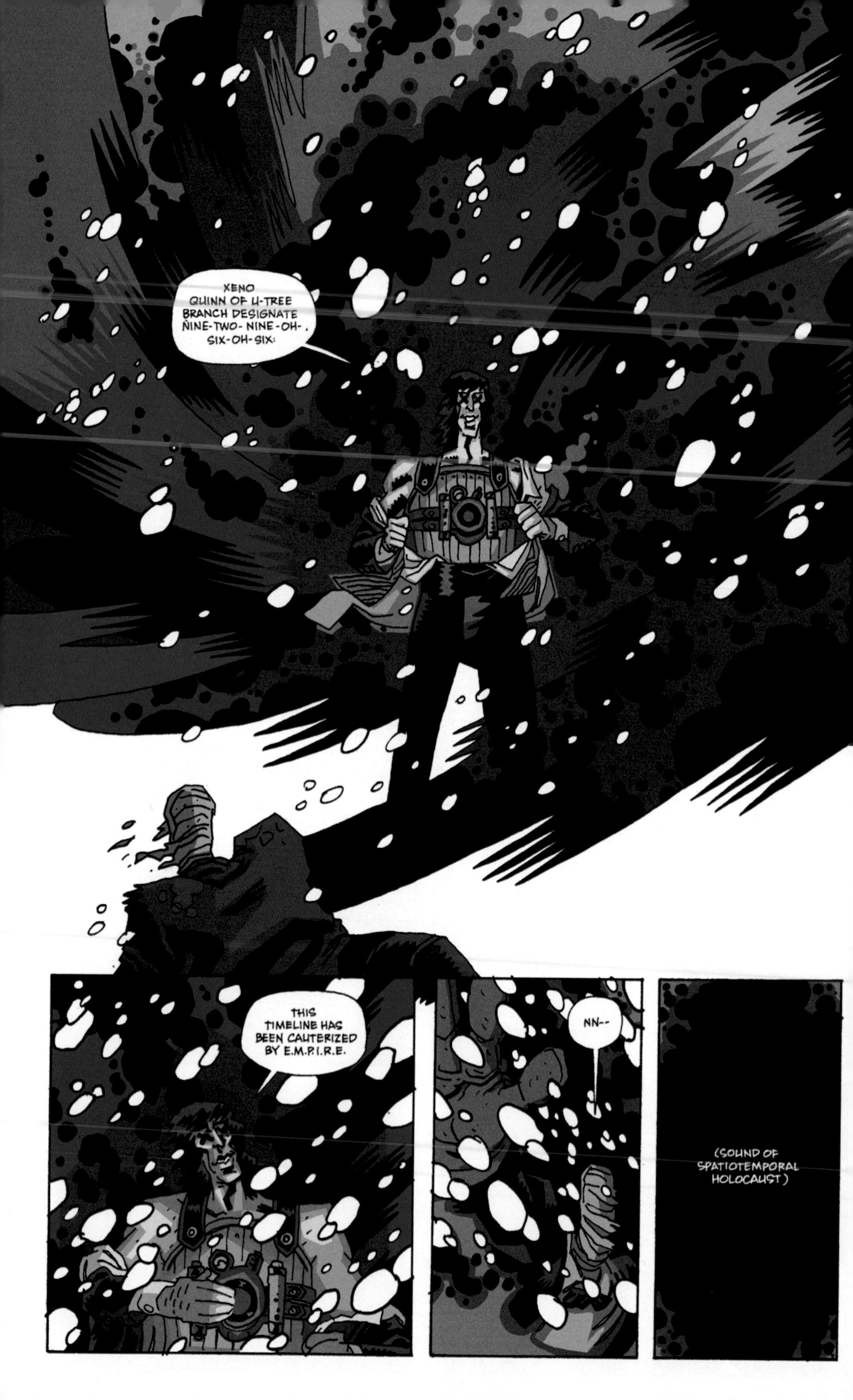
XENO QUINN OF U-TREE BRANCH DESIGNATE ÑINE-TWO-NINE-OH-SIX-OH-SIX:
THIS TIMELINE HAS BEEN CAUTERIZED BY E.M.P.I.R.E.
NN--
(SOUND OF SPATIOTEMPORAL HOLOCAUST)

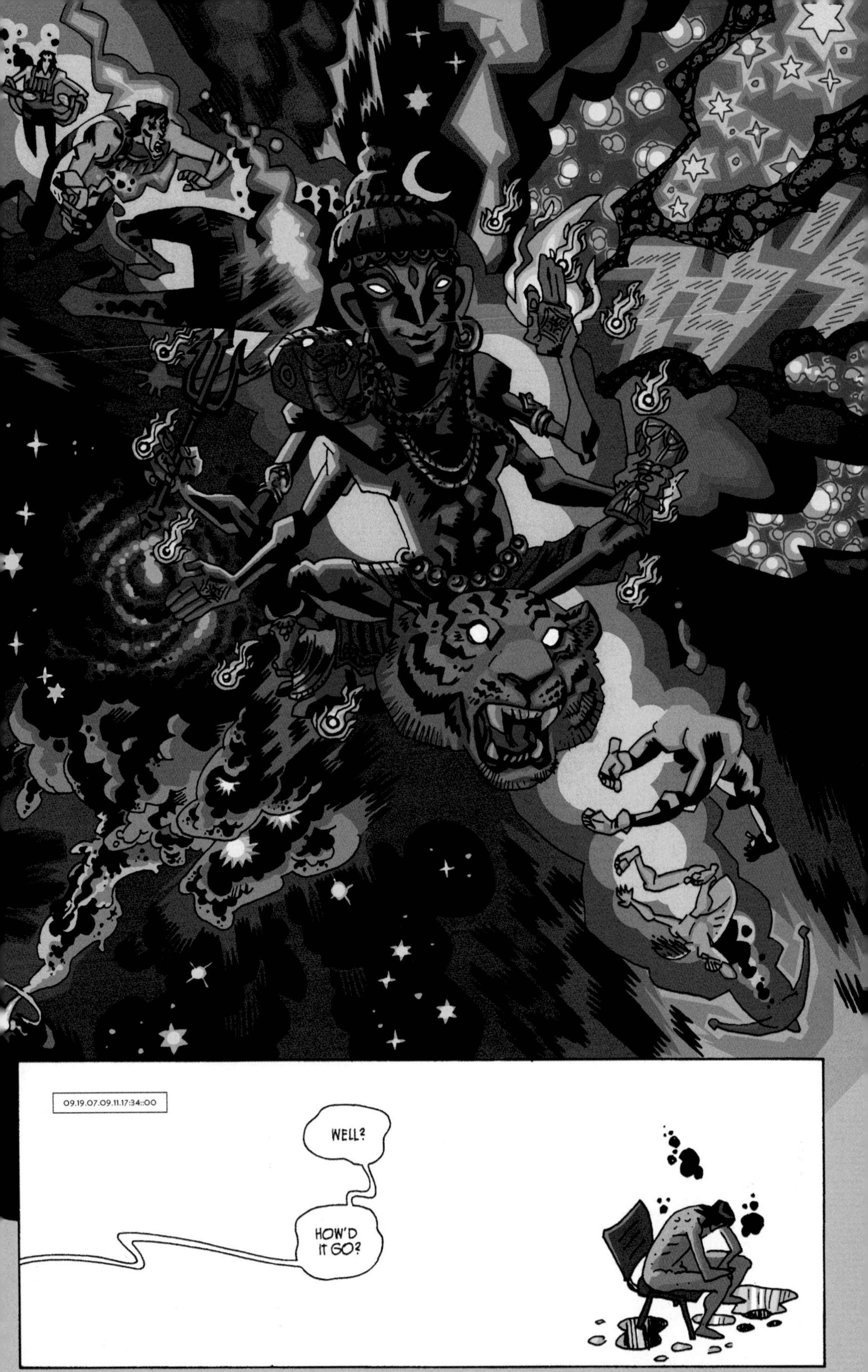
09.19.07.09.11.17:34::00
WELL?
HOW'D IT GO?

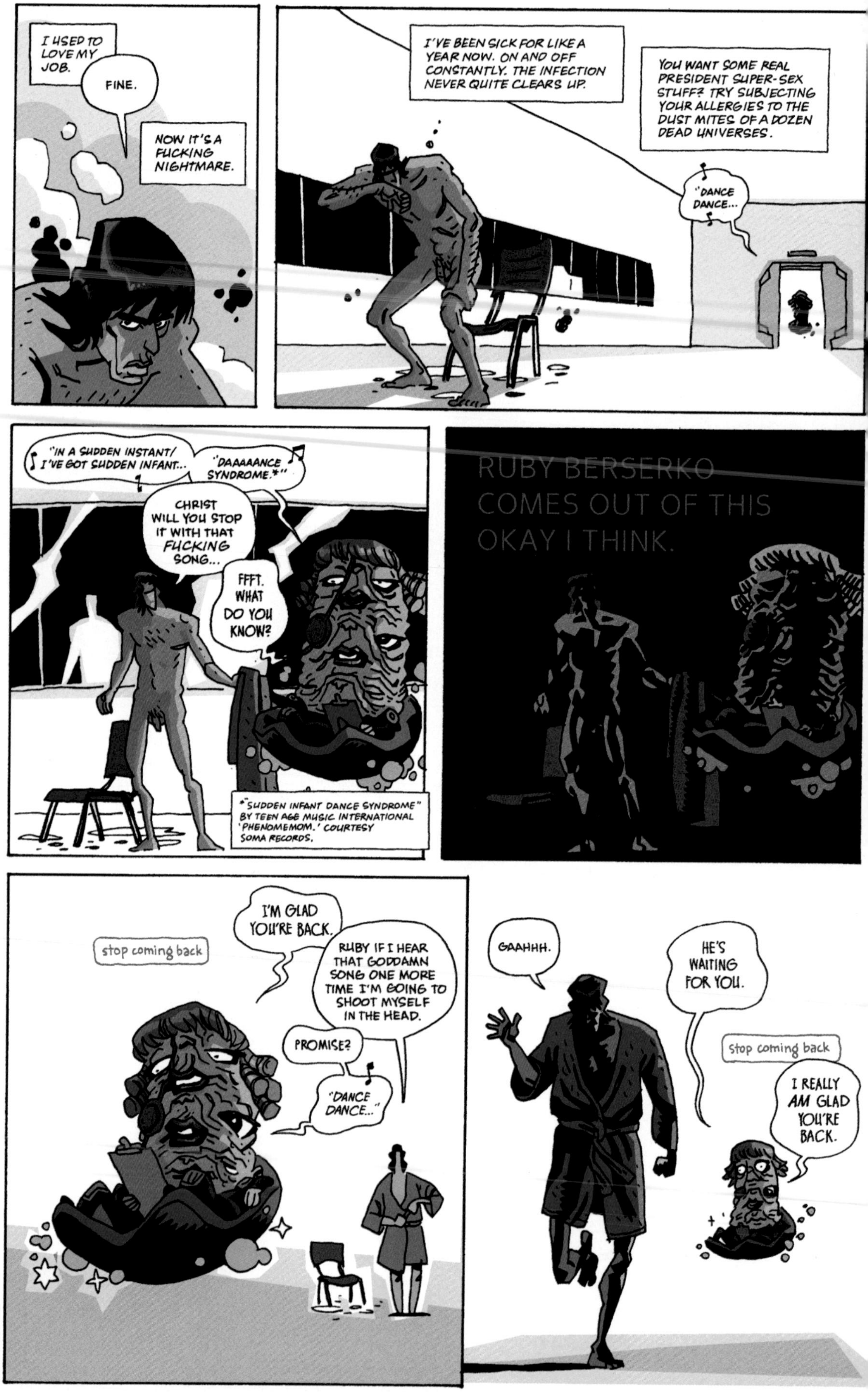
I USED TO LOVE MY JOB.
FINE.
NOW IT'S A FUCKING NIGHTMARE.
I'VE BEEN SICK FOR LIKE A YEAR NOW. ON AND OFF CONSTANTLY. THE INFECTION NEVER QUITE CLEARS UP.
YOU WANT SOME REAL PRESIDENT SUPER-SEX STUFF? TRY SUBJECTING YOUR ALLERGIES TO THE DUST MITES OF A DOZEN DEAD UNIVERSES.
"DANCE DANCE...
"IN A SUDDEN INSTANT/ I'VE GOT SUDDEN INFANT...
"DAAAAAANCE SYNDROME.*"
CHRIST WILL YOU STOP IT WITH THAT FUCKING SONG...
FFFT. WHAT DO YOU KNOW?
*"SUDDEN INFANT DANCE SYNDROME" BY TEEN AGE MUSIC INTERNATIONAL 'PHENOMEMOM.' COURTESY SOMA RECORDS.
RUBY BERSERKO COMES OUT OF THIS OKAY I THINK.
I'M GLAD YOU'RE BACK.
stop coming back
RUBY IF I HEAR THAT GODDAMN SONG ONE MORE TIME I'M GOING TO SHOOT MYSELF IN THE HEAD.
PROMISE?
"DANCE DANCE..."
GAAHHH.
HE'S WAITING FOR YOU.
stop coming back
I REALLY AM GLAD YOU'RE BACK.

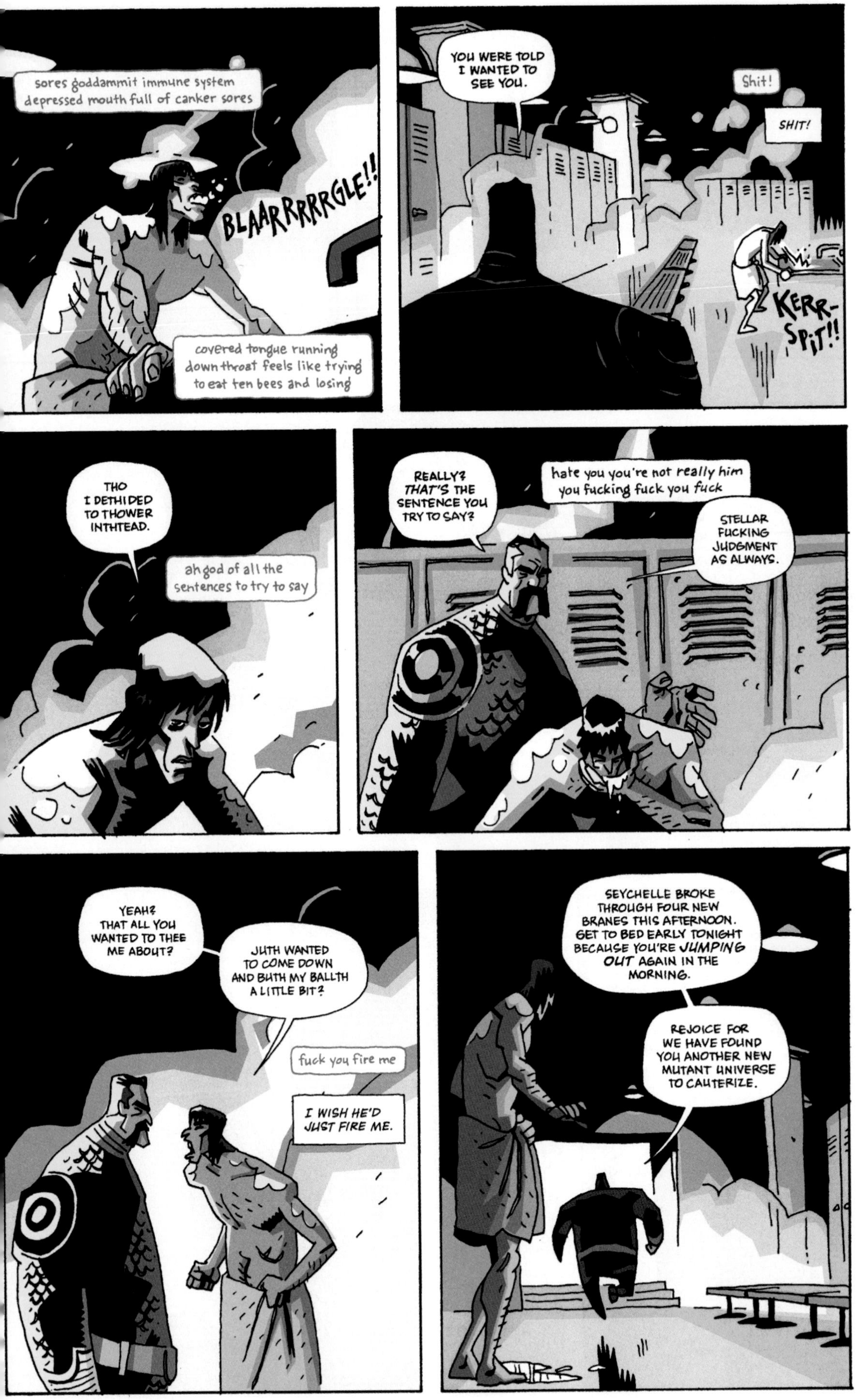
sores goddammit immune system depressed mouth full of canker sores
BLAARRRRRGLE!!
covered tongue running down throat feels like trying to eat ten bees and losing
YOU WERE TOLD I WANTED TO SEE YOU.
Shit!
SHIT!
KERR-SPIT!!
THO I DETHIDED TO THOWER INTHTEAD.
ah god of all the sentences to try to say
REALLY? THAT'S THE SENTENCE YOU TRY TO SAY?
hate you you're not really him you fucking fuck you fuck
STELLAR FUCKING JUDGMENT AS ALWAYS.
YEAH? THAT ALL YOU WANTED TO THEE ME ABOUT?
JUTH WANTED TO COME DOWN AND BUTH MY BALLTH A LITTLE BIT?
fuck you fire me
I WISH HE'D JUST FIRE ME.
SEYCHELLE BROKE THROUGH FOUR NEW BRANES THIS AFTERNOON. GET TO BED EARLY TONIGHT BECAUSE YOU'RE JUMPING OUT AGAIN IN THE MORNING.
REJOICE FOR WE HAVE FOUND YOU ANOTHER NEW MUTANT UNIVERSE TO CAUTERIZE.

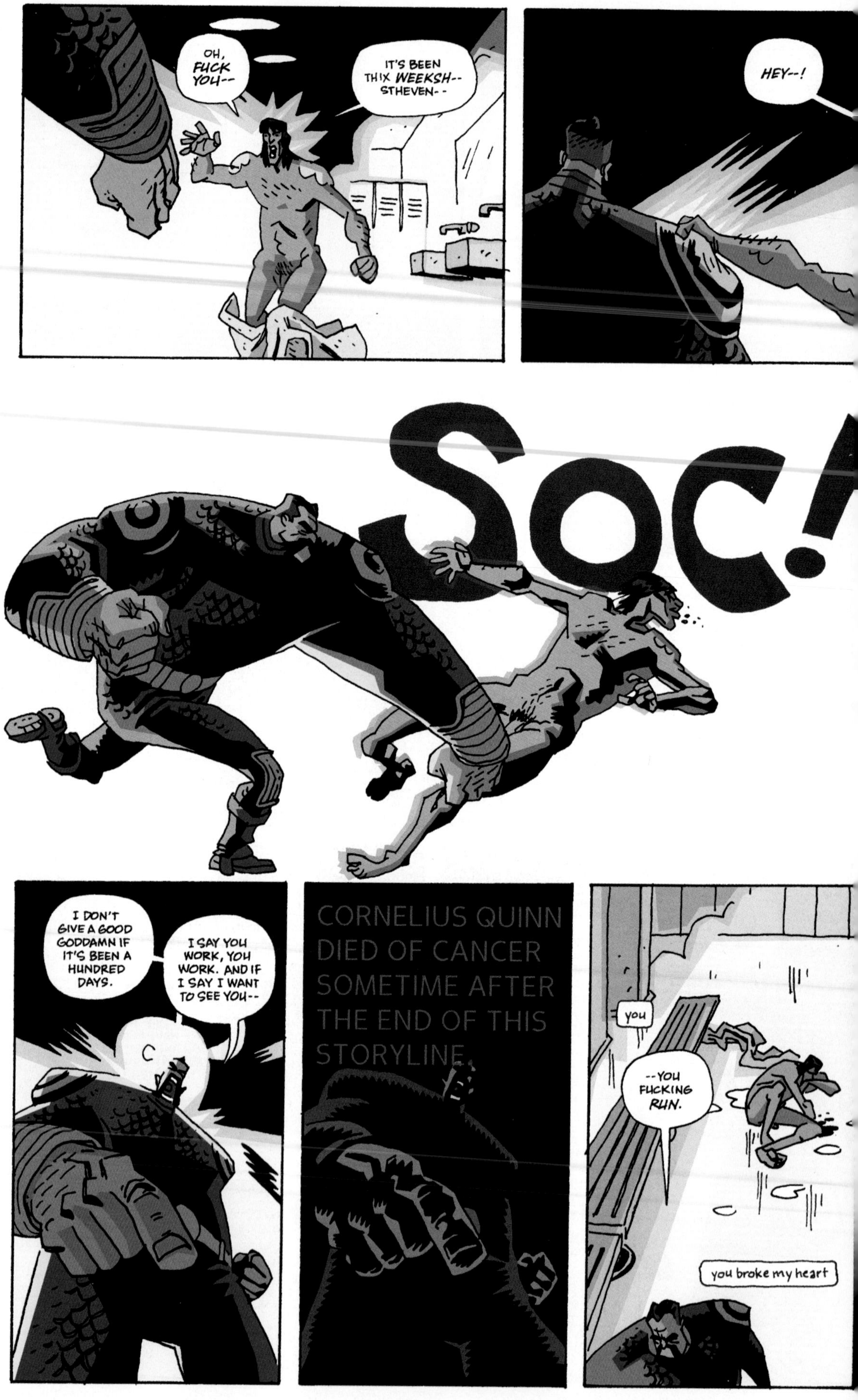
OH, FUCK YOU--
IT'S BEEN THIX WEEKSH-- STHEVEN--
HEY--!
SOC!
I DON'T GIVE A GOOD GODDAMN IF IT'S BEEN A HUNDRED DAYS.
I SAY YOU WORK, YOU WORK. AND IF I SAY I WANT TO SEE YOU--
CORNELIUS QUINN DIED OF CANCER SOMETIME AFTER THE END OF THIS STORYLINE.
you
--YOU FUCKING RUN.
you broke my heart

IT'S BEEN THREE YEARS, FOUR MONTHS, THREE WEEKS, AND ONE DAY.
...

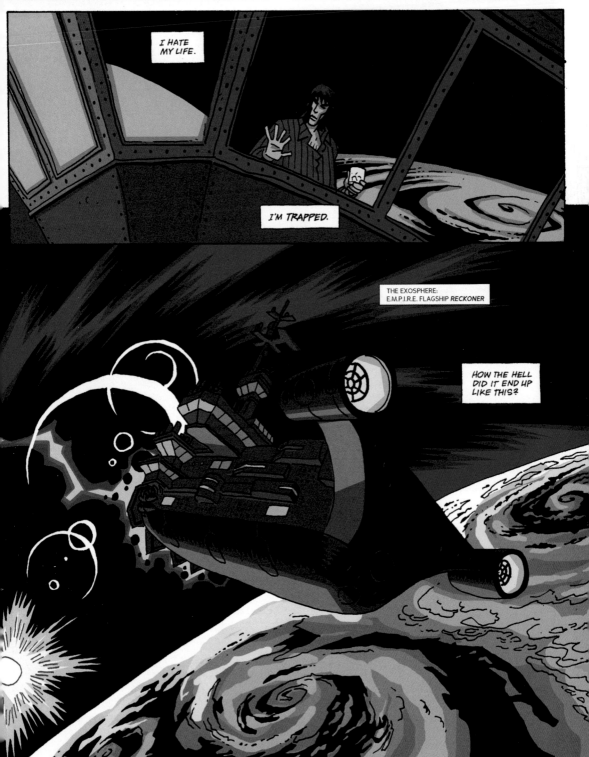

I HATE MY LIFE.

I'M TRAPPED.

THE EXOSPHERE:
E.M.P.I.R.E. FLAGSHIP *RECKONER*

HOW THE HELL DID IT END UP LIKE THIS?

2. I'M IN LOVE WITH MY CAR

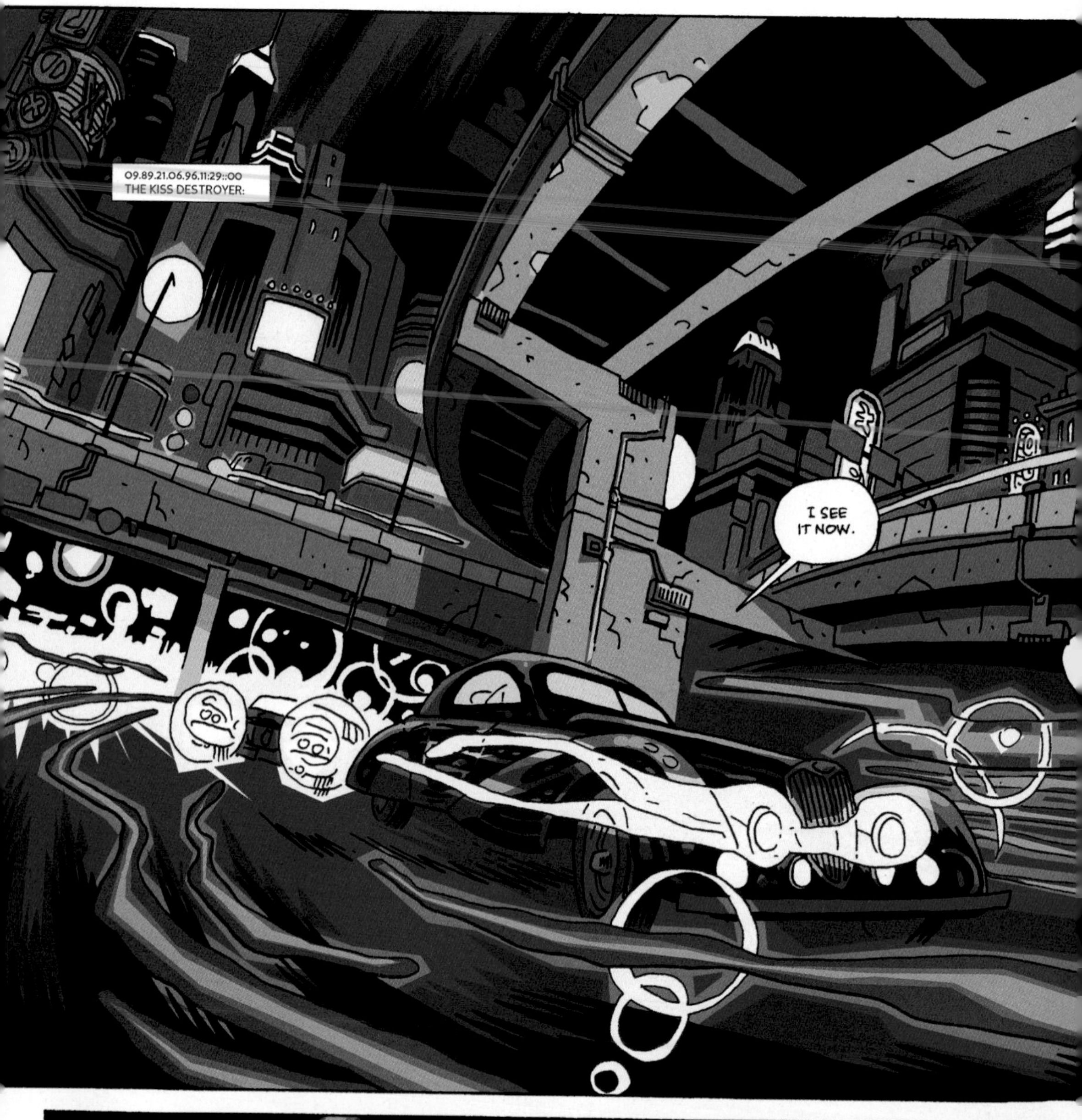

09.89.21.06.96.11:29::00
THE KISS DESTROYER:
I SEE IT NOW.

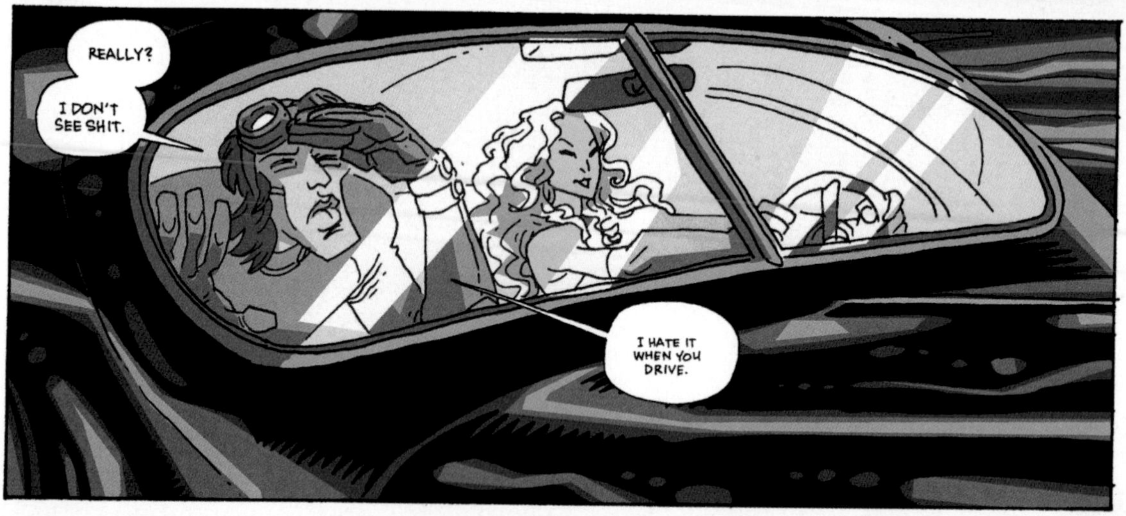

REALLY?
I DON'T SEE SHIT.
I HATE IT WHEN YOU DRIVE.

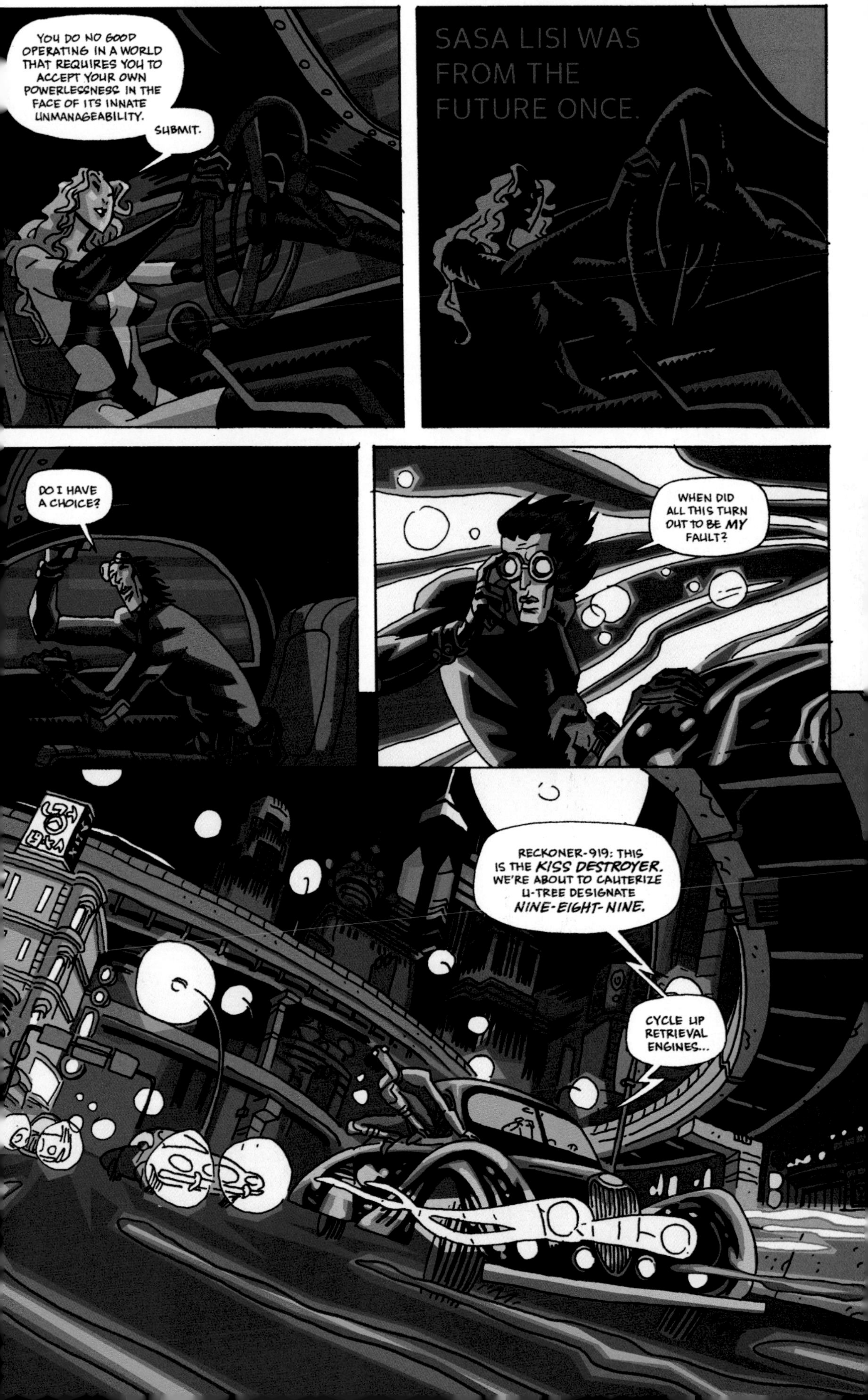
YOU DO NO GOOD OPERATING IN A WORLD THAT REQUIRES YOU TO ACCEPT YOUR OWN POWERLESSNESS IN THE FACE OF ITS INNATE UNMANAGEABILITY.
SUBMIT.
SASA LISI WAS FROM THE FUTURE ONCE.
DO I HAVE A CHOICE?
WHEN DID ALL THIS TURN OUT TO BE MY FAULT?
RECKONER-919: THIS IS THE KISS DESTROYER. WE'RE ABOUT TO CAUTERIZE U-TREE DESIGNATE NINE-EIGHT-NINE.
CYCLE UP RETRIEVAL ENGINES...

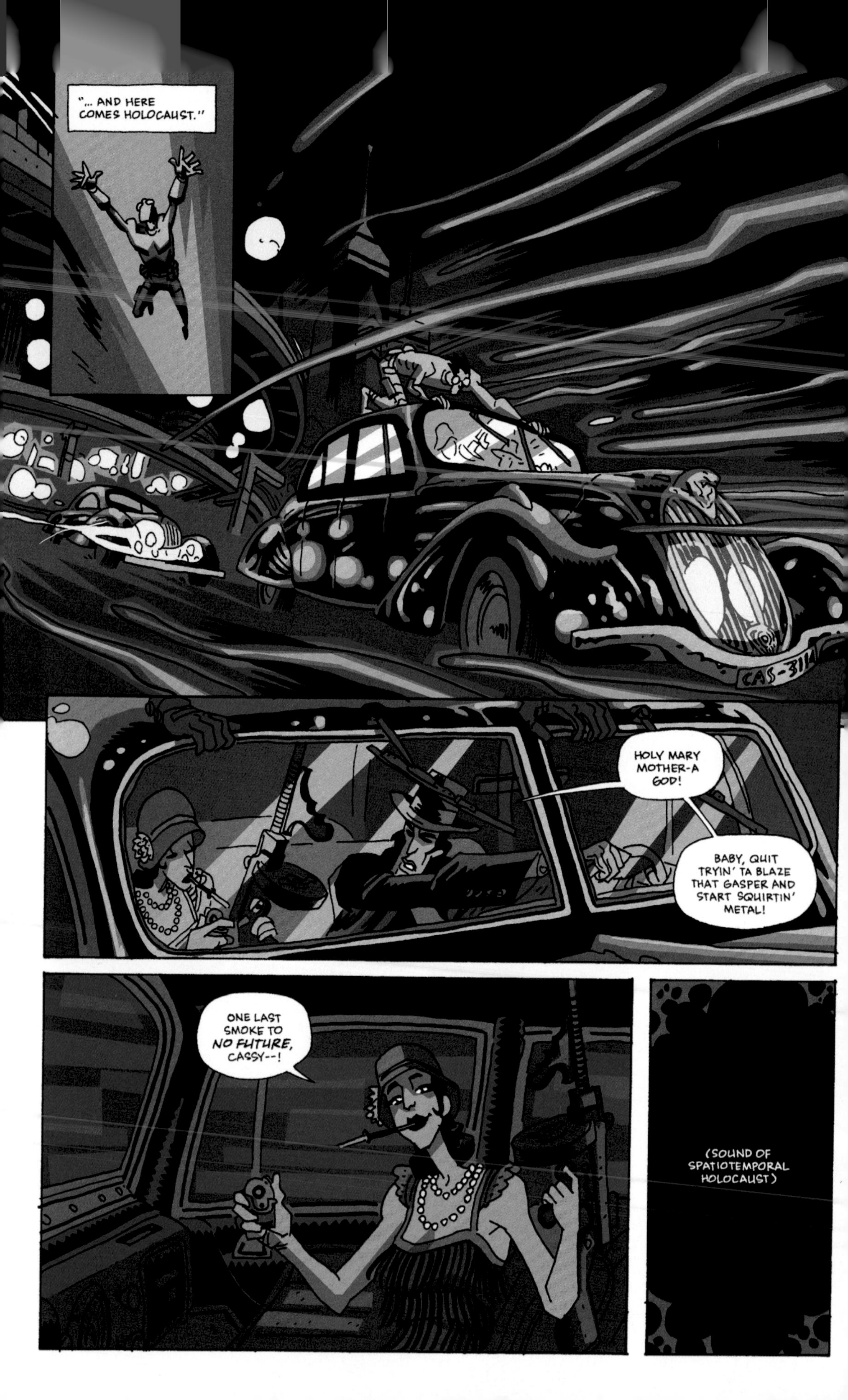
"... AND HERE COMES HOLOCAUST."
CAS-3114
HOLY MARY MOTHER-A GOD!
BABY, QUIT TRYIN' TA BLAZE THAT GASPER AND START SQUIRTIN' METAL!
ONE LAST SMOKE TO *NO FUTURE,* CASSY--!
(SOUND OF SPATIOTEMPORAL HOLOCAUST)

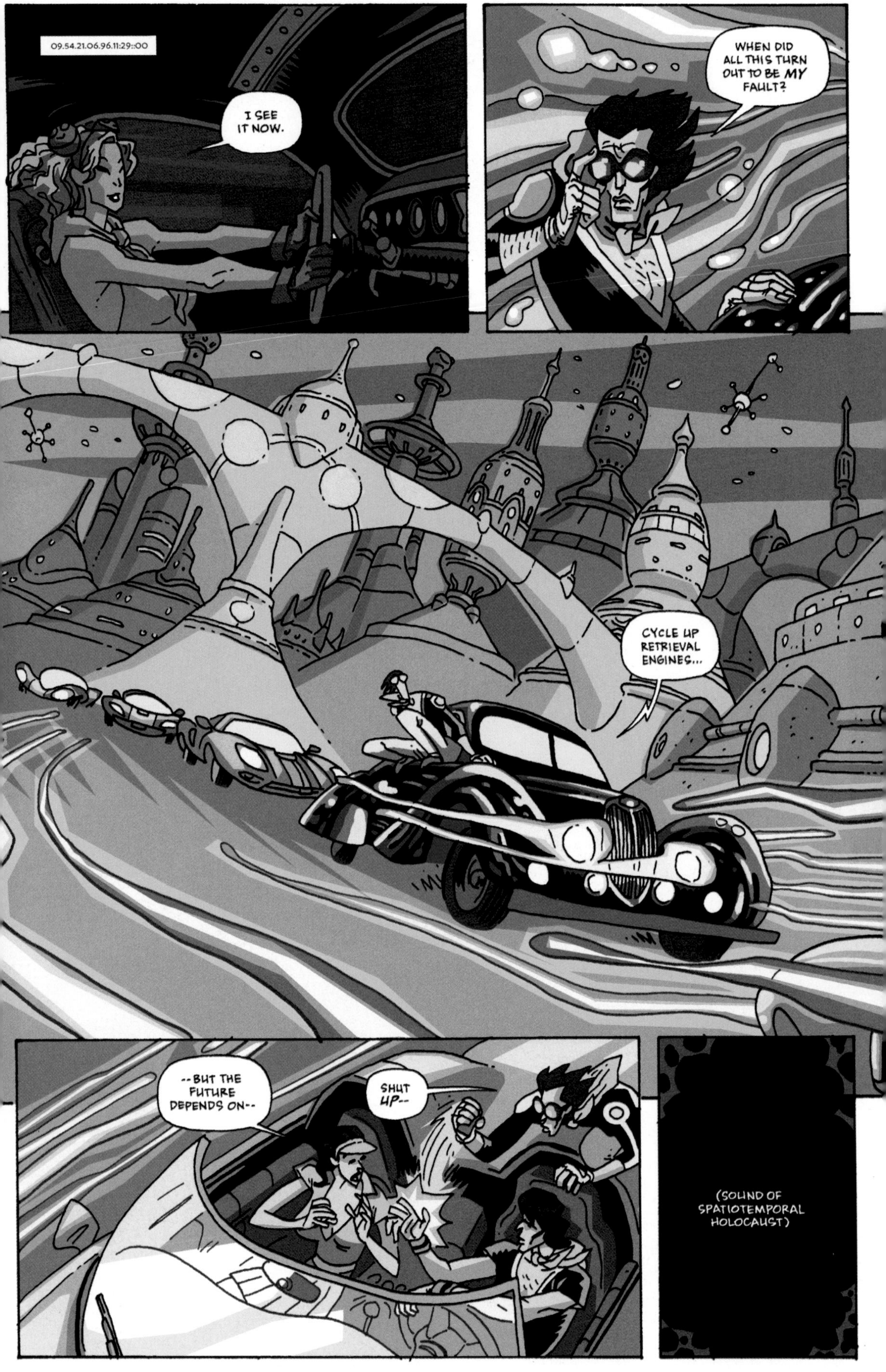
09.54.21.06.96.11:29::00
I SEE IT NOW.
WHEN DID ALL THIS TURN OUT TO BE MY FAULT?
CYCLE UP RETRIEVAL ENGINES...
--BUT THE FUTURE DEPENDS ON--
SHUT UP--
(SOUND OF SPATIOTEMPORAL HOLOCAUST)

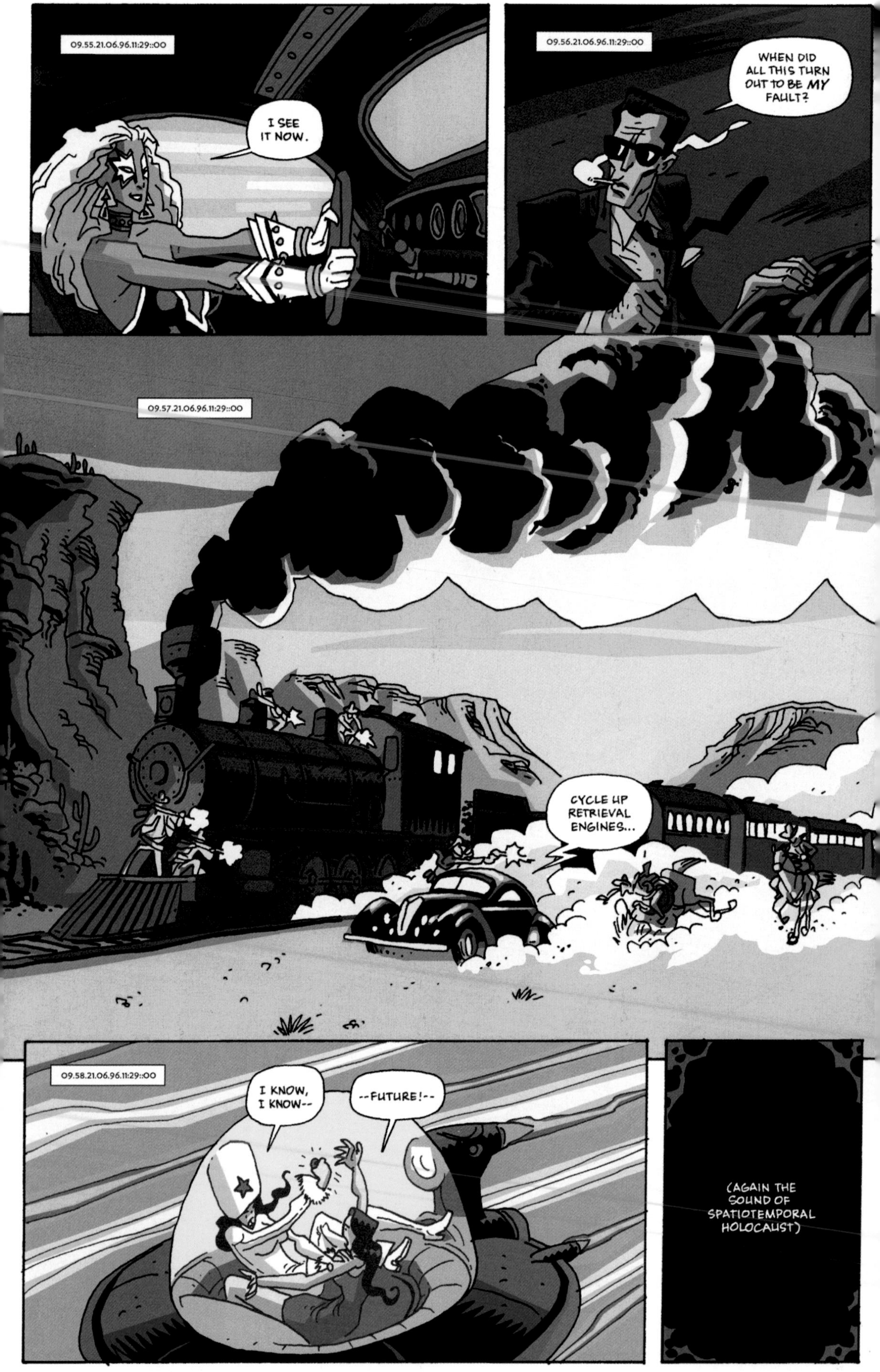
09.55.21.06.96.11:29::00
I SEE IT NOW.
09.56.21.06.96.11:29::00
WHEN DID ALL THIS TURN OUT TO BE MY FAULT?
09.57.21.06.96.11:29::00
CYCLE UP RETRIEVAL ENGINES...
09.58.21.06.96.11:29::00
I KNOW, I KNOW--
--FUTURE!--
(AGAIN THE SOUND OF SPATIOTEMPORAL HOLOCAUST)

09.59.21.06.96.11:29::OO

I

09.50.21.06.96.11:29::OO

W

09.51.21.06.96.11:29::OO

CYCLE

09.52.21.06.96.11:29::OO

--FUTURE--

(SOUND OF SPATIOTEMPORAL HOLOCAUST)

09.53.21.06.96.11:29::OO

SEE

09.60.21.06.96.11:29::OO

H

09.49.21.06.96.11:29::OO

UP

09.48.21.06.96.11:29::OO

--FUTURE--

(SOUND OF SPATIOTEMPORAL HOLOCAUST)

09.40.21.06.96.11:29::OO

IT

96.11:29::OO

E

09.31.21.06.96.11:29::OO

RETRIEVAL

29::OO

FOOOCHA

(SOUND OF SPATIOTEMPORAL HOLOCAUST)

09.22.21.06.96.11:29::OO

NOW.

09.20.21.06.96.11:29::OO

N

09.69.21.06.96.11:29::OO

ENGINES.

11:29::OO

FUTURE!

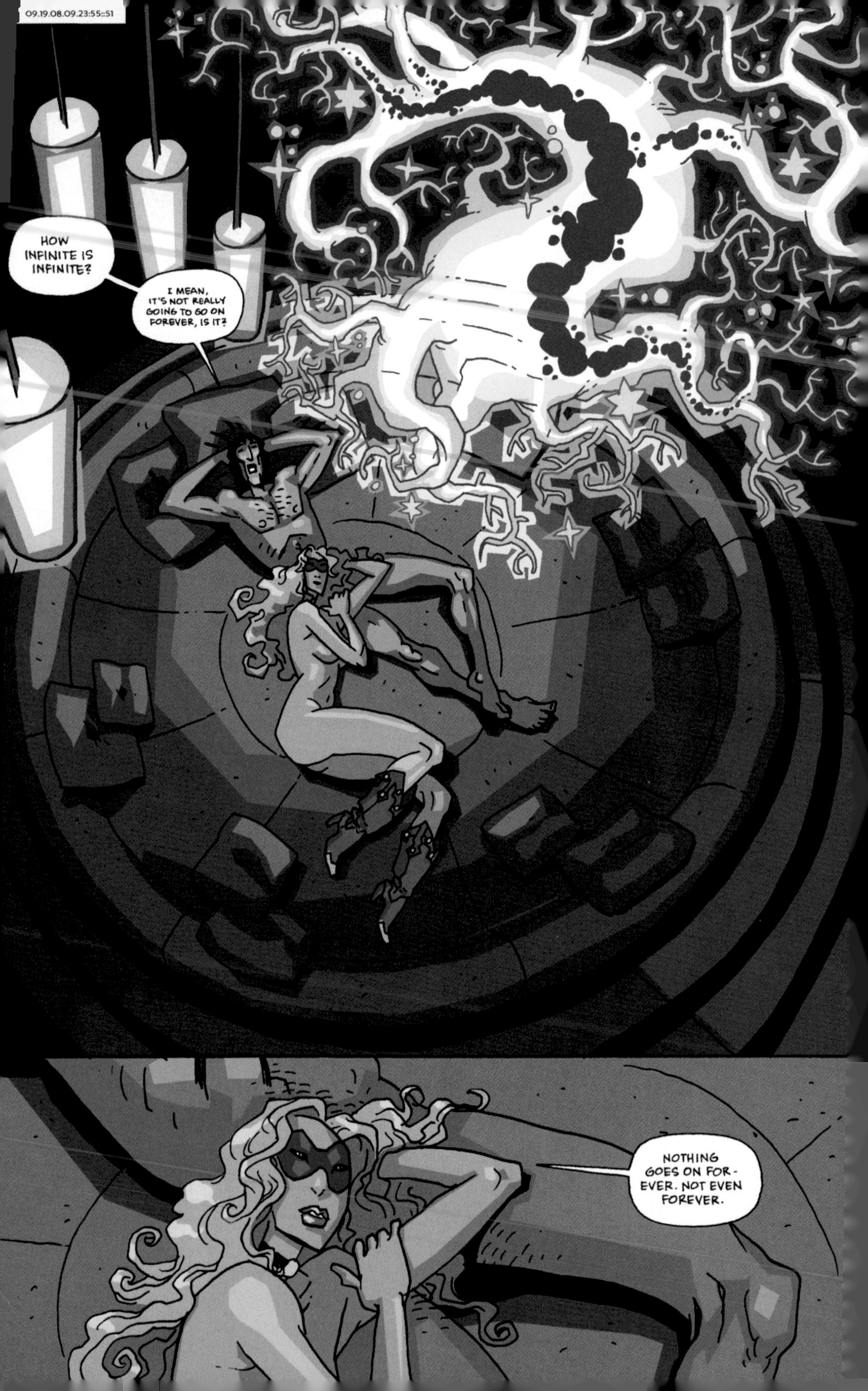
09.19.08.09.23:55::51
HOW INFINITE IS INFINITE?
I MEAN, IT'S NOT REALLY GOING TO GO ON FOREVER, IS IT?
NOTHING GOES ON FOR-EVER. NOT EVEN FOREVER.

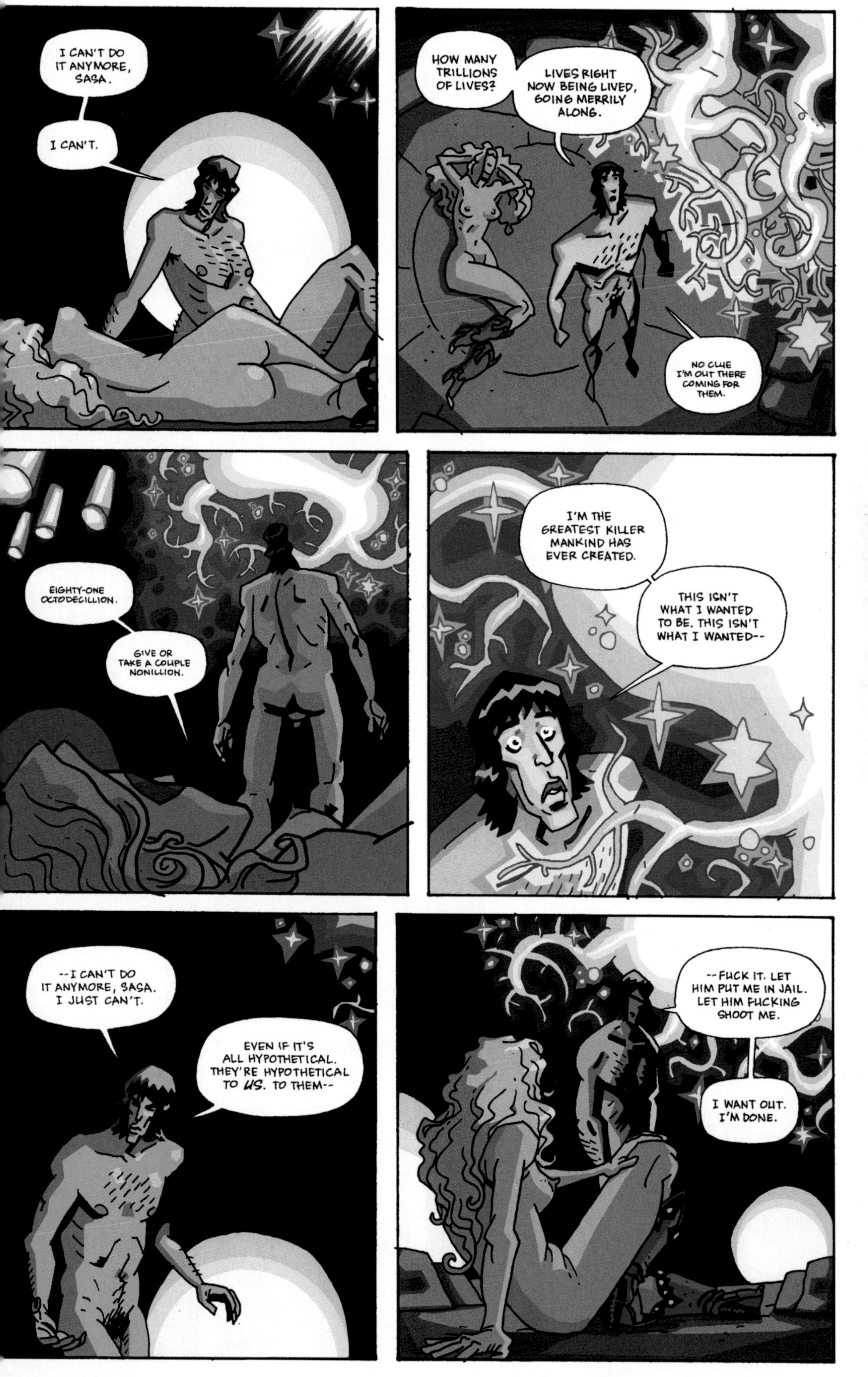
I CAN'T DO IT ANYMORE, SASA.
I CAN'T.
HOW MANY TRILLIONS OF LIVES?
LIVES RIGHT NOW BEING LIVED, GOING MERRILY ALONG.
NO CLUE I'M OUT THERE COMING FOR THEM.
EIGHTY-ONE OCTODECILLION.
GIVE OR TAKE A COUPLE NONILLION.
I'M THE GREATEST KILLER MANKIND HAS EVER CREATED.
THIS ISN'T WHAT I WANTED TO BE. THIS ISN'T WHAT I WANTED--
--I CAN'T DO IT ANYMORE, SASA. I JUST CAN'T.
EVEN IF IT'S ALL HYPOTHETICAL. THEY'RE HYPOTHETICAL TO *US*. TO THEM--
--FUCK IT. LET HIM PUT ME IN JAIL. LET HIM FUCKING SHOOT ME.
I WANT OUT. I'M DONE.

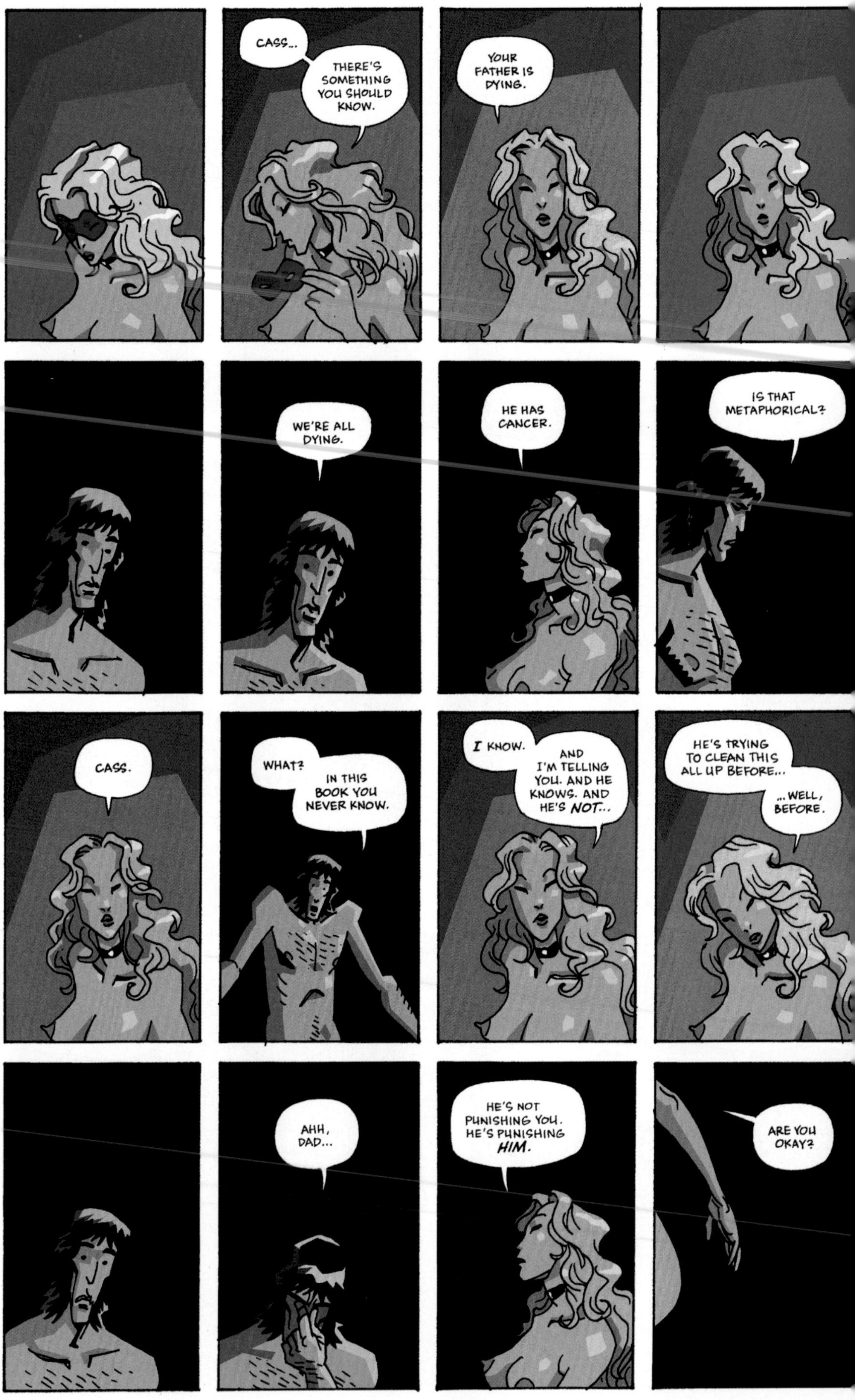
CASS...
THERE'S SOMETHING YOU SHOULD KNOW.
YOUR FATHER IS DYING.
WE'RE ALL DYING.
HE HAS CANCER.
IS THAT METAPHORICAL?
CASS.
WHAT?
IN THIS BOOK YOU NEVER KNOW.
I KNOW.
AND I'M TELLING YOU. AND HE KNOWS. AND HE'S NOT...
HE'S TRYING TO CLEAN THIS ALL UP BEFORE...
...WELL, BEFORE.
AHH, DAD...
HE'S NOT PUNISHING YOU. HE'S PUNISHING HIM.
ARE YOU OKAY?

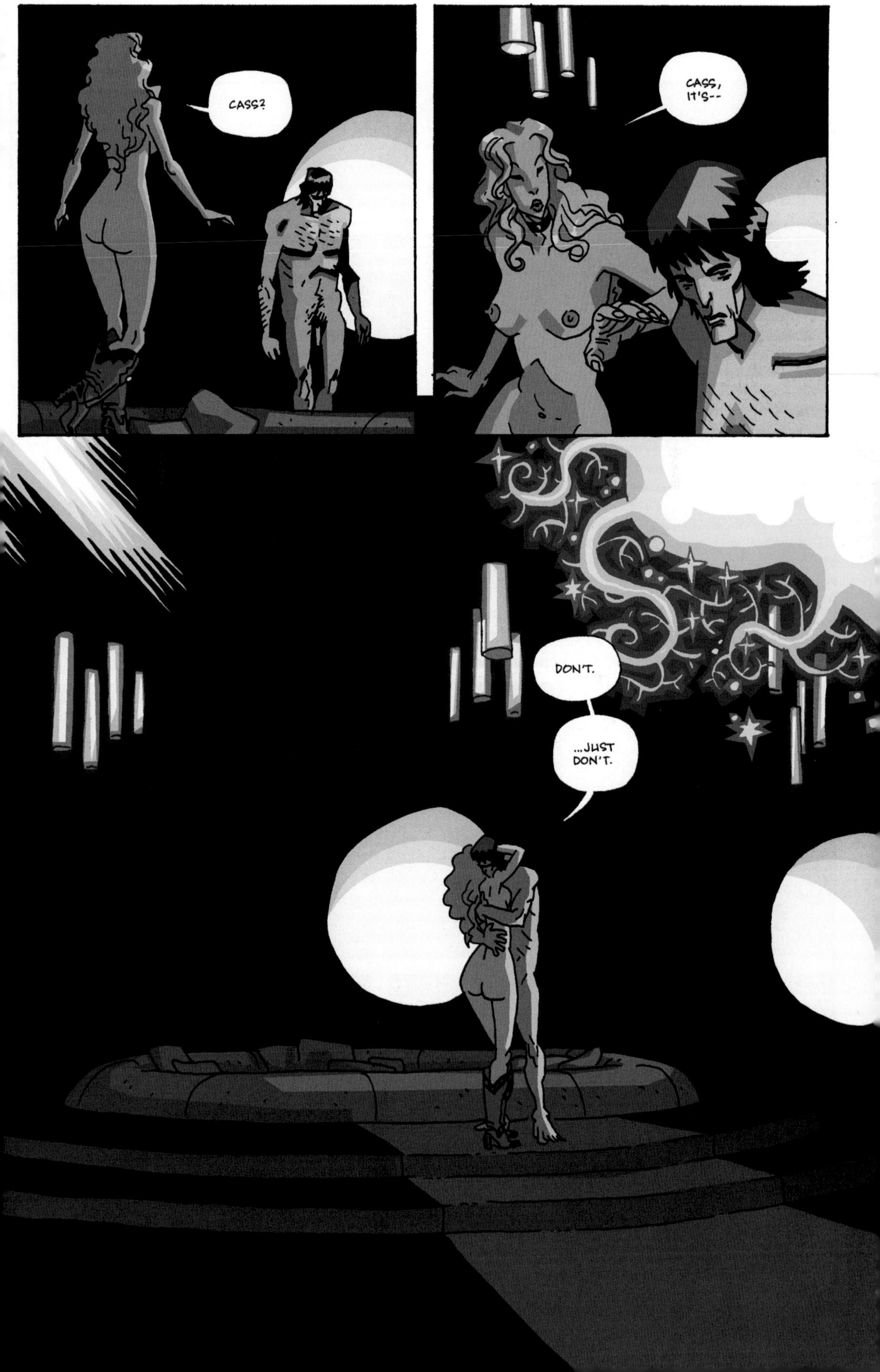
CASS?
CASS, IT'S--
DON'T.
...JUST DON'T.

3. EVERYTHING IS OVER

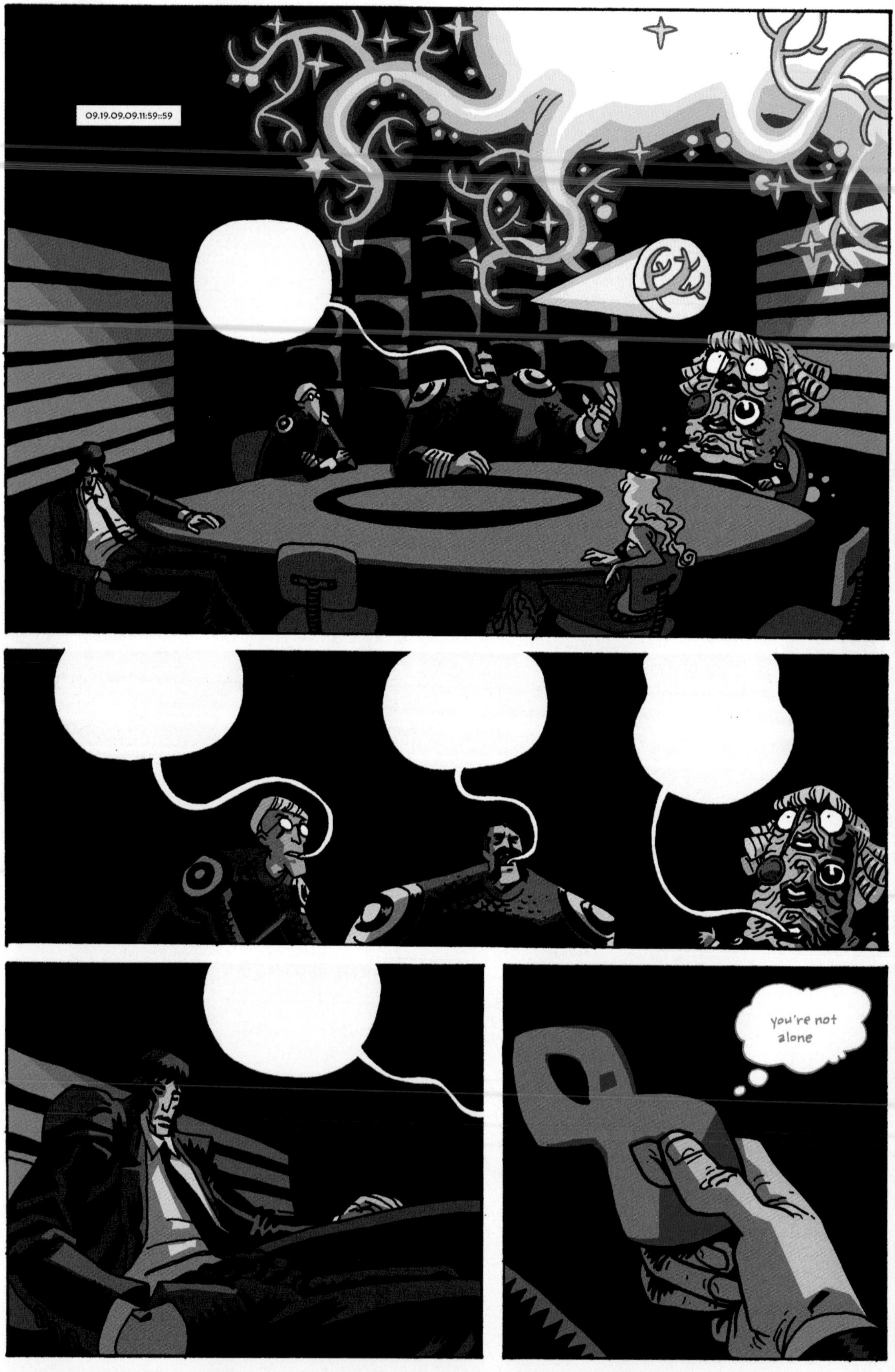

09.19.09.09.11:59::59
you're not alone

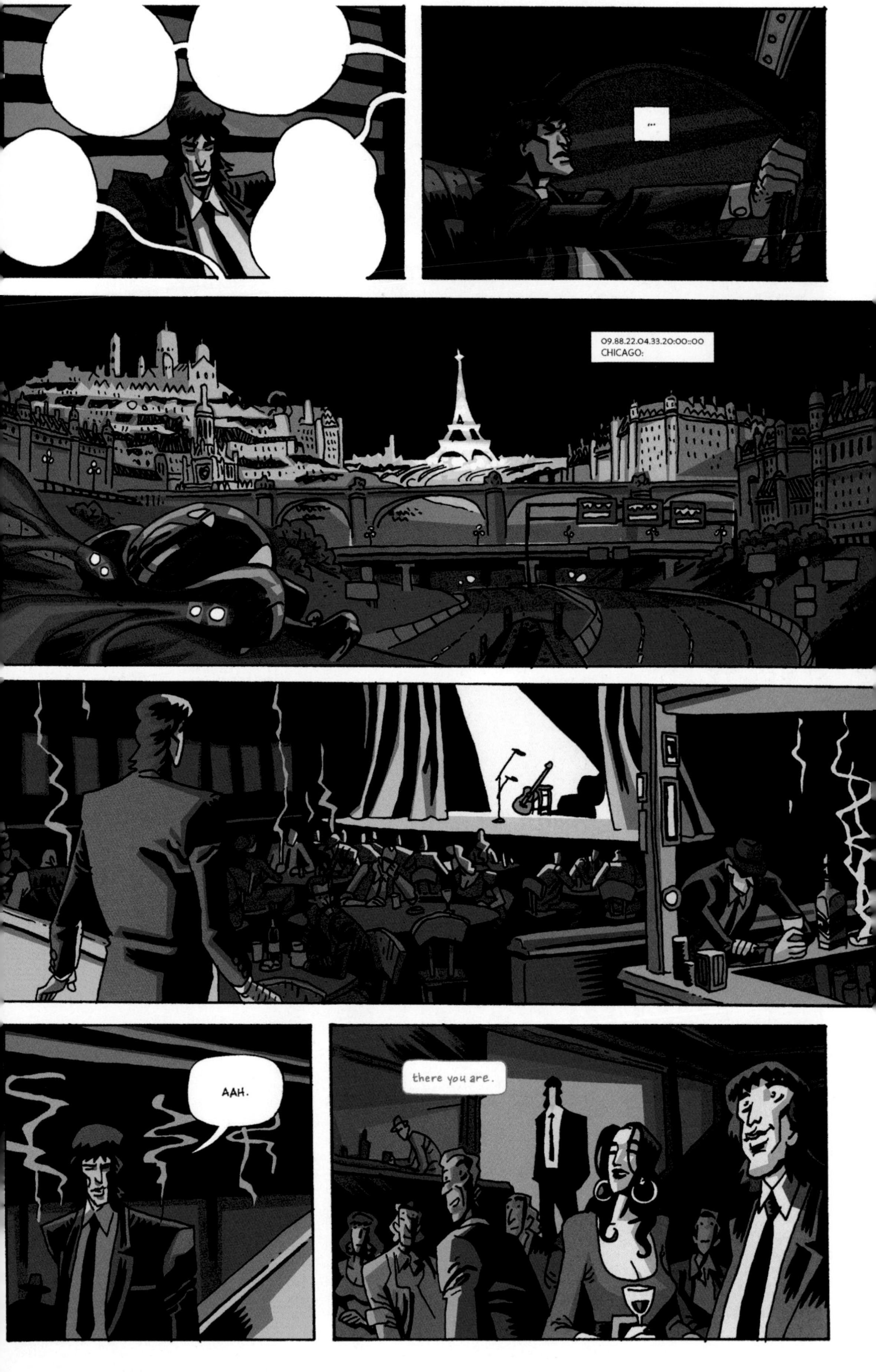
...
09.88.22.04.33.20:00::00
CHICAGO:
AAH.
there you are.

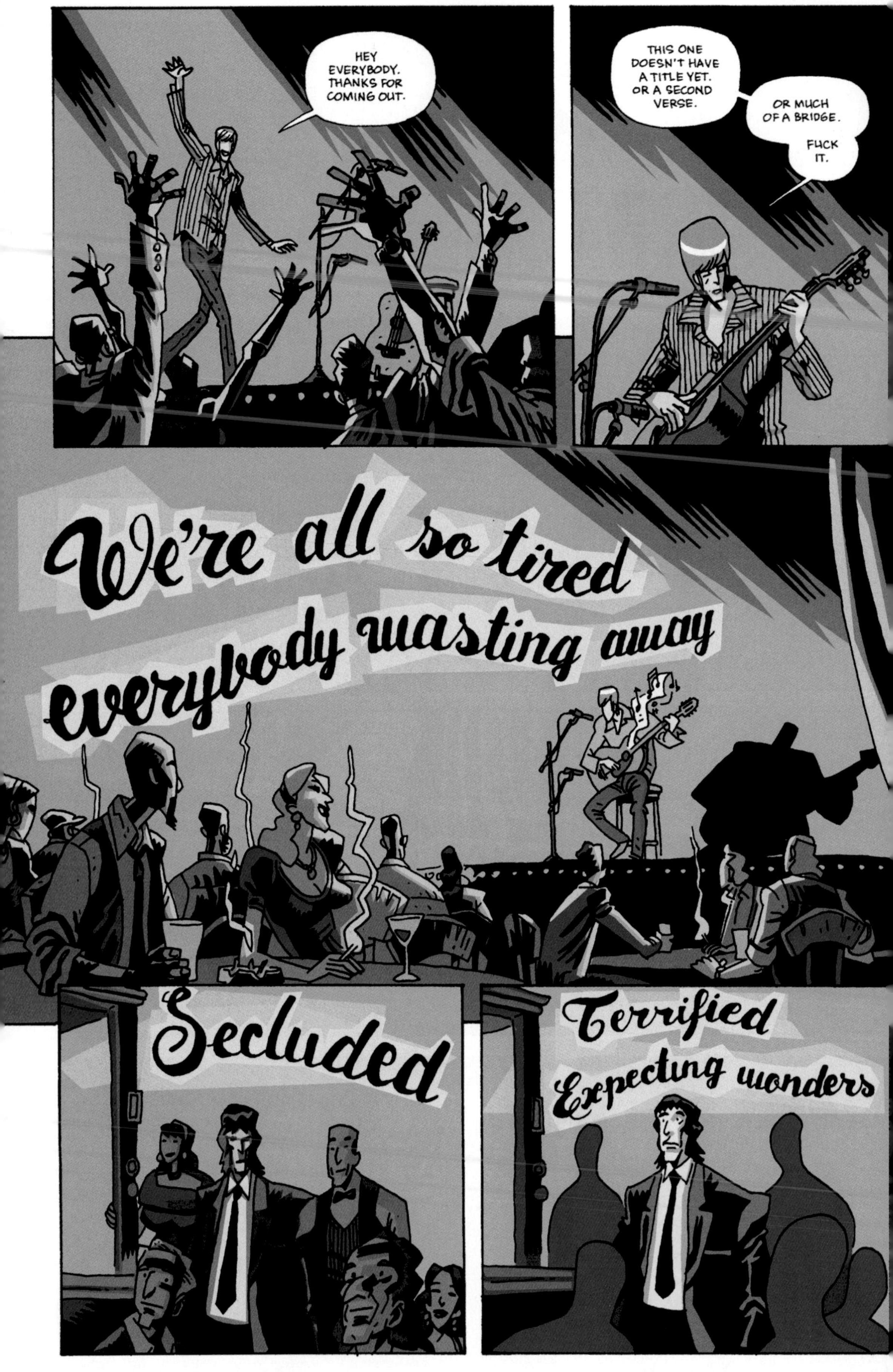
HEY EVERYBODY. THANKS FOR COMING OUT.
THIS ONE DOESN'T HAVE A TITLE YET. OR A SECOND VERSE.
OR MUCH OF A BRIDGE.
FUCK IT.
We're all so tired
everybody wasting away
Secluded
Terrified
Expecting wonders

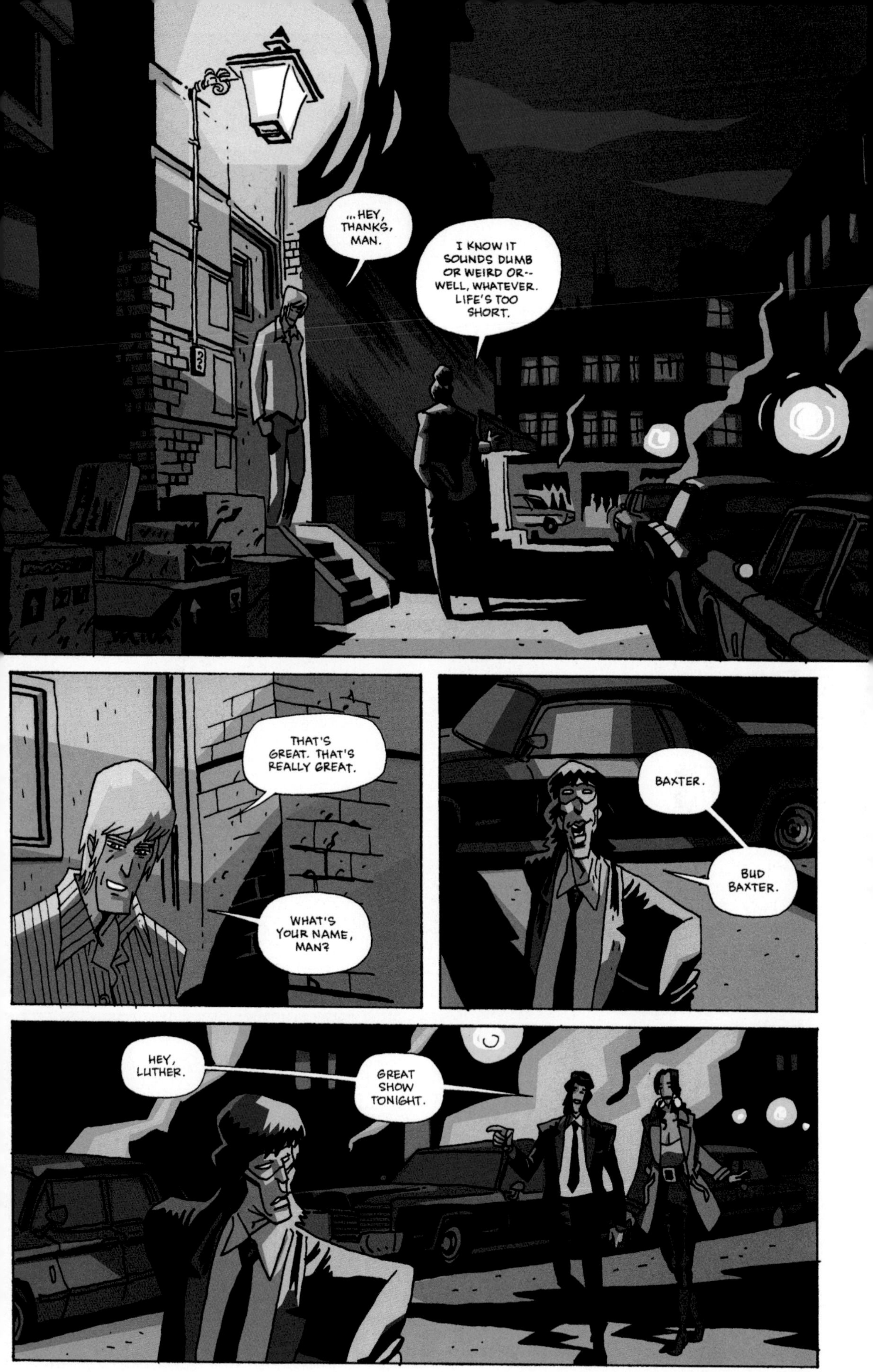
...HEY, THANKS, MAN.
I KNOW IT SOUNDS DUMB OR WEIRD OR-- WELL, WHATEVER. LIFE'S TOO SHORT.
THAT'S GREAT. THAT'S REALLY GREAT.
WHAT'S YOUR NAME, MAN?
BAXTER.
BUD BAXTER.
HEY, LUTHER.
GREAT SHOW TONIGHT.

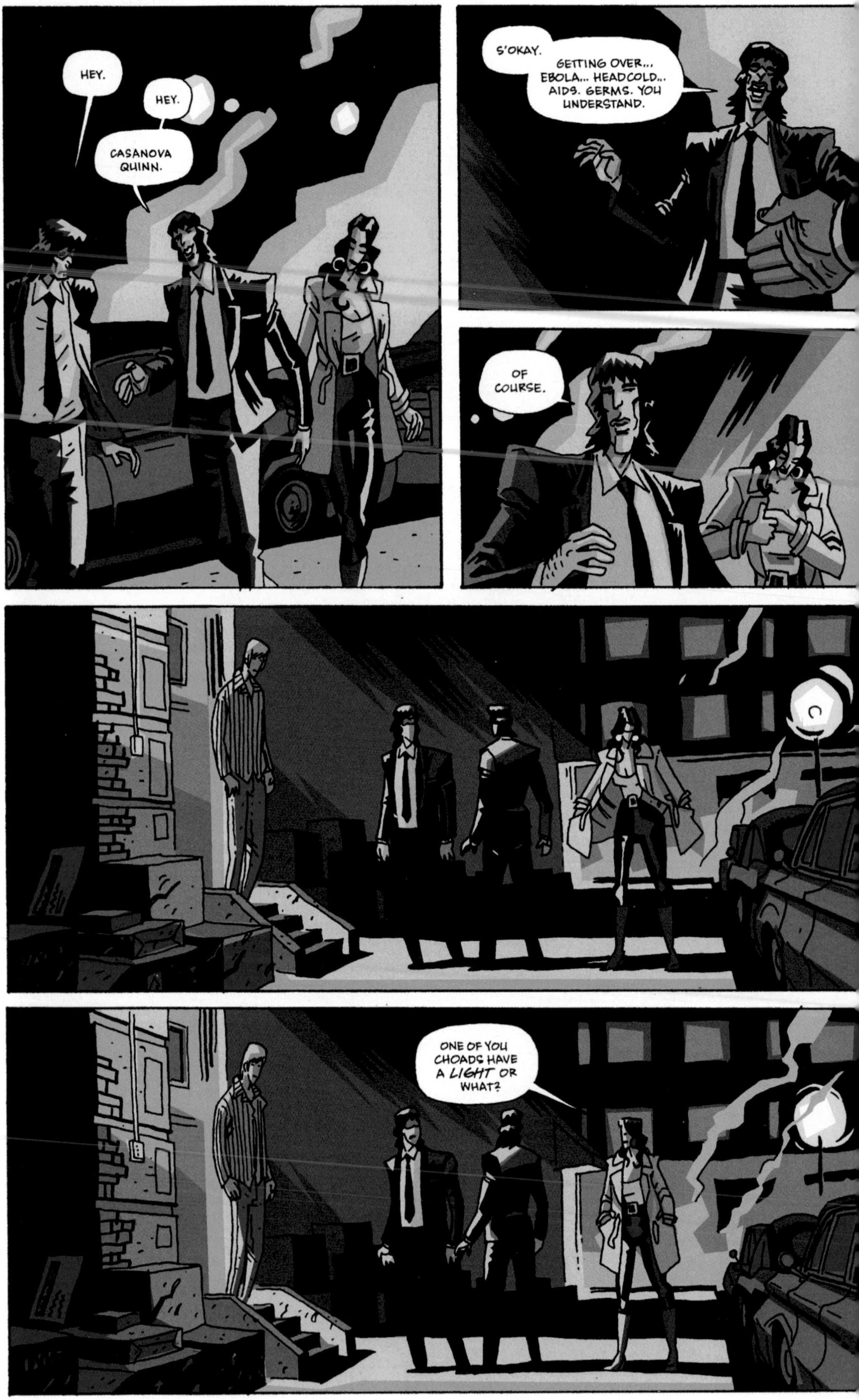
HEY.
HEY.
CASANOVA QUINN.
S'OKAY.
GETTING OVER... EBOLA... HEADCOLD... AIDS. GERMS. YOU UNDERSTAND.
OF COURSE.
ONE OF YOU CHOADS HAVE A *LIGHT* OR WHAT?

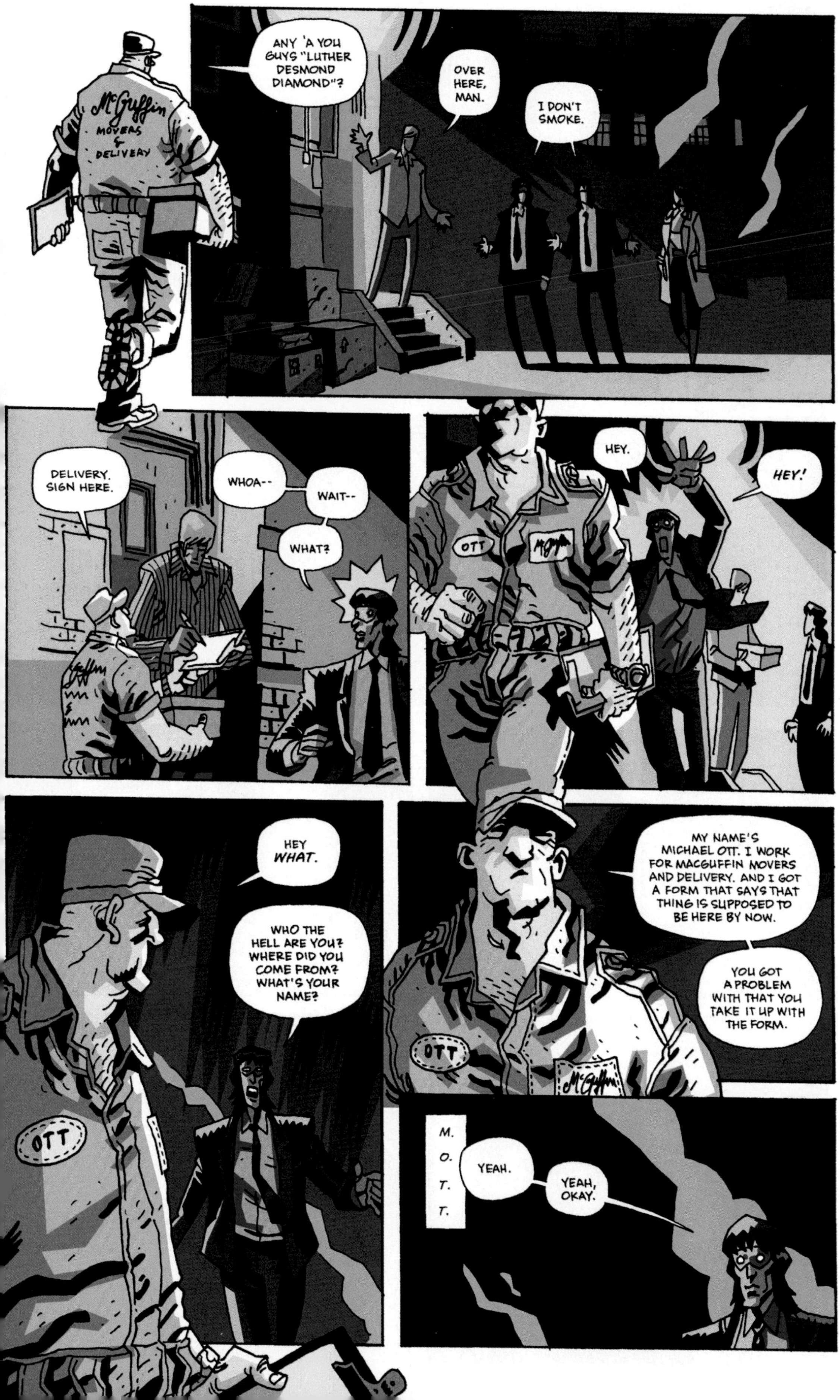
McGuffin MOVERS & DELIVERY
ANY 'A YOU GUYS "LUTHER DESMOND DIAMOND"?
OVER HERE, MAN.
I DON'T SMOKE.
DELIVERY. SIGN HERE.
WHOA--
WAIT--
WHAT?
HEY.
HEY!
OTT
HEY WHAT.
WHO THE HELL ARE YOU? WHERE DID YOU COME FROM? WHAT'S YOUR NAME?
OTT
MY NAME'S MICHAEL OTT. I WORK FOR MACGUFFIN MOVERS AND DELIVERY. AND I GOT A FORM THAT SAYS THAT THING IS SUPPOSED TO BE HERE BY NOW.
YOU GOT A PROBLEM WITH THAT YOU TAKE IT UP WITH THE FORM.
OTT
M. O. T. T.
YEAH.
YEAH, OKAY.

M.O.T.T.

SO, LOOK, I NEED TO GO DO MY SECOND SET BUT LATER, YOU GUYS SHOULD COME BY THE HOTEL AND HANG OUT,...

I'M STAYING UNDER MY ALIAS OF "NEWMAN XENO."

GET IT?

...WHAT?

MY ROCK STAR ALIAS.

"NEWMAN XENO." NEW MAN. XENO, ALIEN. MR. X. Y'KNOW.

IT'S FUN?

WHAT?

WHAT'S IN THE BOX, EARTHMAN?

OH. UH...

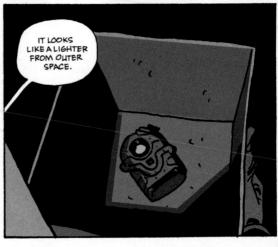

IT LOOKS LIKE A LIGHTER FROM OUTER SPACE.

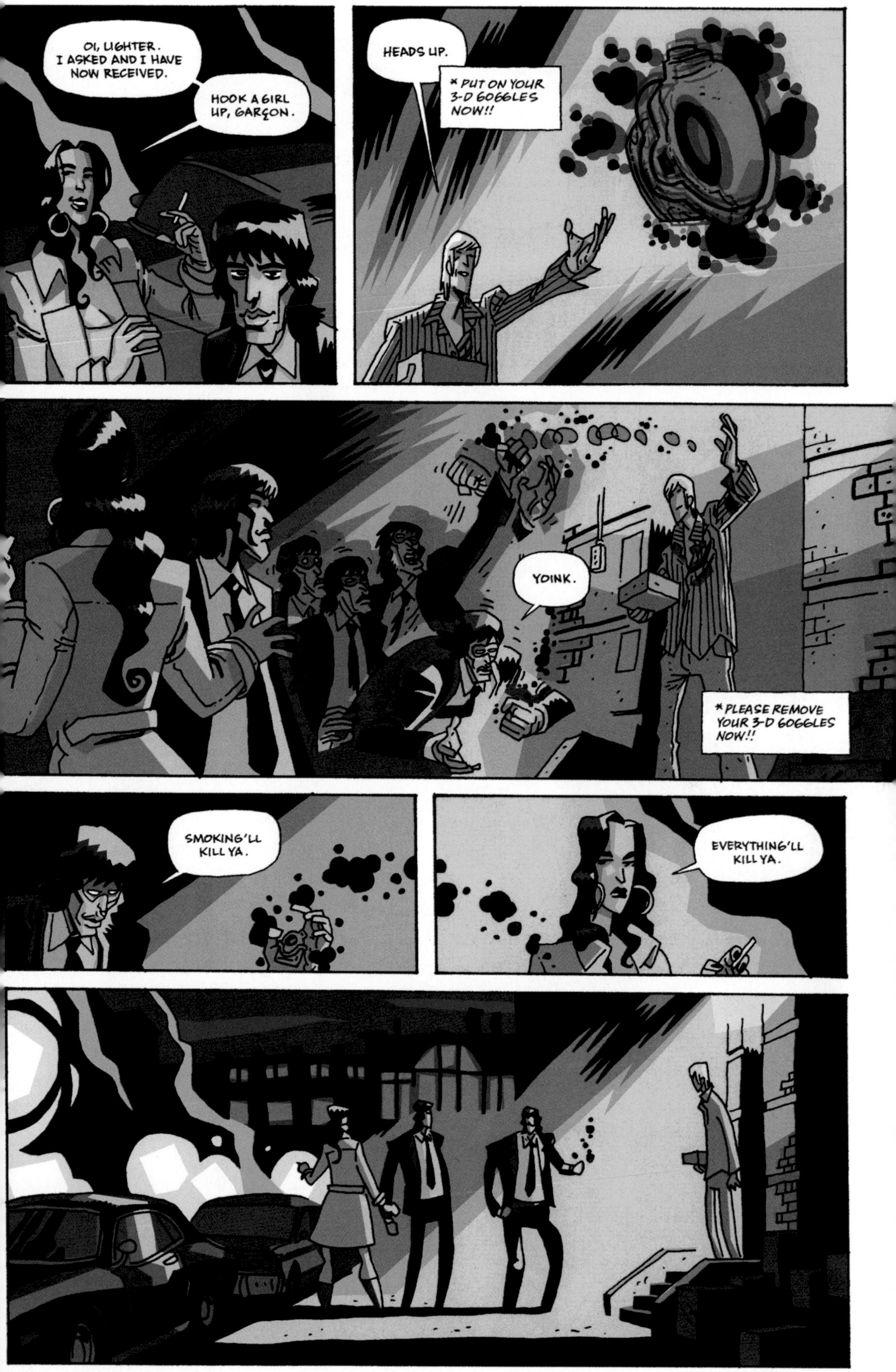
OI, LIGHTER. I ASKED AND I HAVE NOW RECEIVED.
HOOK A GIRL UP, GARÇON.
HEADS UP.
* PUT ON YOUR 3-D GOGGLES NOW!!
YOINK.
* PLEASE REMOVE YOUR 3-D GOGGLES NOW!!
SMOKING'LL KILL YA.
EVERYTHING'LL KILL YA.

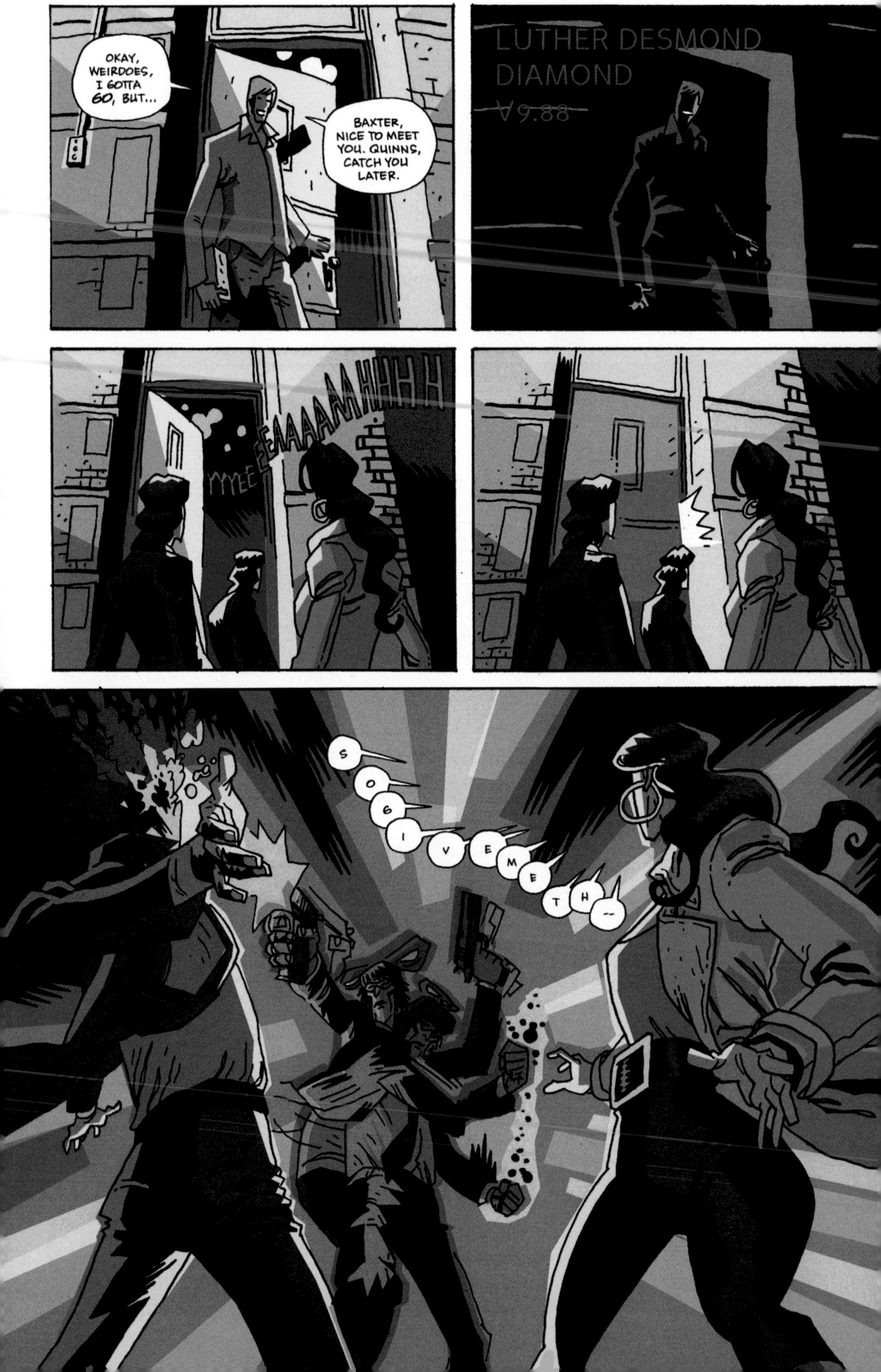
OKAY, WEIRDOES, I GOTTA GO, BUT...
BAXTER, NICE TO MEET YOU. QUINNS, CATCH YOU LATER.
LUTHER DESMOND DIAMOND
V9.88
YYYEEEAAAAAAHHHHH
S O G I V E M E T H--

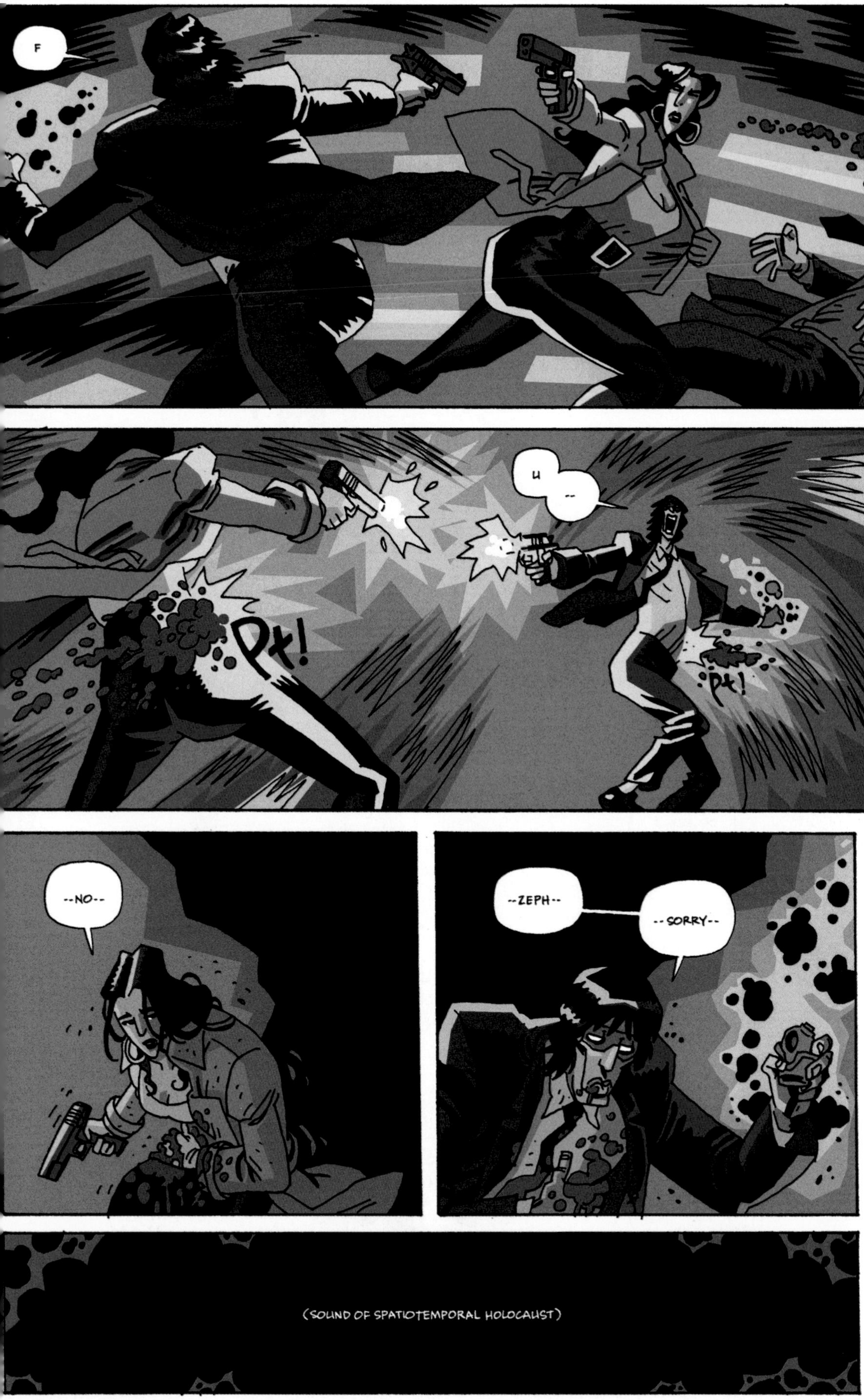
F
U
--
Pt!
Pt!
--NO--
--ZEPH--
--SORRY--
(SOUND OF SPATIOTEMPORAL HOLOCAUST)

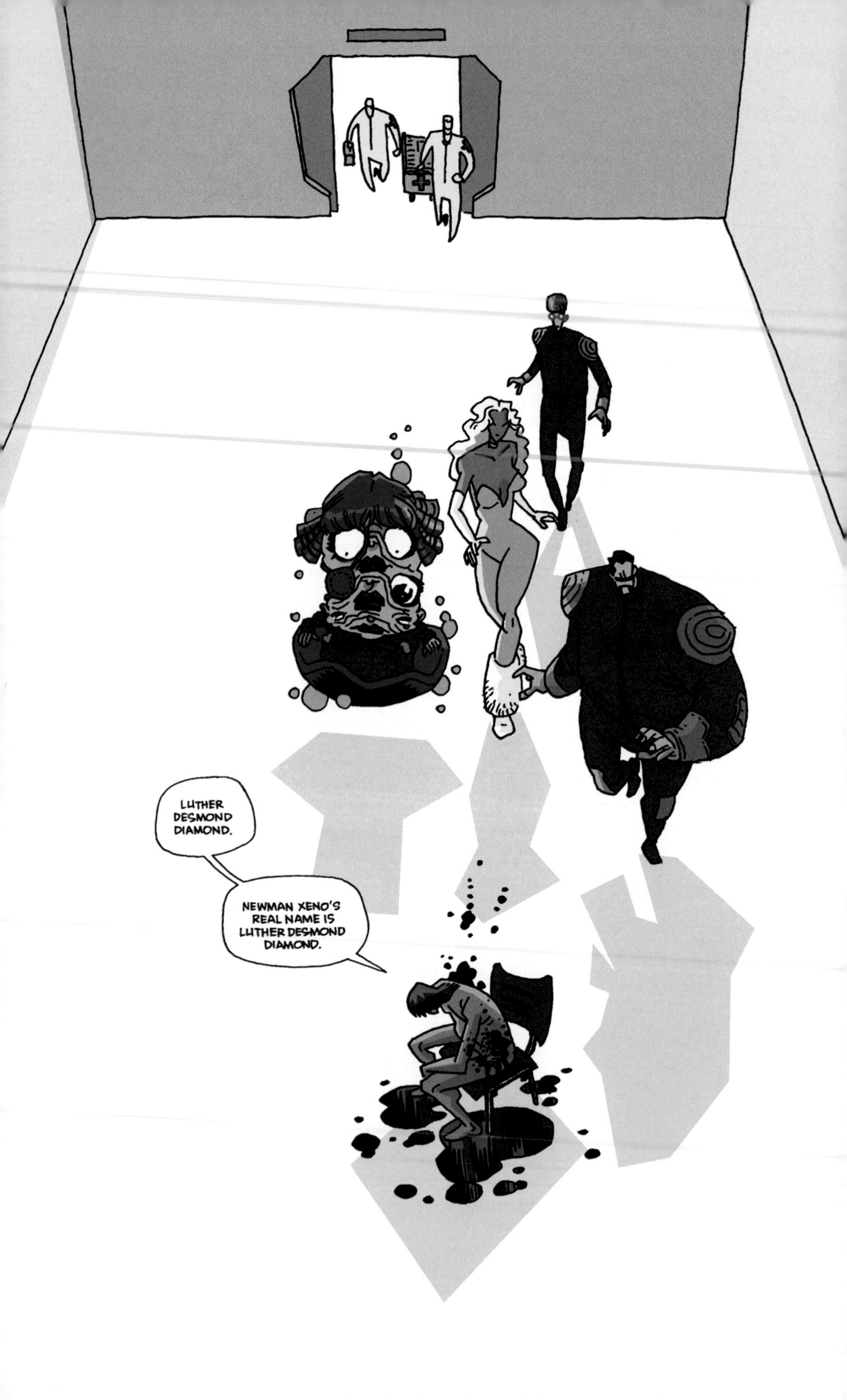
LUTHER DESMOND DIAMOND.
NEWMAN XENO'S REAL NAME IS LUTHER DESMOND DIAMOND.

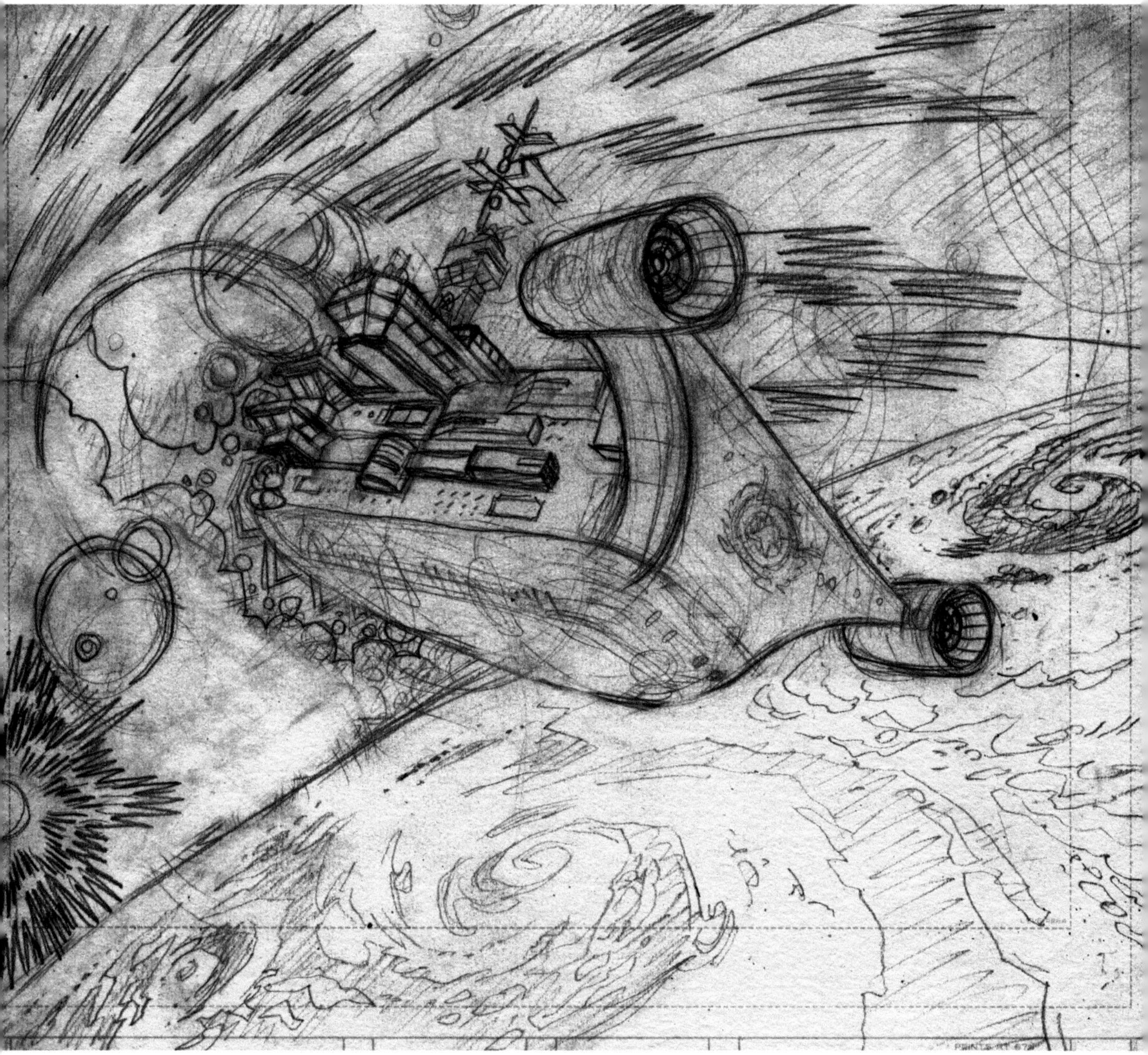

4. 'TIL I DIE

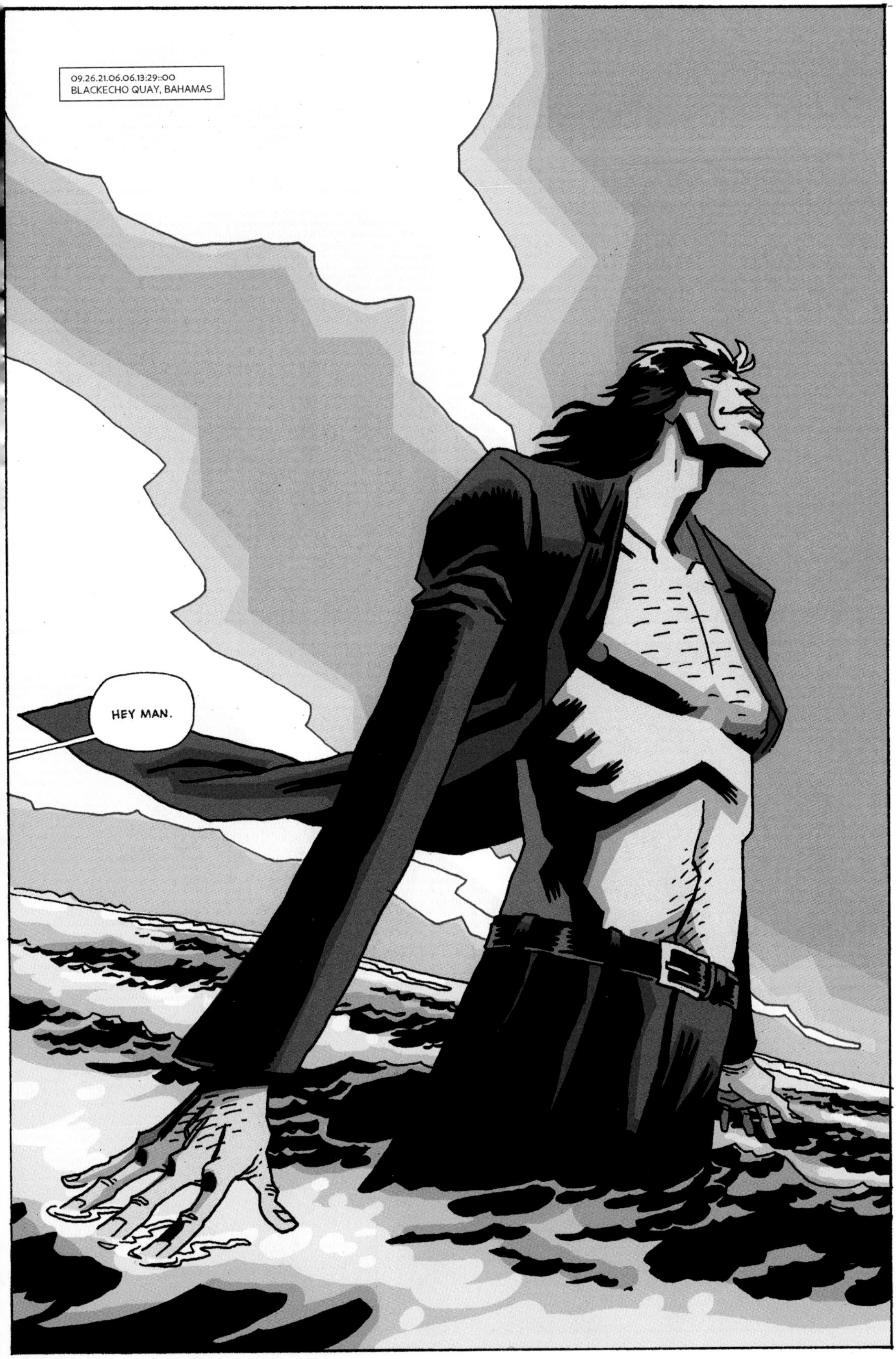
09.26.21.06.06.13:29::00
BLACKECHO QUAY, BAHAMAS
HEY MAN.

YOU'RE KIND OF COMPLICATING MY THING, MAN.
WHAT THE HELL ARE YOU DOING HERE?
NOT TO BE A COCK BUT IF YOU KNEW HOW MUCH MONEY IT COST ME TO BUY A WHOLE ISLAND JUST SO I COULD MAKE MY MUSIC ALONE...
...WHAT ARE YOU, PRESS? A FAN?
LUTHER DESMOND DIAMOND v9.26
OI, FUCKO! I SAID --
--I--
KER SPLASH
THIS IS IT.
THIS IS THE JOB NOW.

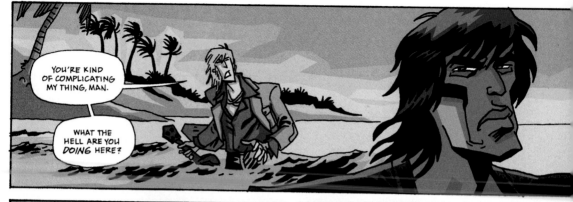

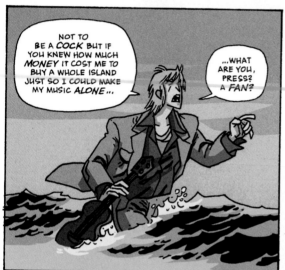

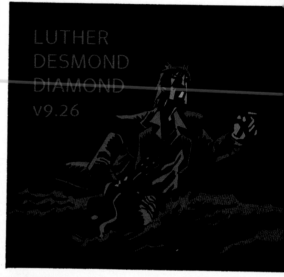

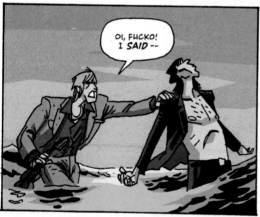

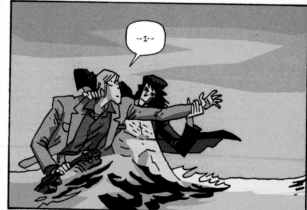

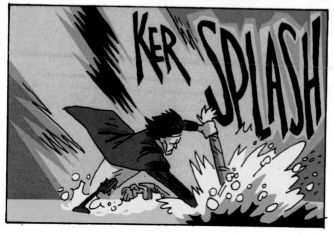

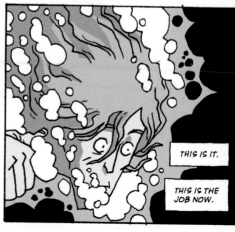

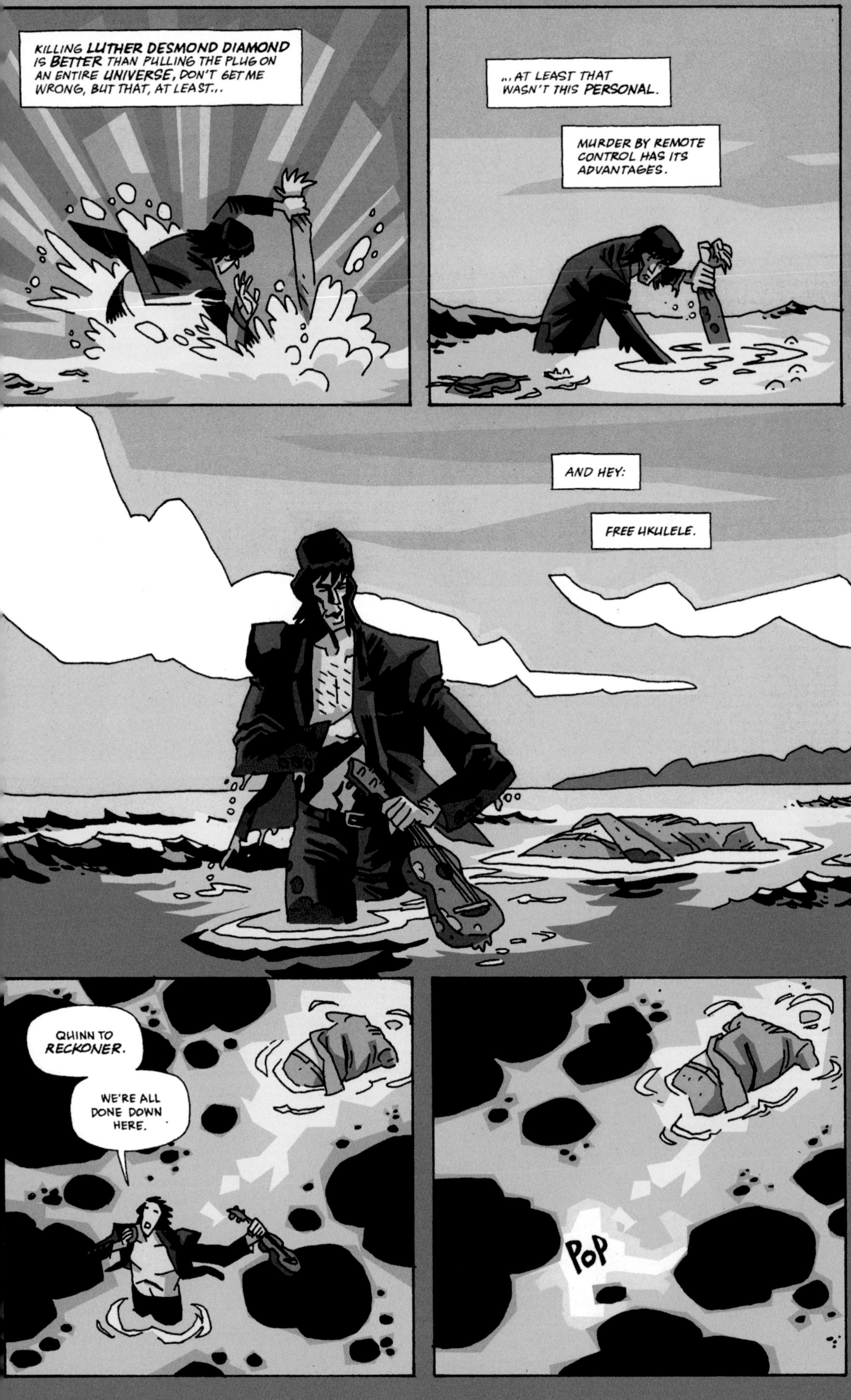
KILLING LUTHER DESMOND DIAMOND IS BETTER THAN PULLING THE PLUG ON AN ENTIRE UNIVERSE, DON'T GET ME WRONG, BUT THAT, AT LEAST...
...AT LEAST THAT WASN'T THIS PERSONAL.
MURDER BY REMOTE CONTROL HAS ITS ADVANTAGES.
AND HEY:
FREE UKULELE.
QUINN TO RECKONER.
WE'RE ALL DONE DOWN HERE.
POP

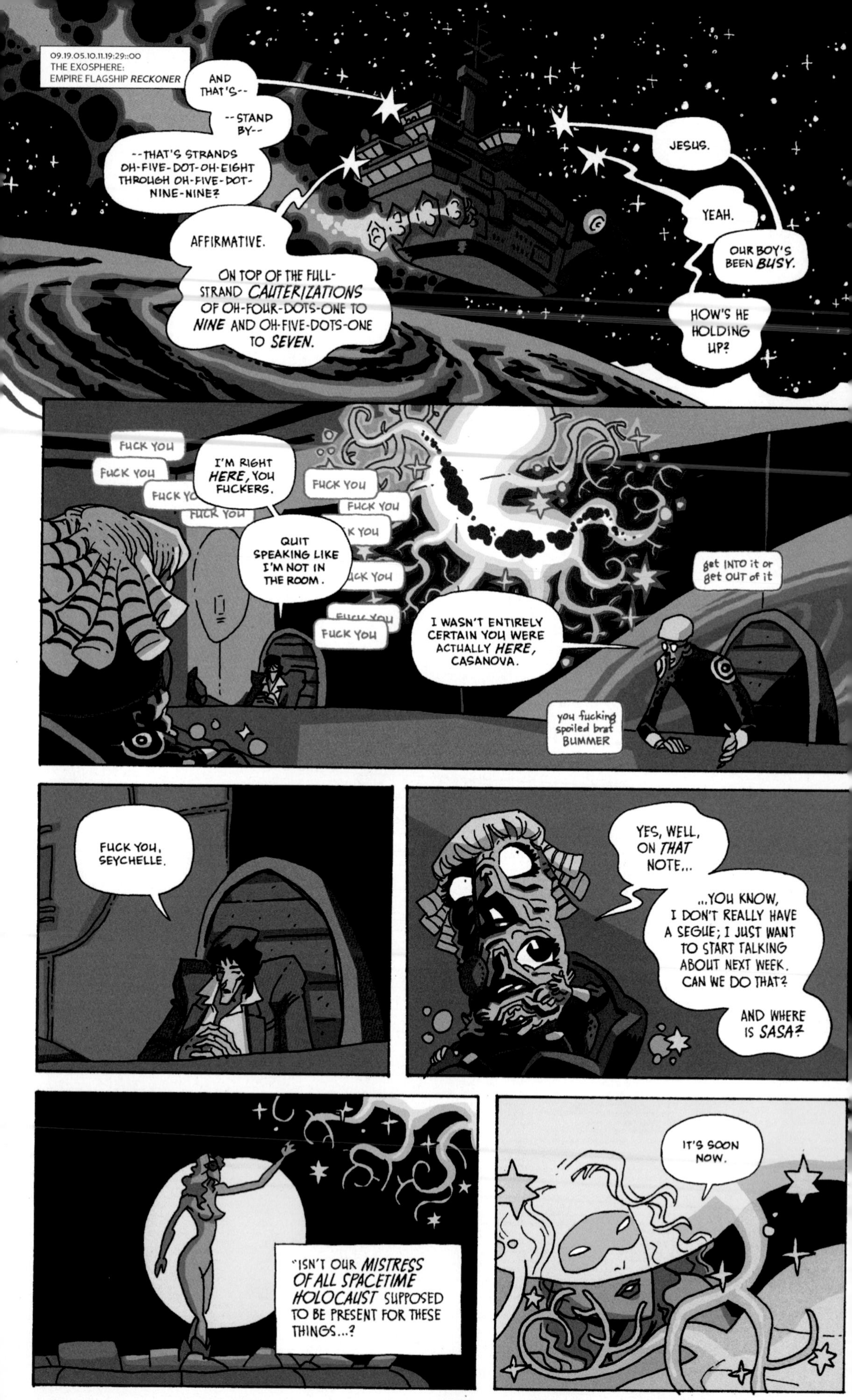
09.19.05.10.11.19:29::00
THE EXOSPHERE:
EMPIRE FLAGSHIP RECKONER
AND THAT'S--
--STAND BY--
--THAT'S STRANDS OH-FIVE-DOT-OH-EIGHT THROUGH OH-FIVE-DOT-NINE-NINE?
AFFIRMATIVE.
ON TOP OF THE FULL-STRAND CAUTERIZATIONS OF OH-FOUR-DOTS-ONE TO NINE AND OH-FIVE-DOTS-ONE TO SEVEN.
JESUS.
YEAH.
OUR BOY'S BEEN BUSY.
HOW'S HE HOLDING UP?
FUCK YOU
FUCK YOU
I'M RIGHT HERE, YOU FUCKERS.
FUCK YOU
FUCK YOU
QUIT SPEAKING LIKE I'M NOT IN THE ROOM.
FUCK YOU
FUCK YOU
get INTO it or get OUT of it
I WASN'T ENTIRELY CERTAIN YOU WERE ACTUALLY HERE, CASANOVA.
you fucking spoiled brat BUMMER
FUCK YOU, SEYCHELLE.
YES, WELL, ON THAT NOTE...
...YOU KNOW, I DON'T REALLY HAVE A SEGUE; I JUST WANT TO START TALKING ABOUT NEXT WEEK. CAN WE DO THAT?
AND WHERE IS SASA?
"ISN'T OUR MISTRESS OF ALL SPACETIME HOLOCAUST SUPPOSED TO BE PRESENT FOR THESE THINGS...?
IT'S SOON NOW.

WHAT?

WHAT?

WHAT?

SASA?

WHAT.

OH.

HEULLLLLLLO.

IIIIIIIIIIT'SSSSSOOOOOOONNNOW

BILLY PILGRIM'S PRECIOUS LITTLE *LIFE*.

HOW ARE YOU HOLDING UP?

FINE.

I'M FINE.

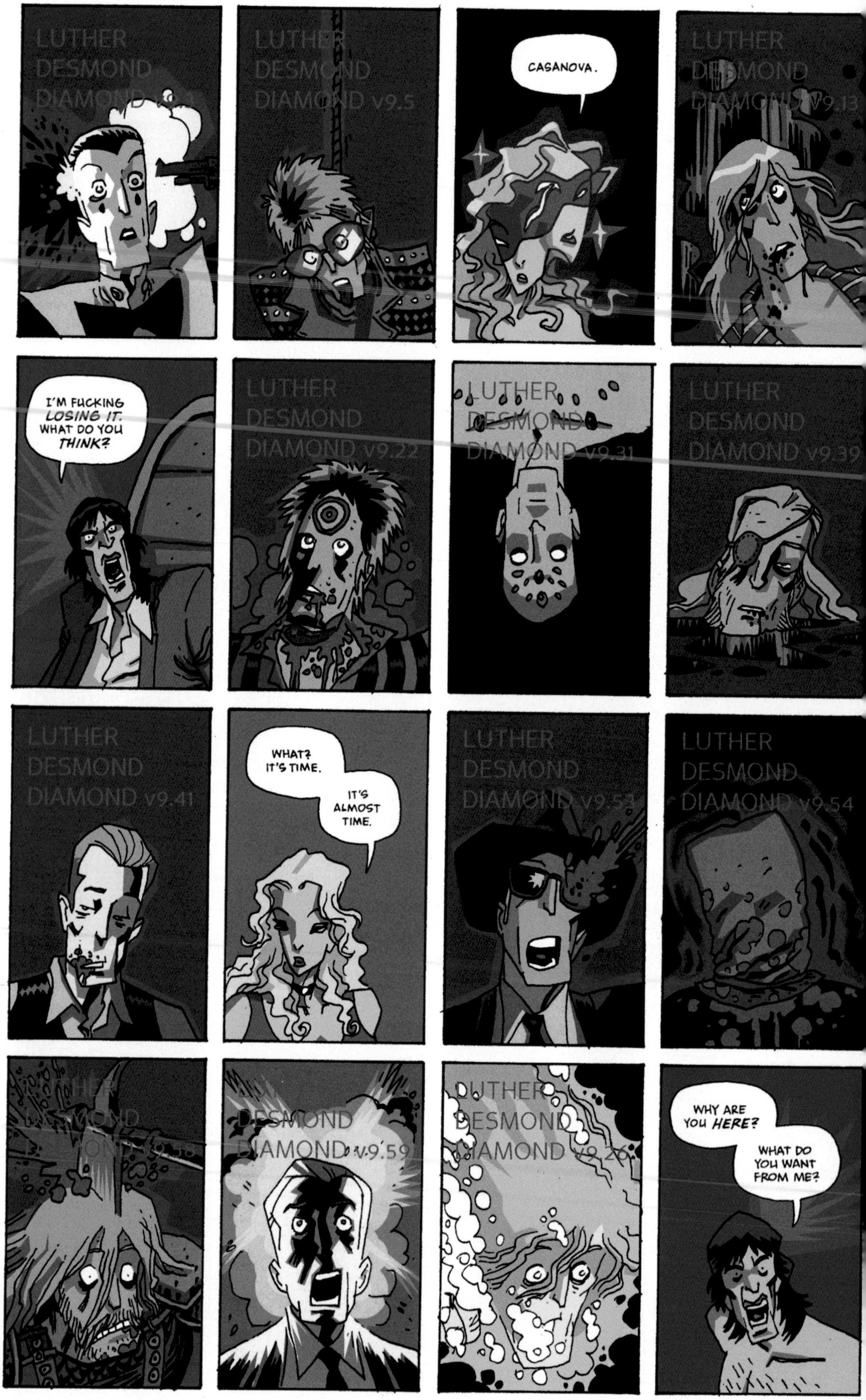
LUTHER DESMOND DIAMOND
LUTHER DESMOND DIAMOND v9.5
CASANOVA.
LUTHER DESMOND DIAMOND v9.13
I'M FUCKING *LOSING IT.* WHAT DO YOU *THINK?*
LUTHER DESMOND DIAMOND v9.22
LUTHER DESMOND DIAMOND v9.31
LUTHER DESMOND DIAMOND v9.39
LUTHER DESMOND DIAMOND v9.41
WHAT? IT'S TIME.
IT'S ALMOST TIME.
LUTHER DESMOND DIAMOND v9.53
LUTHER DESMOND DIAMOND v9.54
DESMOND DIAMOND v9.59
LUTHER DESMOND DIAMOND v9.26
WHY ARE YOU *HERE?*
WHAT DO YOU WANT FROM ME?

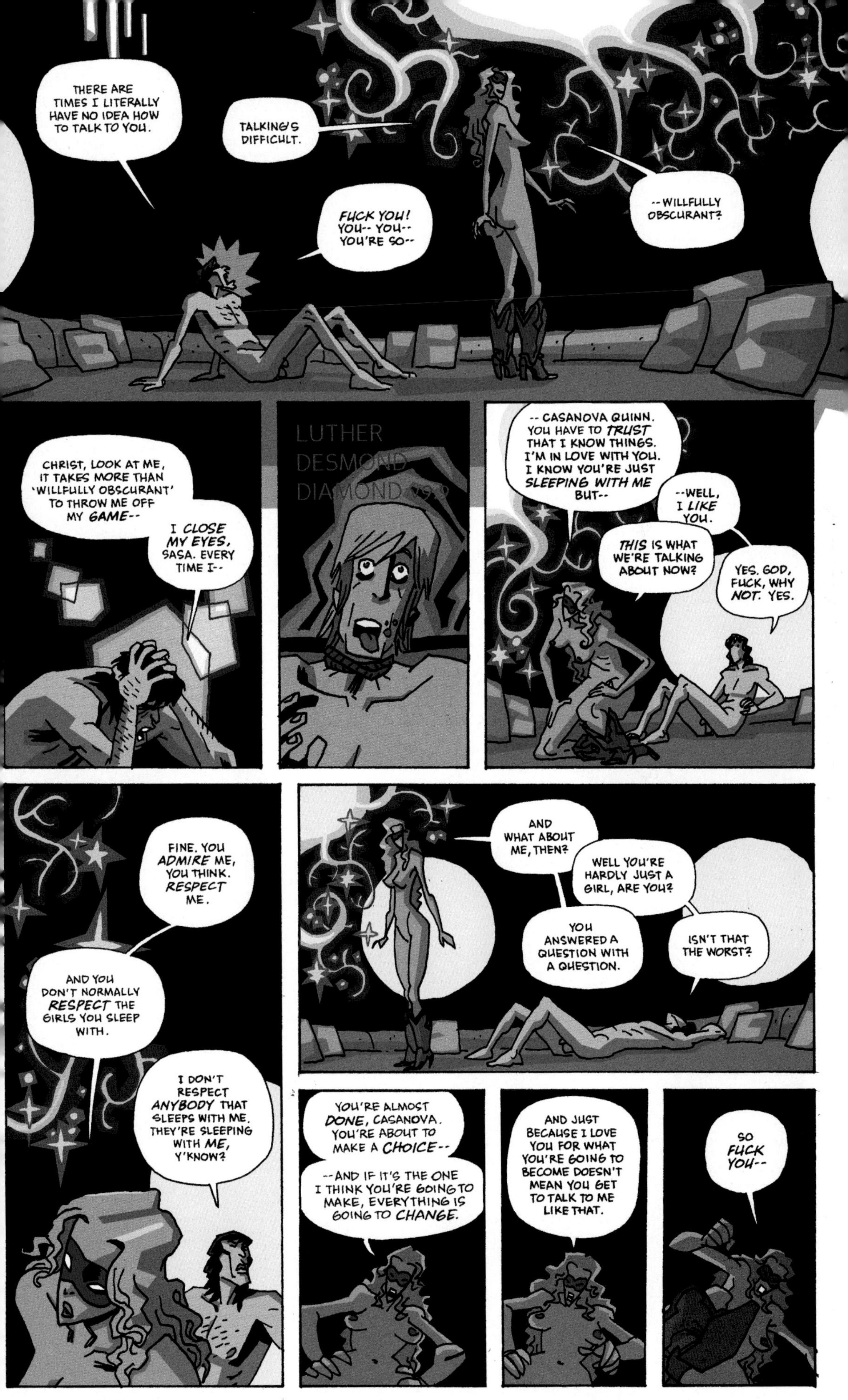
THERE ARE TIMES I LITERALLY HAVE NO IDEA HOW TO TALK TO YOU.
TALKING'S DIFFICULT.
FUCK YOU! YOU-- YOU-- YOU'RE SO--
--WILLFULLY OBSCURANT?
CHRIST, LOOK AT ME, IT TAKES MORE THAN 'WILLFULLY OBSCURANT' TO THROW ME OFF MY GAME--
I CLOSE MY EYES, SASA. EVERY TIME I--
-- CASANOVA QUINN. YOU HAVE TO TRUST THAT I KNOW THINGS. I'M IN LOVE WITH YOU. I KNOW YOU'RE JUST SLEEPING WITH ME BUT--
--WELL, I LIKE YOU.
THIS IS WHAT WE'RE TALKING ABOUT NOW?
YES. GOD, FUCK, WHY NOT. YES.
FINE. YOU ADMIRE ME, YOU THINK. RESPECT ME.
AND YOU DON'T NORMALLY RESPECT THE GIRLS YOU SLEEP WITH.
I DON'T RESPECT ANYBODY THAT SLEEPS WITH ME. THEY'RE SLEEPING WITH ME, Y'KNOW?
AND WHAT ABOUT ME, THEN?
WELL YOU'RE HARDLY JUST A GIRL, ARE YOU?
YOU ANSWERED A QUESTION WITH A QUESTION.
ISN'T THAT THE WORST?
YOU'RE ALMOST DONE, CASANOVA. YOU'RE ABOUT TO MAKE A CHOICE--
--AND IF IT'S THE ONE I THINK YOU'RE GOING TO MAKE, EVERYTHING IS GOING TO CHANGE.
AND JUST BECAUSE I LOVE YOU FOR WHAT YOU'RE GOING TO BECOME DOESN'T MEAN YOU GET TO TALK TO ME LIKE THAT.
SO FUCK YOU--

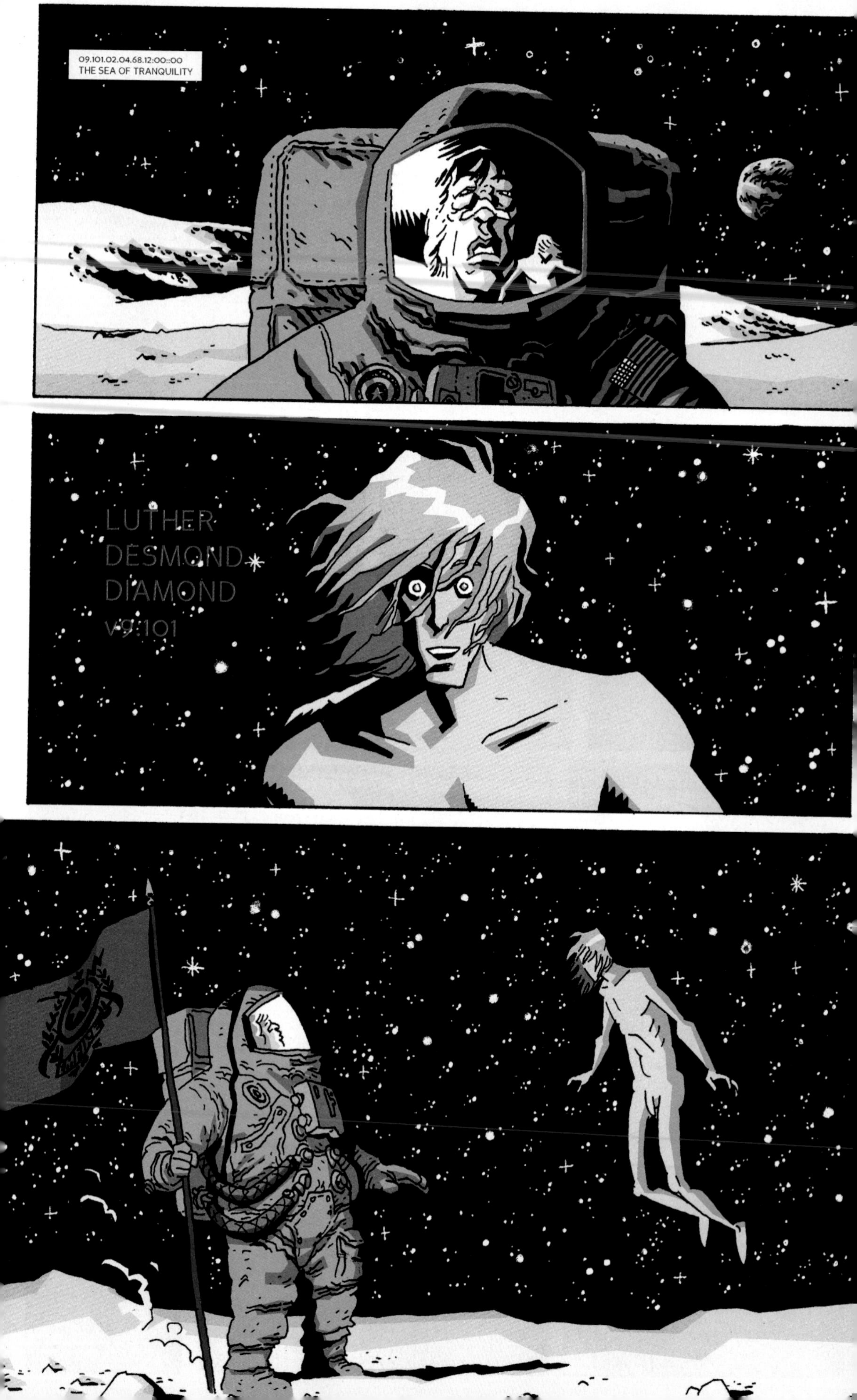
09.101.02.04.68.12:00::00
THE SEA OF TRANQUILITY
LUTHER
DESMOND
DIAMOND
V9:101

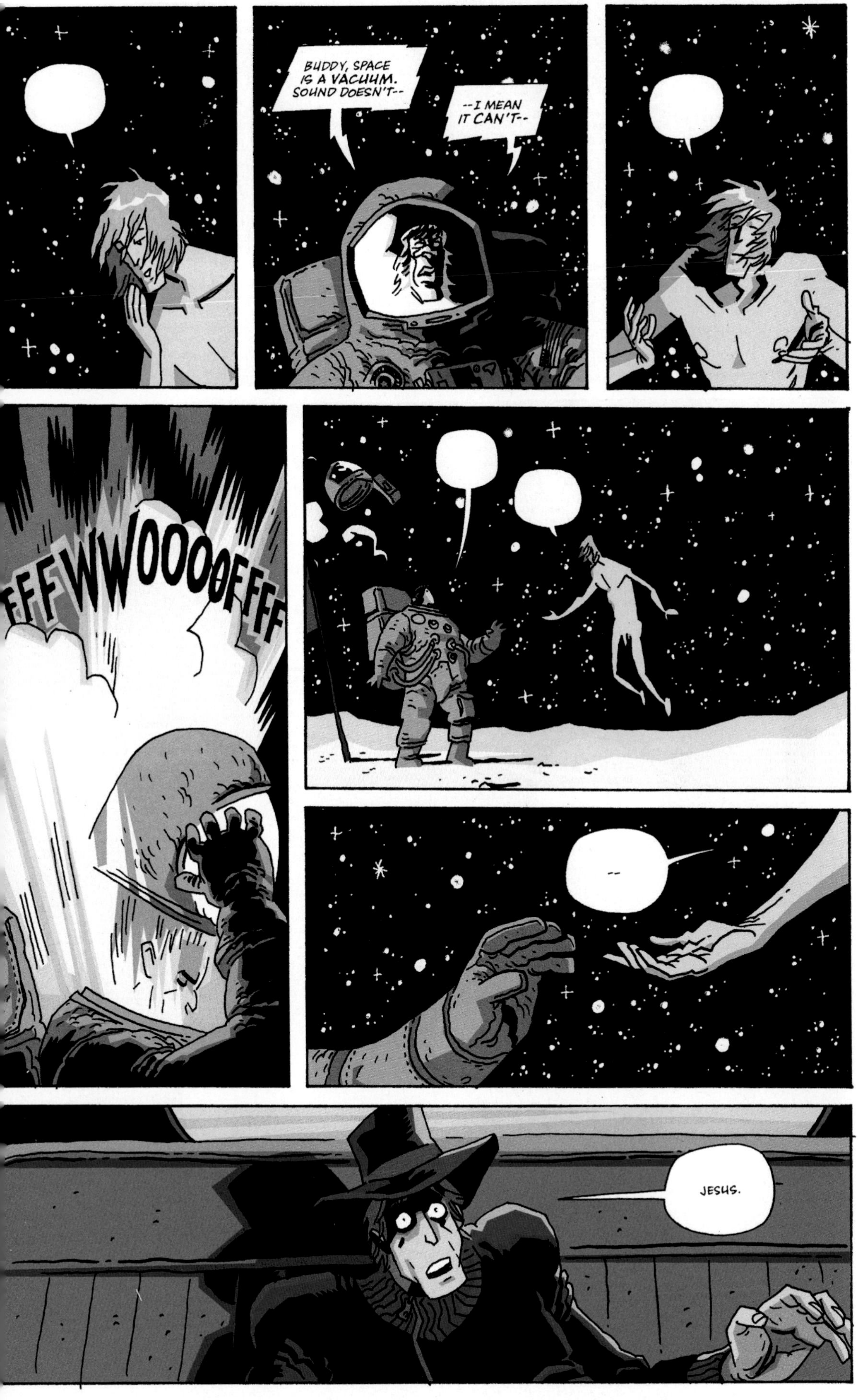
BUDDY, SPACE IS A VACUUM. SOUND DOESN'T--
--I MEAN IT CAN'T--
FFFWWOOOOFFFF
--
JESUS.

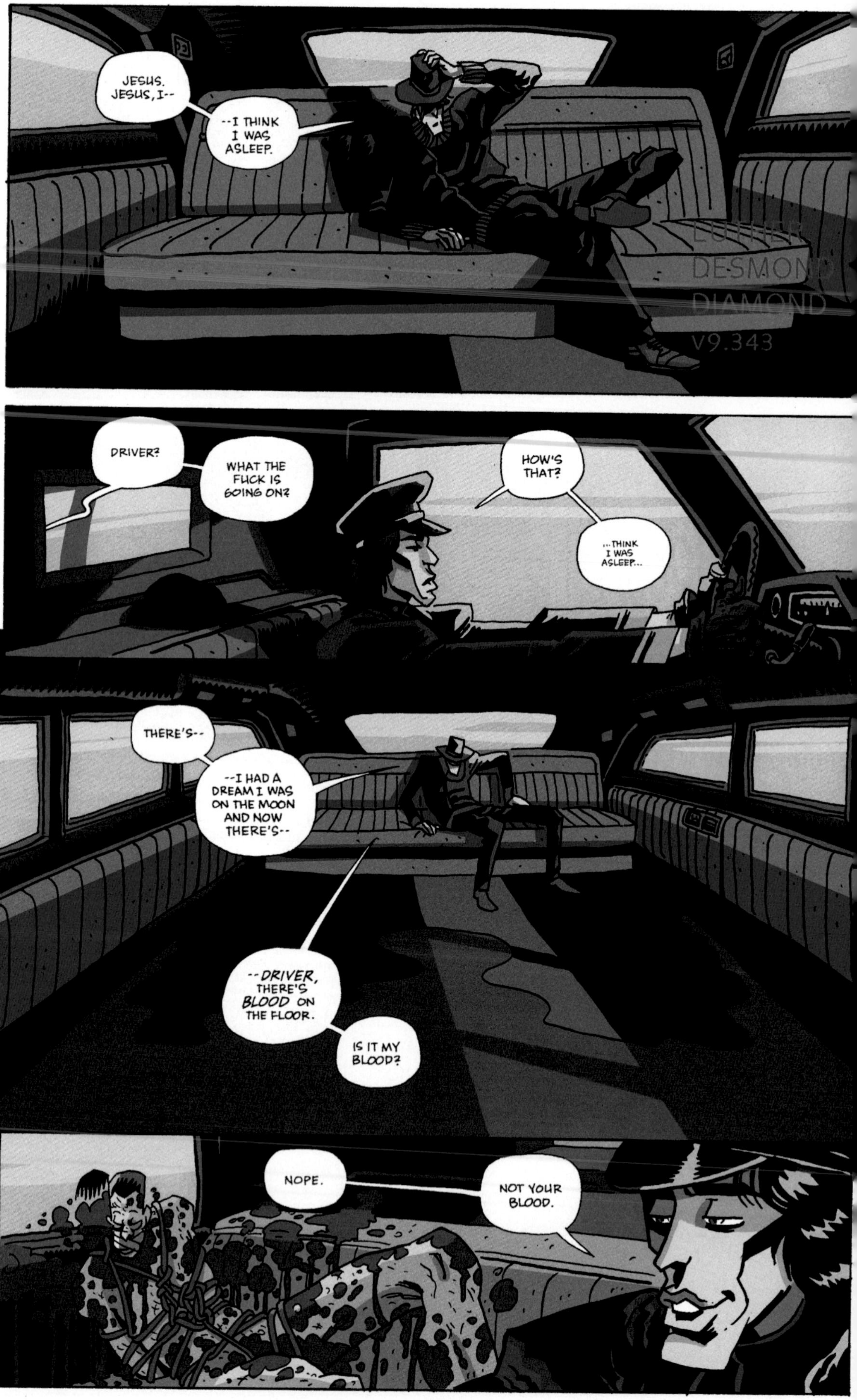
JESUS. JESUS, I--
--I THINK I WAS ASLEEP.
LUTHER
DESMOND
DIAMOND
V9.343
DRIVER?
WHAT THE FUCK IS GOING ON?
HOW'S THAT?
...THINK I WAS ASLEEP...
THERE'S--
--I HAD A DREAM I WAS ON THE MOON AND NOW THERE'S--
--DRIVER, THERE'S BLOOD ON THE FLOOR.
IS IT MY BLOOD?
NOPE.
NOT YOUR BLOOD.

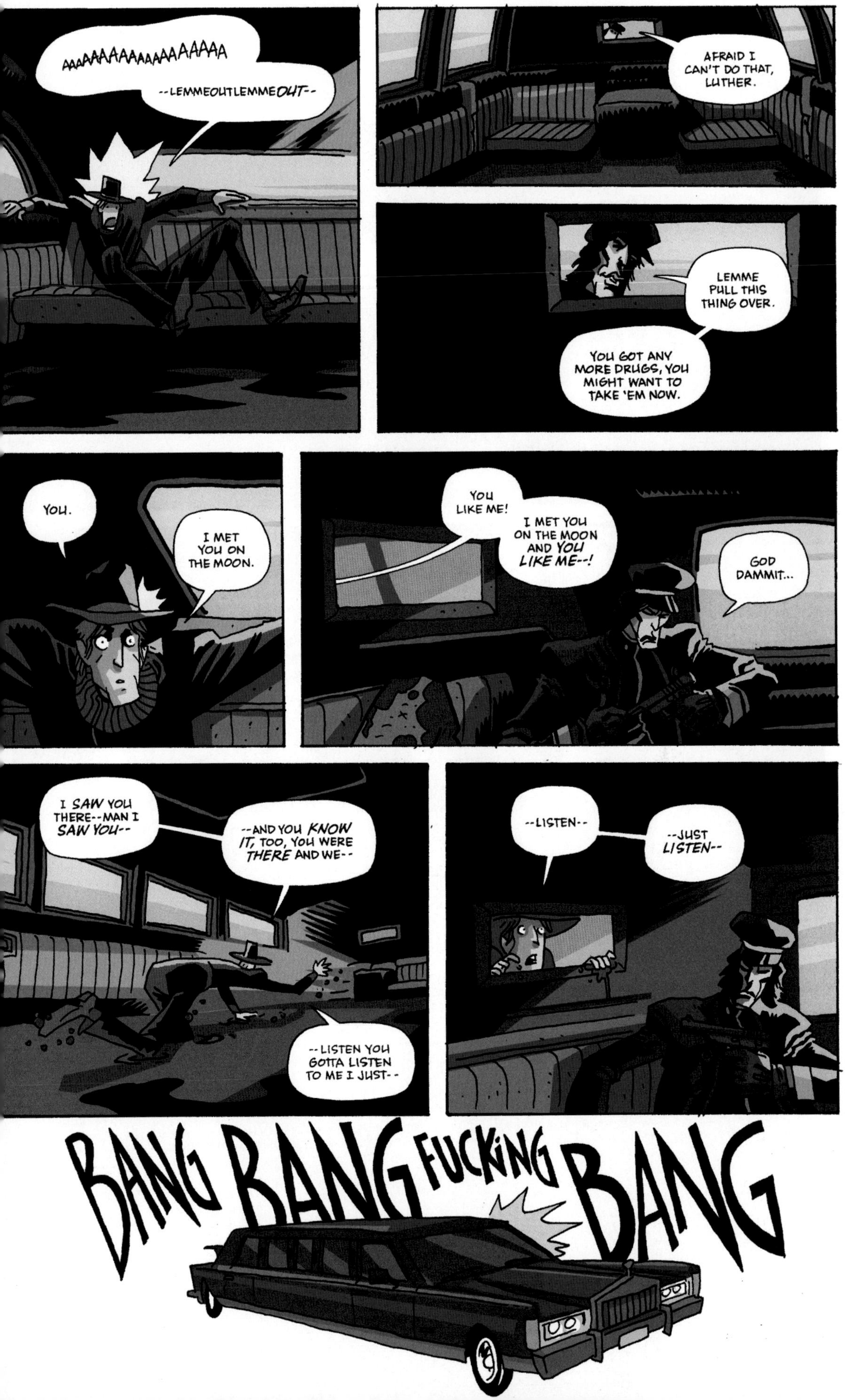
AAAAAAAAAAAAAAAAAA
--LEMMEOUTLEMMEOUT--
AFRAID I CAN'T DO THAT, LUTHER.
LEMME PULL THIS THING OVER.
YOU GOT ANY MORE DRUGS, YOU MIGHT WANT TO TAKE 'EM NOW.
YOU.
I MET YOU ON THE MOON.
YOU LIKE ME!
I MET YOU ON THE MOON AND YOU LIKE ME--!
GOD DAMMIT...
I SAW YOU THERE--MAN I SAW YOU--
--AND YOU KNOW IT, TOO, YOU WERE THERE AND WE--
--LISTEN YOU GOTTA LISTEN TO ME I JUST--
--LISTEN--
--JUST LISTEN--
BANG BANG FUCKING BANG

5. MAN ON THE MOON

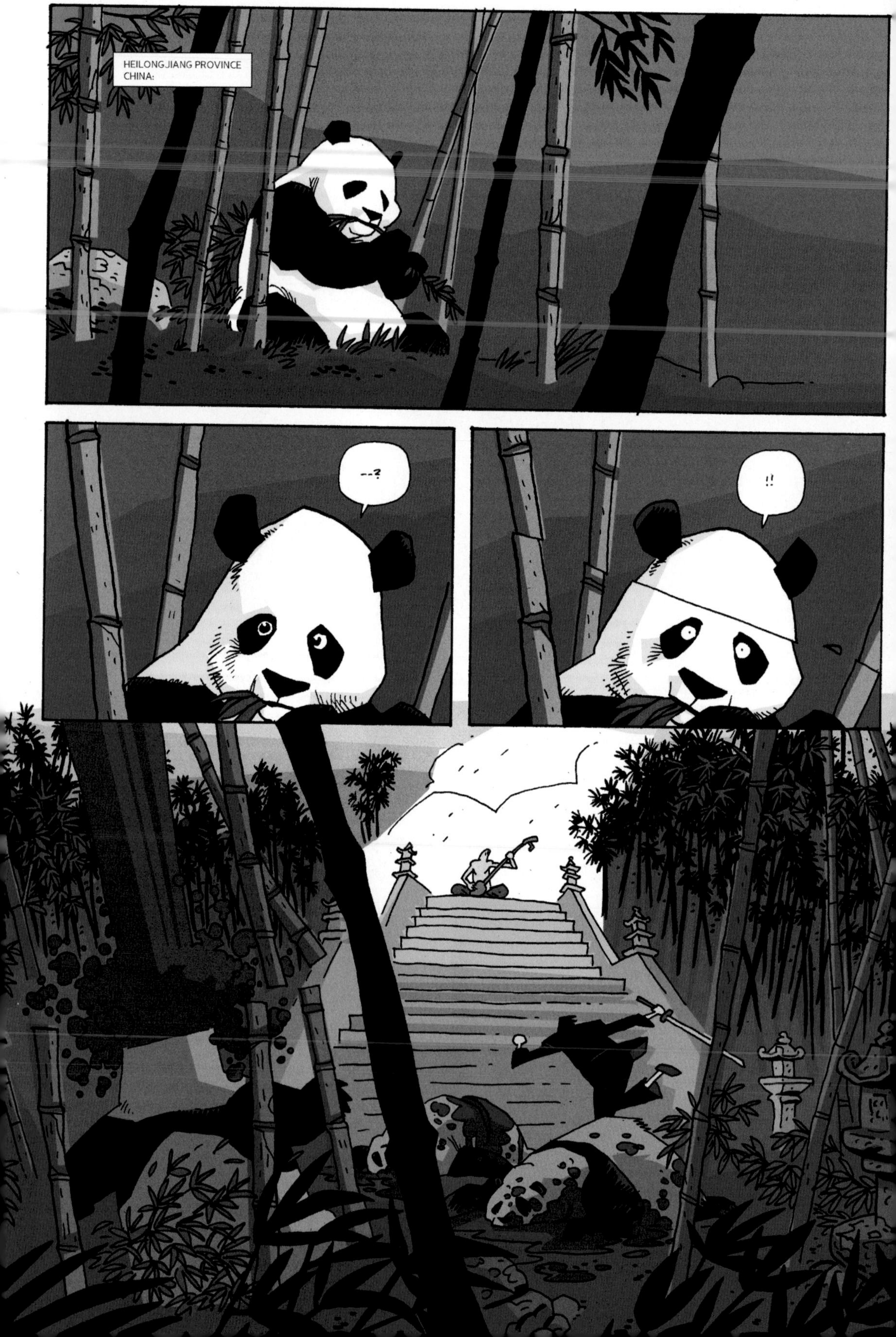
HEILONGJIANG PROVINCE
CHINA:
--?
!!

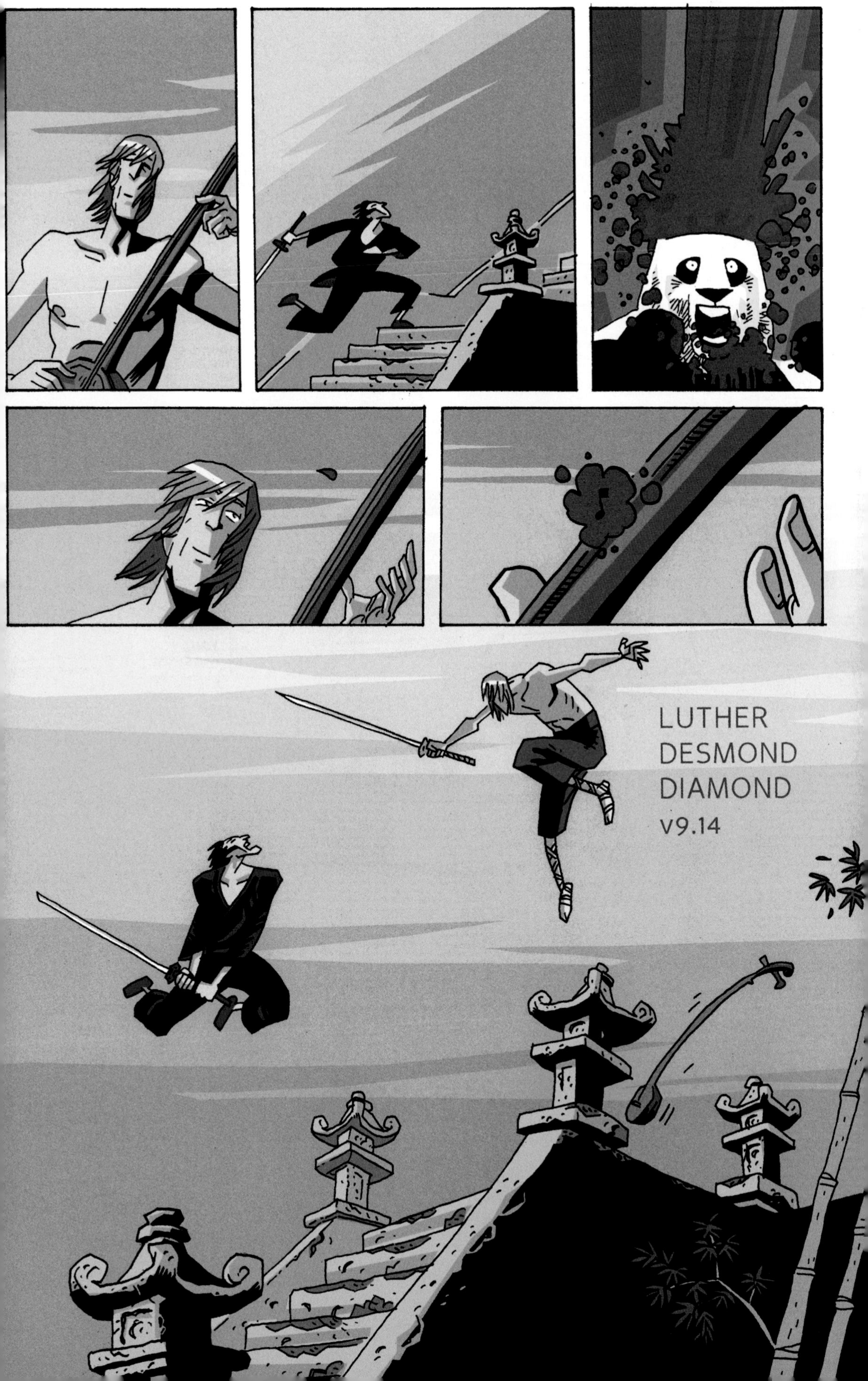
LUTHER
DESMOND
DIAMOND
v9.14

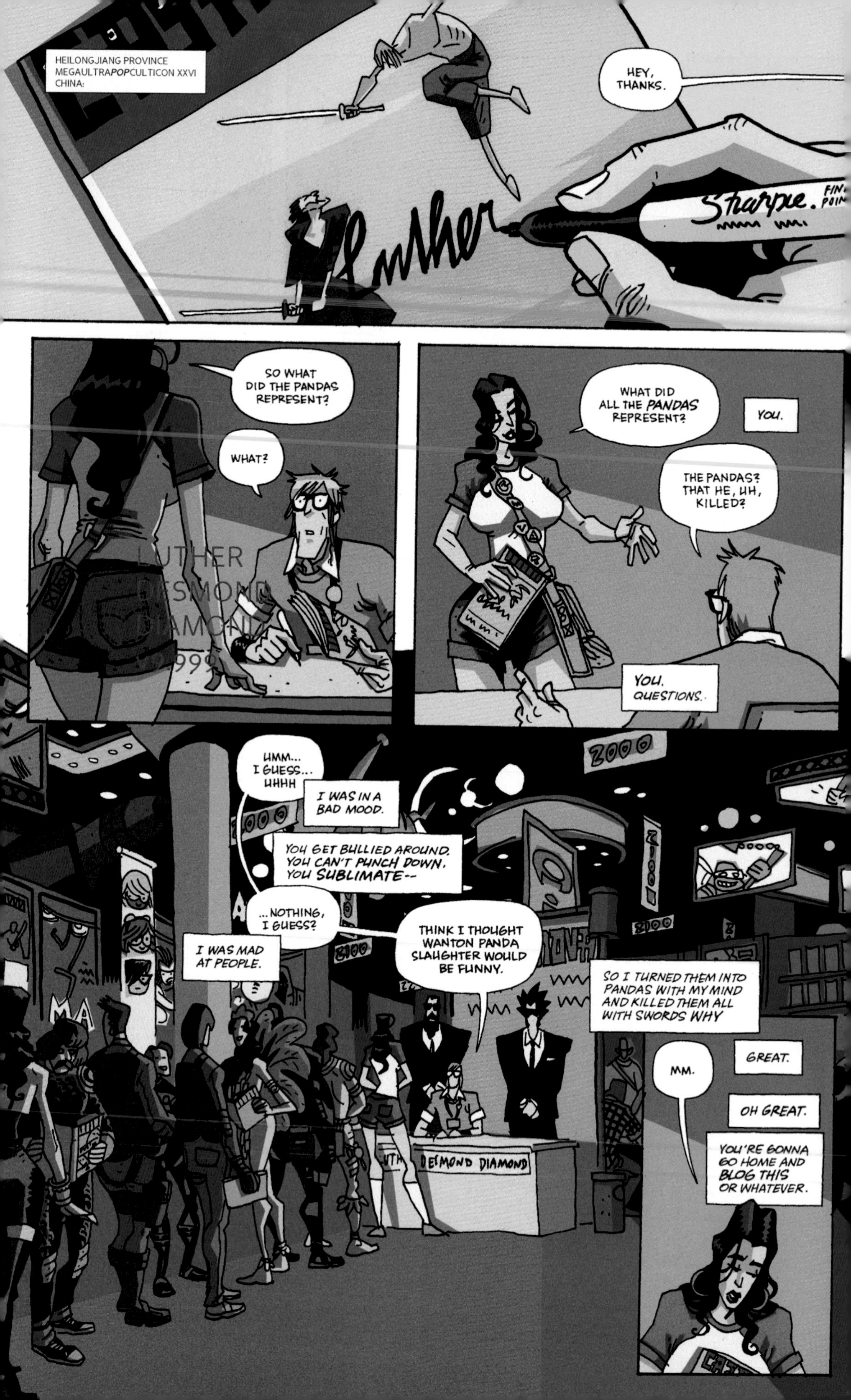
HEILONGJIANG PROVINCE
MEGAULTRAPOPCULTICON XXVI
CHINA:
HEY, THANKS.
Luther
Sharpie.
SO WHAT DID THE PANDAS REPRESENT?
WHAT?
WHAT DID ALL THE PANDAS REPRESENT?
YOU.
THE PANDAS? THAT HE, UH, KILLED?
YOU. QUESTIONS.
UMM... I GUESS... UHHH
I WAS IN A BAD MOOD.
YOU GET BULLIED AROUND. YOU CAN'T PUNCH DOWN. YOU SUBLIMATE--
...NOTHING, I GUESS?
I WAS MAD AT PEOPLE.
THINK I THOUGHT WANTON PANDA SLAUGHTER WOULD BE FUNNY.
SO I TURNED THEM INTO PANDAS WITH MY MIND AND KILLED THEM ALL WITH SWORDS WHY
DESMOND DIAMOND
MM.
GREAT.
OH GREAT.
YOU'RE GONNA GO HOME AND BLOG THIS OR WHATEVER.

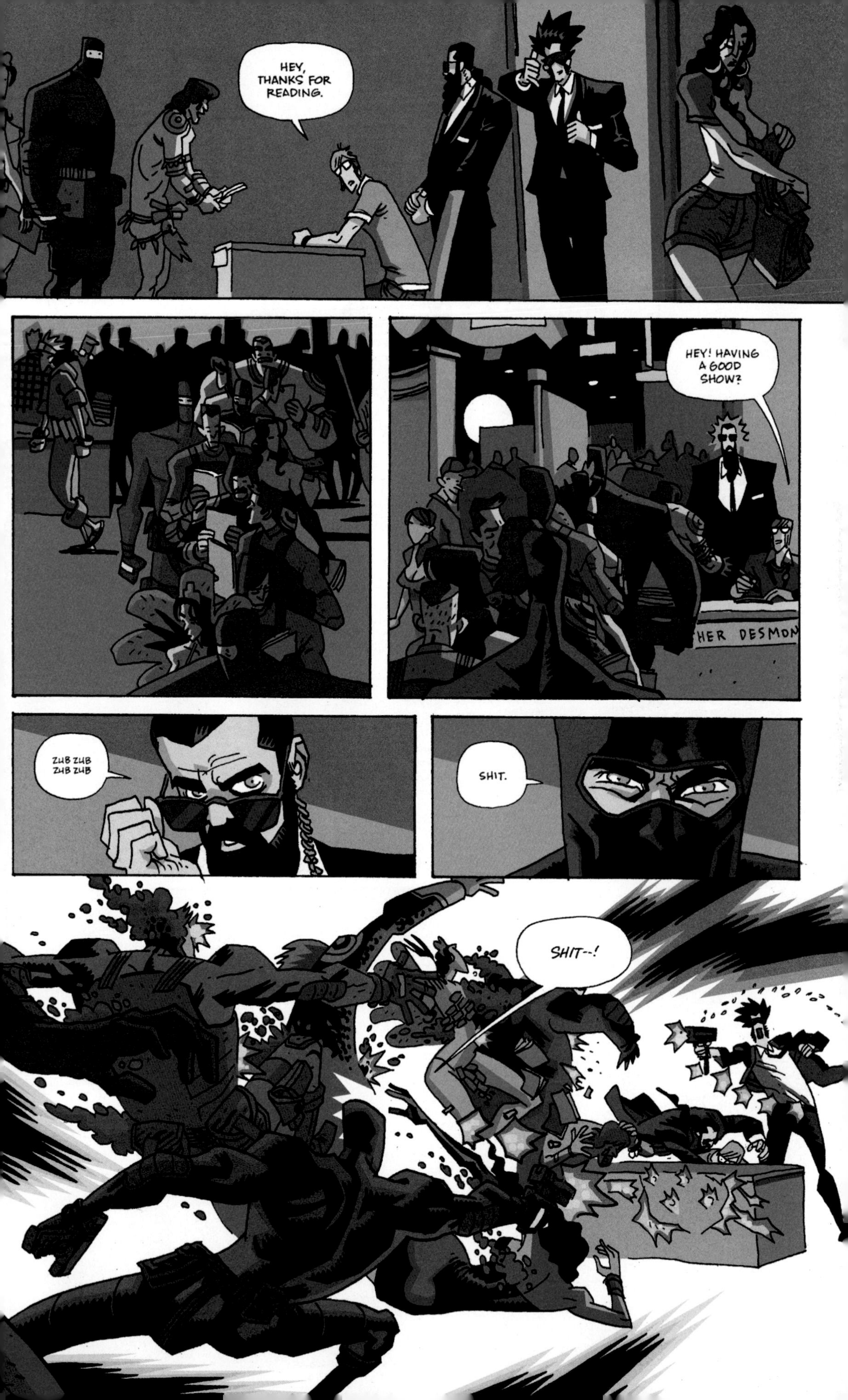
HEY, THANKS FOR READING.
HEY! HAVING A GOOD SHOW?
HER DESMON
ZUB ZUB ZUB ZUB
SHIT.
SHIT--!

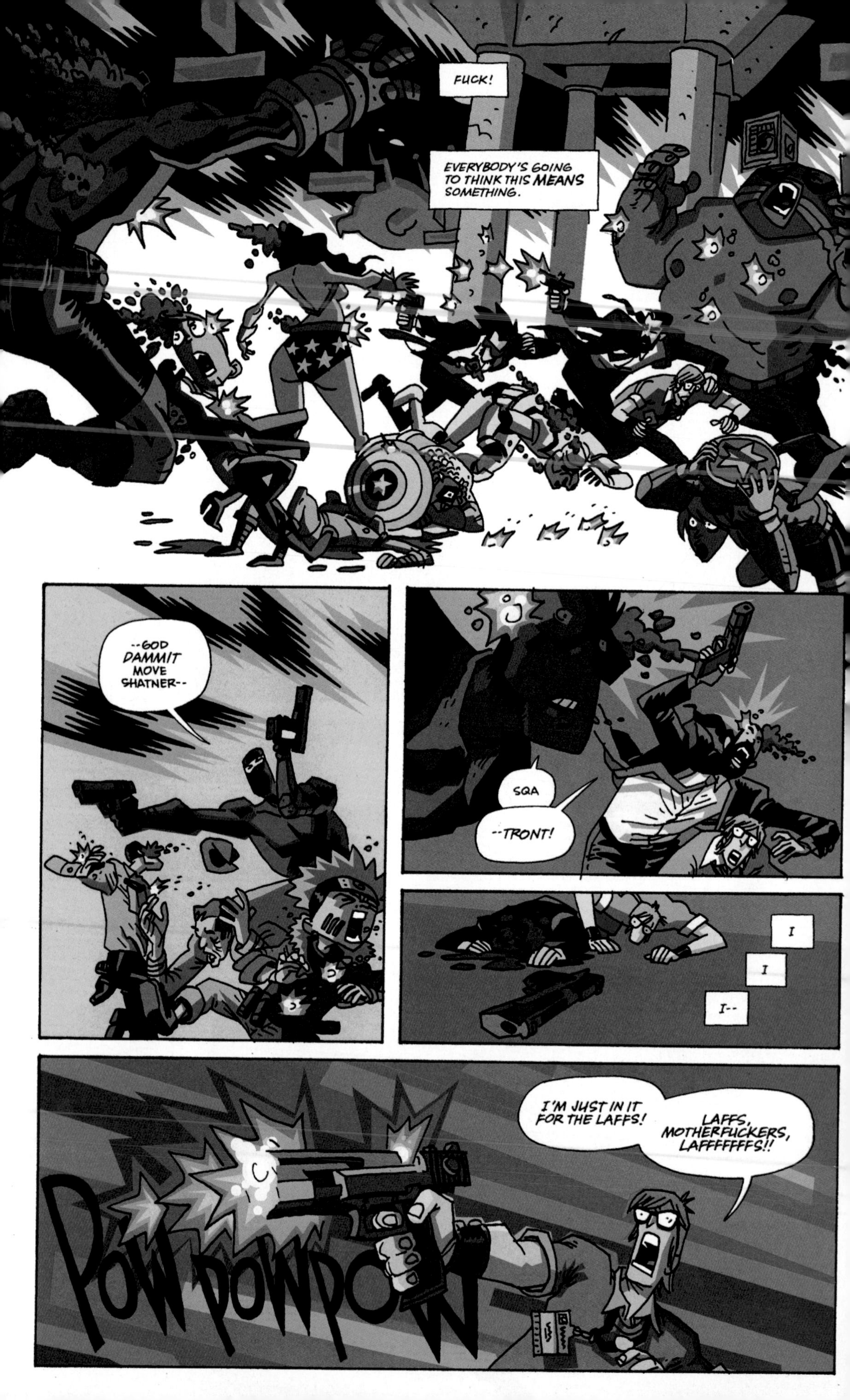
FUCK!
EVERYBODY'S GOING TO THINK THIS MEANS SOMETHING.
--GOD DAMMIT MOVE SHATNER--
SQA
--TRONT!
I
I
I--
I'M JUST IN IT FOR THE LAFFS!
LAFFS, MOTHERFUCKERS, LAFFFFFFFS!!
POW POWPOW

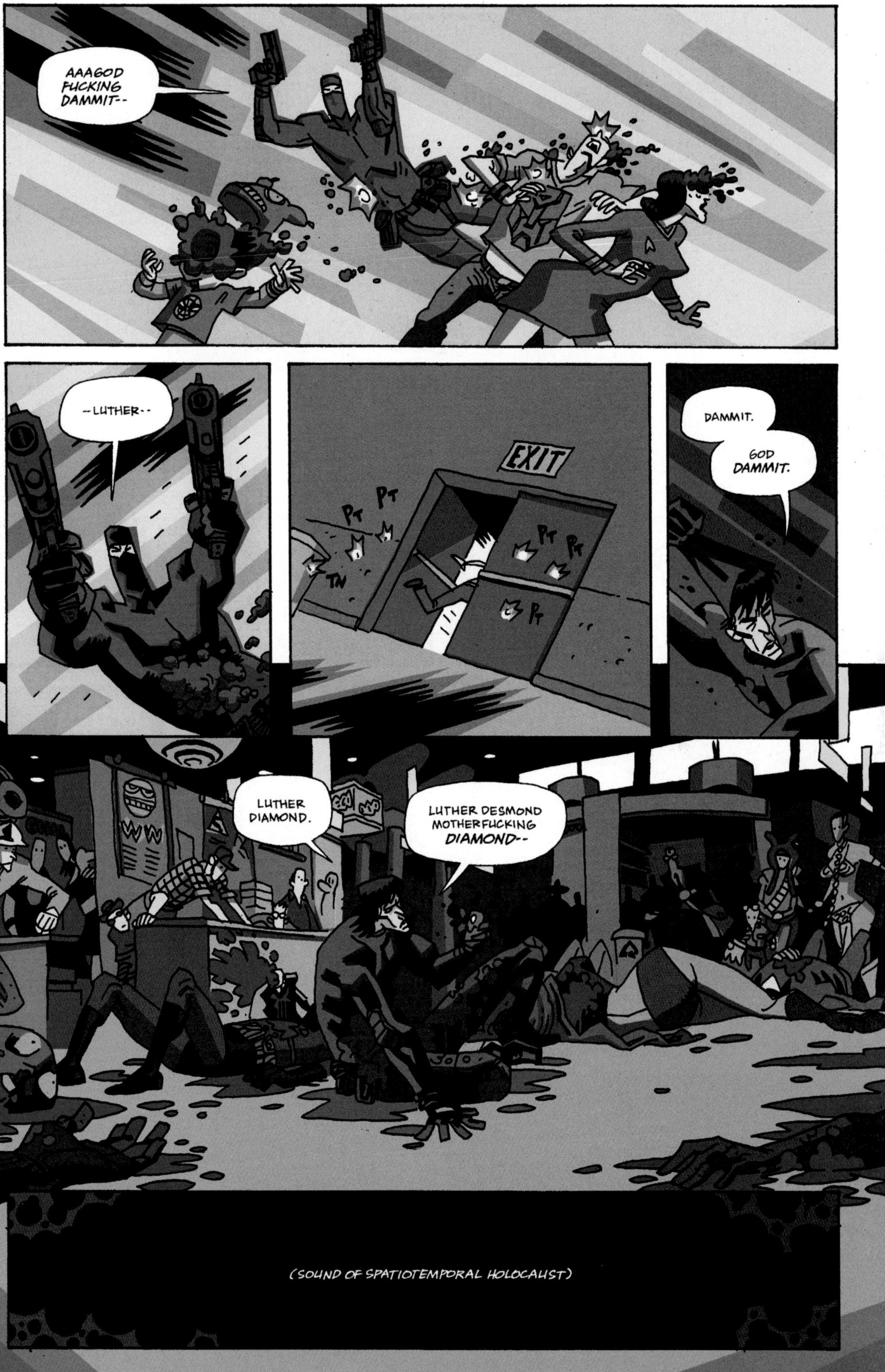
AAAGOD FUCKING DAMMIT--
--LUTHER--
EXIT
Pt
Pt
TN
Pt
Pt
Pt
DAMMIT.
GOD DAMMIT.
LUTHER DIAMOND.
LUTHER DESMOND MOTHERFUCKING DIAMOND--
(SOUND OF SPATIOTEMPORAL HOLOCAUST)

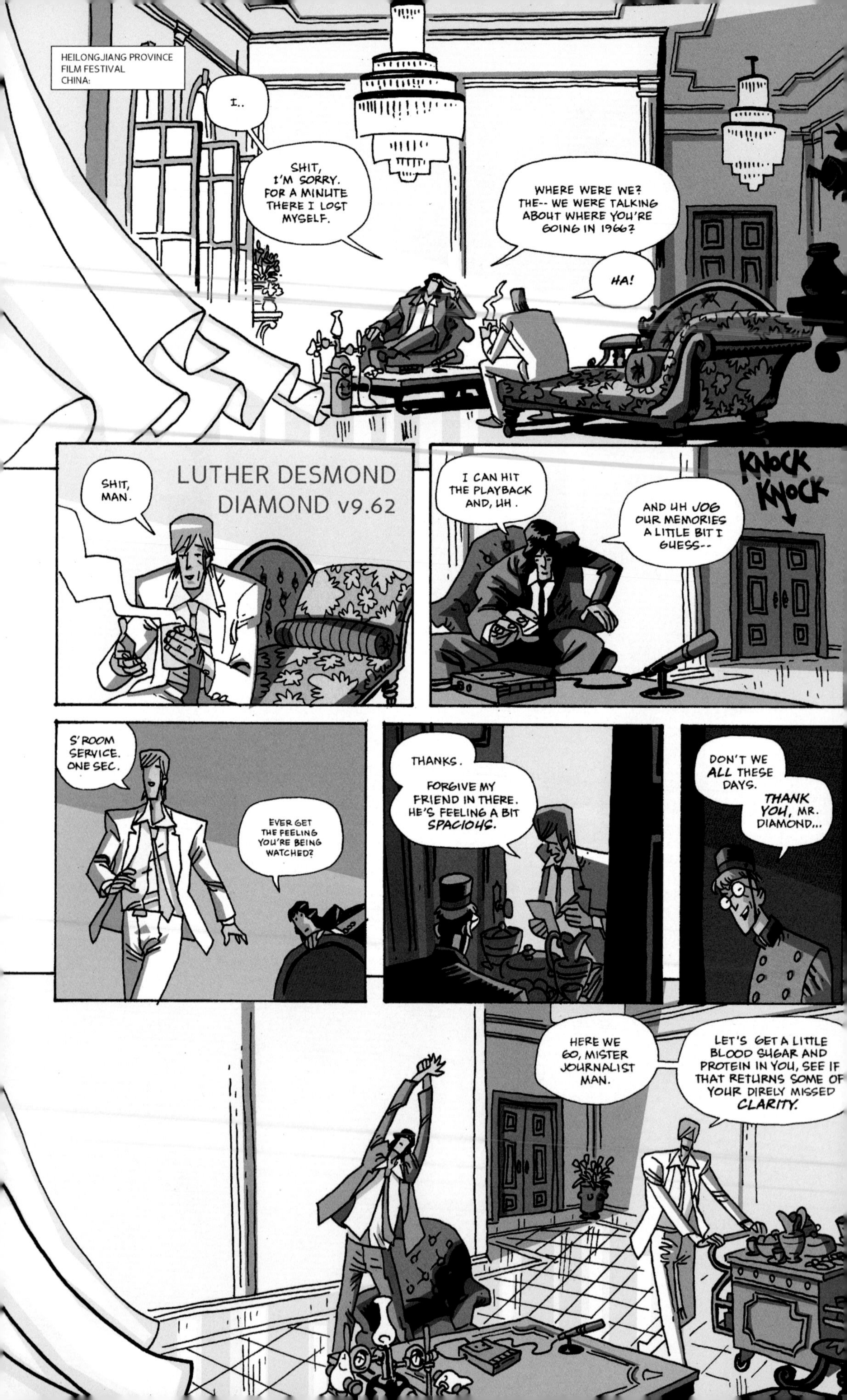
HEILONGJIANG PROVINCE FILM FESTIVAL CHINA:
I..
SHIT, I'M SORRY. FOR A MINUTE THERE I LOST MYSELF.
WHERE WERE WE? THE-- WE WERE TALKING ABOUT WHERE YOU'RE GOING IN 1966?
HA!
SHIT, MAN.
LUTHER DESMOND DIAMOND v9.62
I CAN HIT THE PLAYBACK AND, UH.
AND UH JOG OUR MEMORIES A LITTLE BIT I GUESS--
KNOCK KNOCK
S'ROOM SERVICE. ONE SEC.
EVER GET THE FEELING YOU'RE BEING WATCHED?
THANKS.
FORGIVE MY FRIEND IN THERE. HE'S FEELING A BIT SPACIOUS.
DON'T WE ALL THESE DAYS.
THANK YOU, MR. DIAMOND...
HERE WE GO, MISTER JOURNALIST MAN.
LET'S GET A LITTLE BLOOD SUGAR AND PROTEIN IN YOU, SEE IF THAT RETURNS SOME OF YOUR DIRELY MISSED CLARITY.

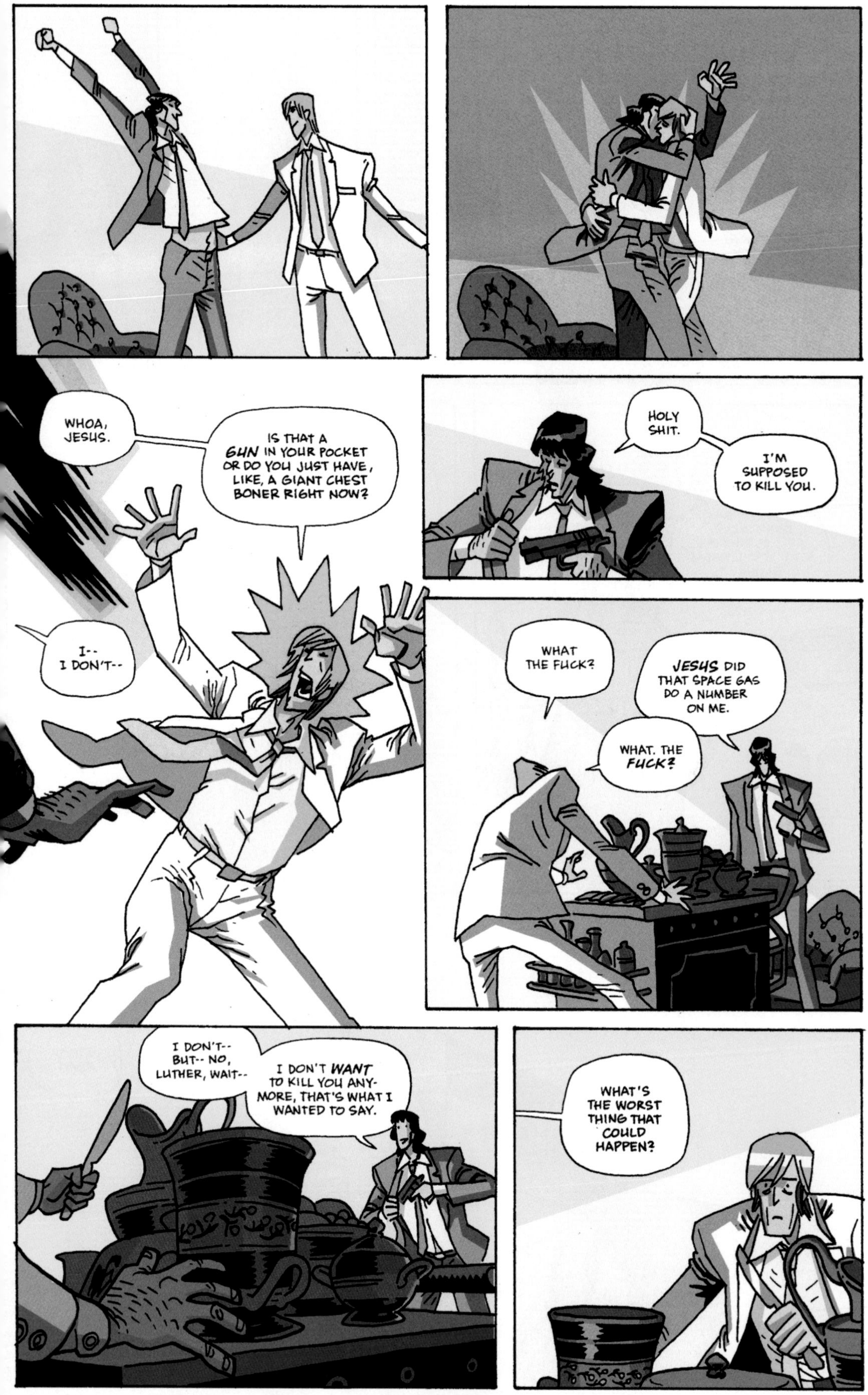
WHOA, JESUS.
IS THAT A GUN IN YOUR POCKET OR DO YOU JUST HAVE, LIKE, A GIANT CHEST BONER RIGHT NOW?
I-- I DON'T--
HOLY SHIT.
I'M SUPPOSED TO KILL YOU.
WHAT THE FUCK?
JESUS DID THAT SPACE GAS DO A NUMBER ON ME.
WHAT. THE FUCK?
I DON'T-- BUT-- NO, LUTHER, WAIT--
I DON'T WANT TO KILL YOU ANY-MORE, THAT'S WHAT I WANTED TO SAY.
WHAT'S THE WORST THING THAT COULD HAPPEN?

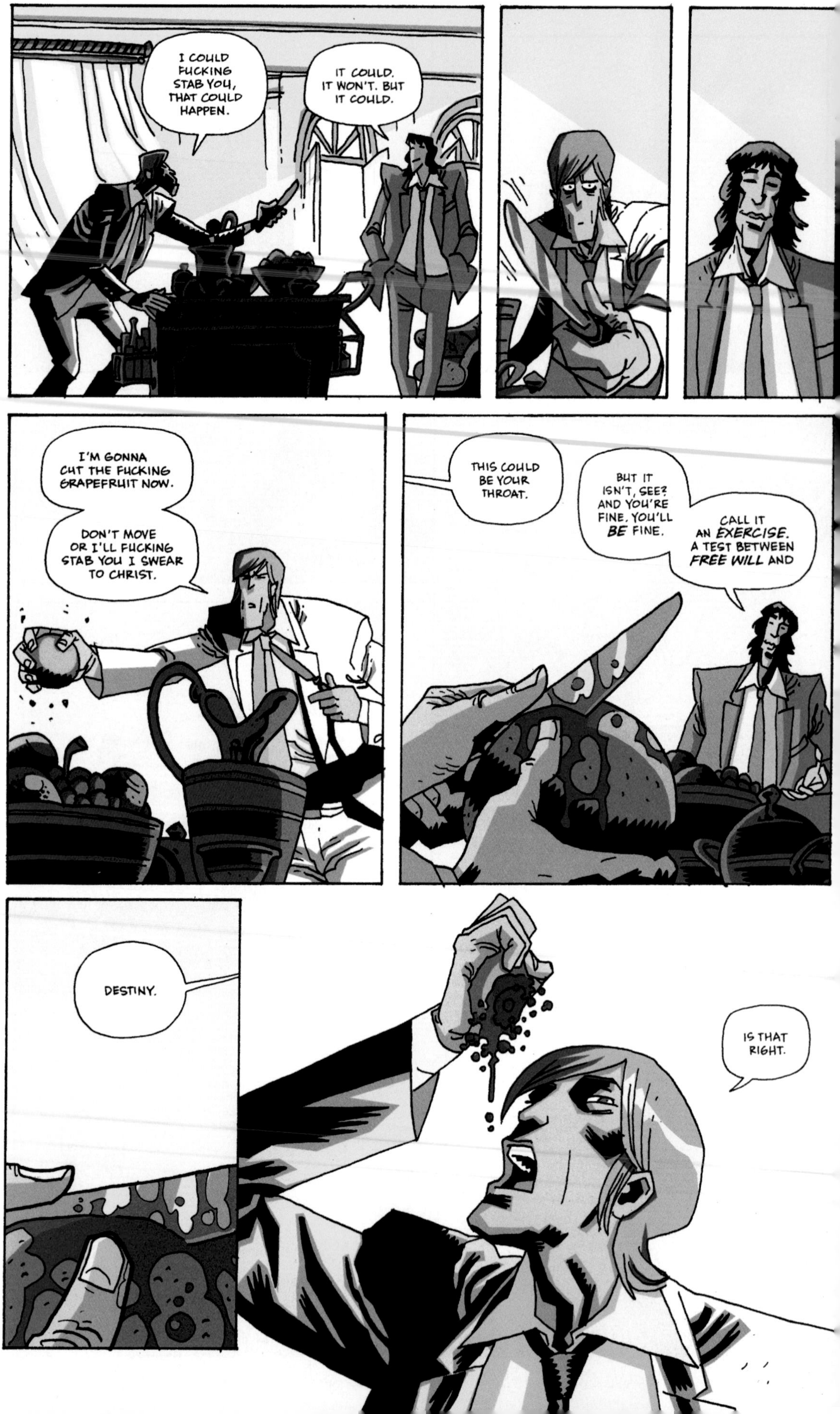
I COULD FUCKING STAB YOU, THAT COULD HAPPEN.
IT COULD. IT WON'T. BUT IT COULD.
I'M GONNA CUT THE FUCKING GRAPEFRUIT NOW.
DON'T MOVE OR I'LL FUCKING STAB YOU I SWEAR TO CHRIST.
THIS COULD BE YOUR THROAT.
BUT IT ISN'T, SEE? AND YOU'RE FINE. YOU'LL *BE* FINE.
CALL IT AN *EXERCISE.* A TEST BETWEEN *FREE WILL* AND
DESTINY.
IS THAT RIGHT.

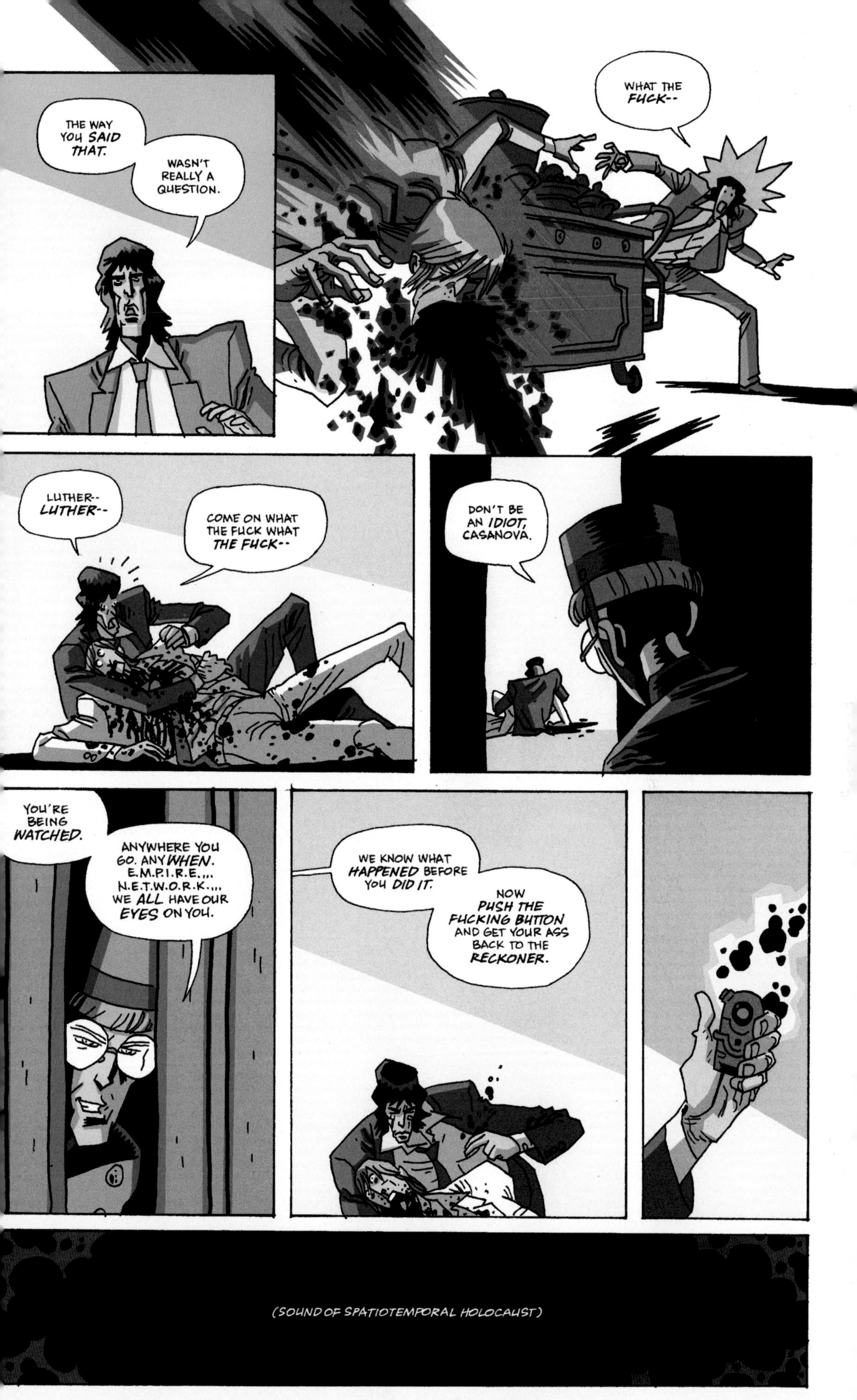
THE WAY YOU SAID THAT.
WASN'T REALLY A QUESTION.
WHAT THE FUCK--
LUTHER-- LUTHER--
COME ON WHAT THE FUCK WHAT THE FUCK--
DON'T BE AN IDIOT, CASANOVA.
YOU'RE BEING WATCHED.
ANYWHERE YOU GO. ANY WHEN. E.M.P.I.R.E.,... N.E.T.W.O.R.K.,... WE ALL HAVE OUR EYES ON YOU.
WE KNOW WHAT HAPPENED BEFORE YOU DID IT.
NOW PUSH THE FUCKING BUTTON AND GET YOUR ASS BACK TO THE RECKONER.
(SOUND OF SPATIOTEMPORAL HOLOCAUST)

6. NIGHT IS OVER

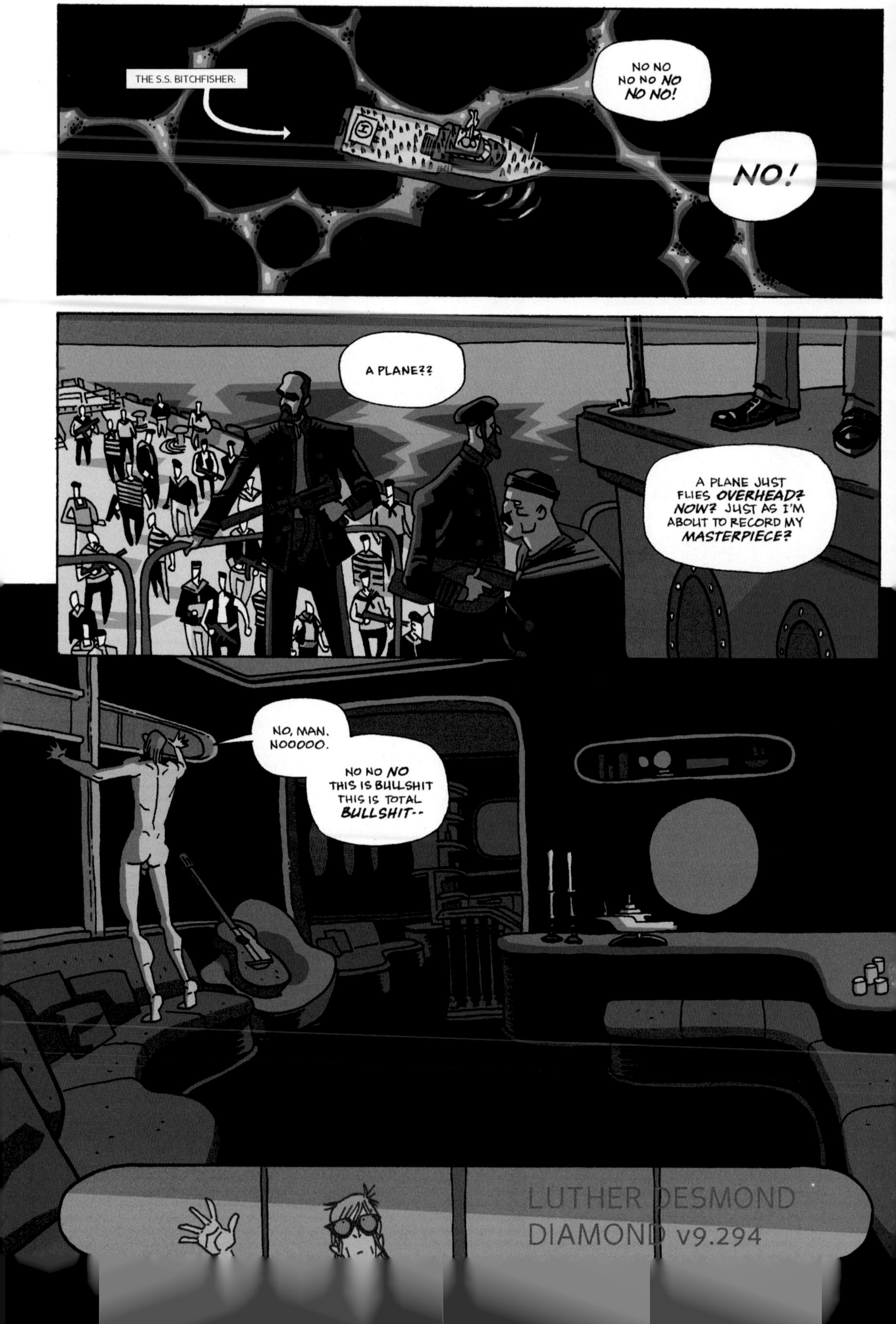
THE S.S. BITCHFISHER:
NO NO
NO NO NO
NO NO!
NO!
A PLANE??
A PLANE JUST FLIES OVERHEAD? NOW? JUST AS I'M ABOUT TO RECORD MY MASTERPIECE?
NO, MAN. NOOOOO.
NO NO NO THIS IS BULLSHIT THIS IS TOTAL BULLSHIT--
LUTHER DESMOND DIAMOND v9.294

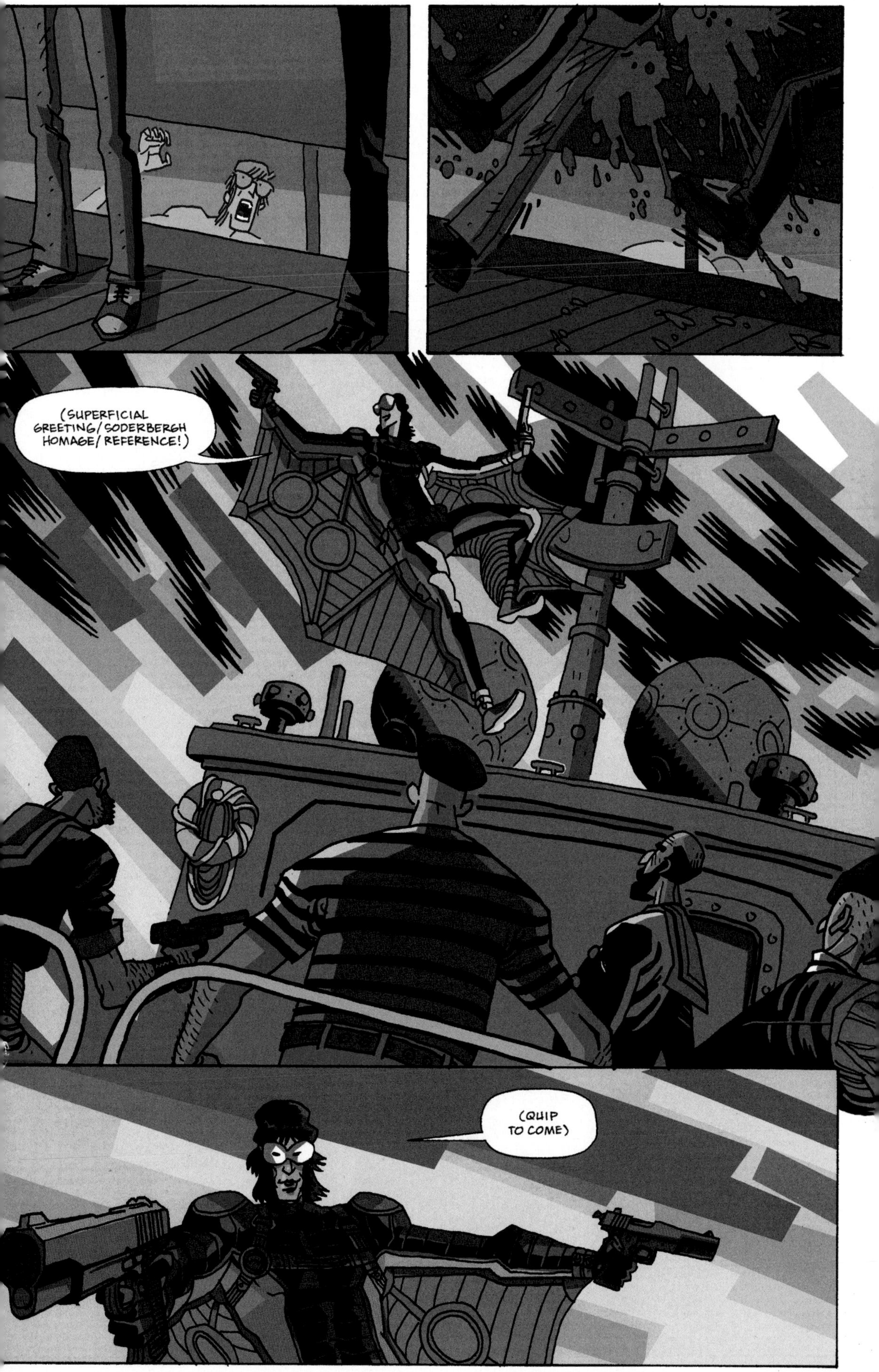
(SUPERFICIAL GREETING/ SODERBERGH HOMAGE/ REFERENCE!)
(QUIP TO COME)

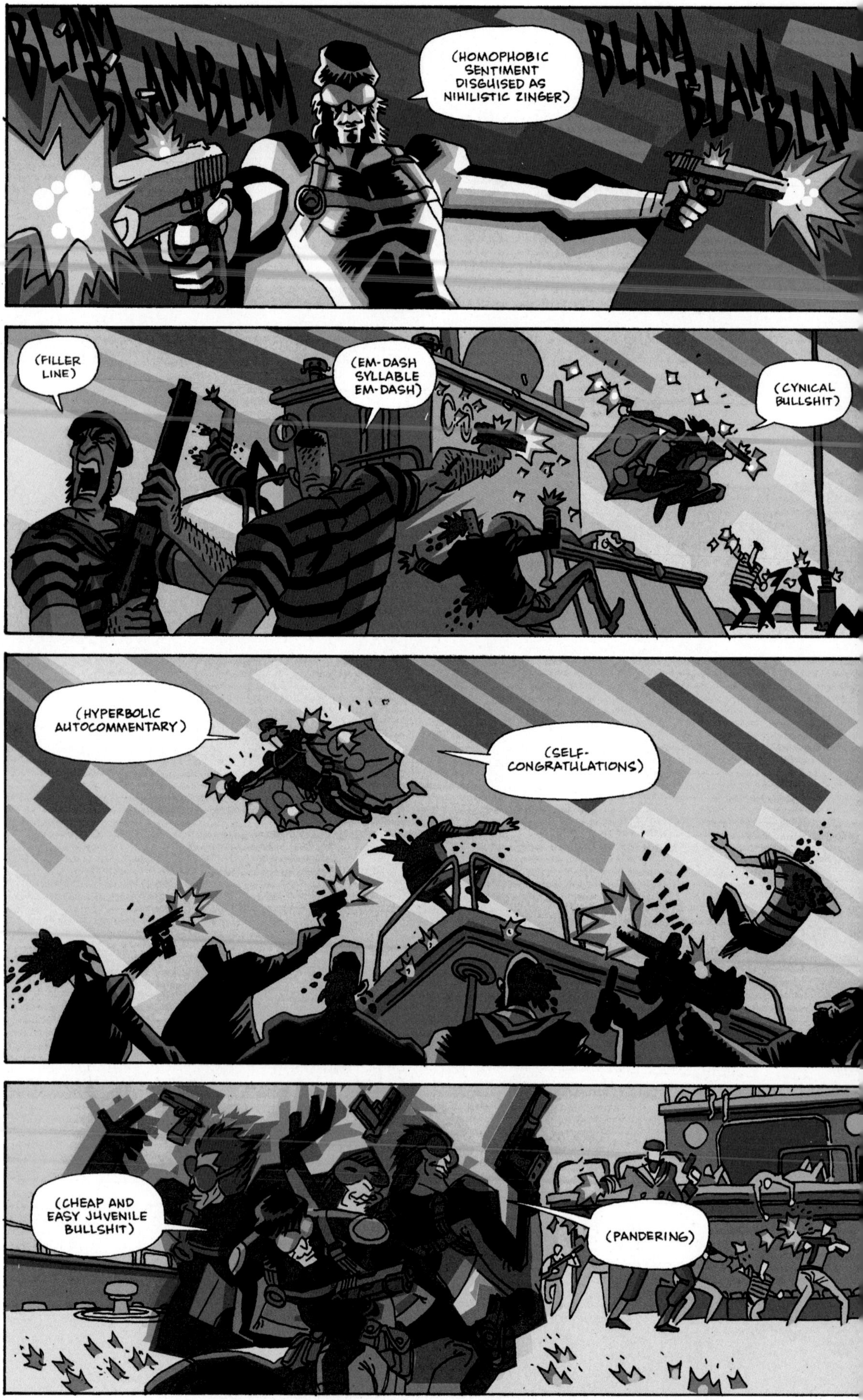
BLAM BLAMBLAM
(HOMOPHOBIC SENTIMENT DISGUISED AS NIHILISTIC ZINGER)
BLAM BLAM BLAM
(FILLER LINE)
(EM-DASH SYLLABLE EM-DASH)
(CYNICAL BULLSHIT)
(HYPERBOLIC AUTOCOMMENTARY)
(SELF-CONGRATULATIONS)
(CHEAP AND EASY JUVENILE BULLSHIT)
(PANDERING)

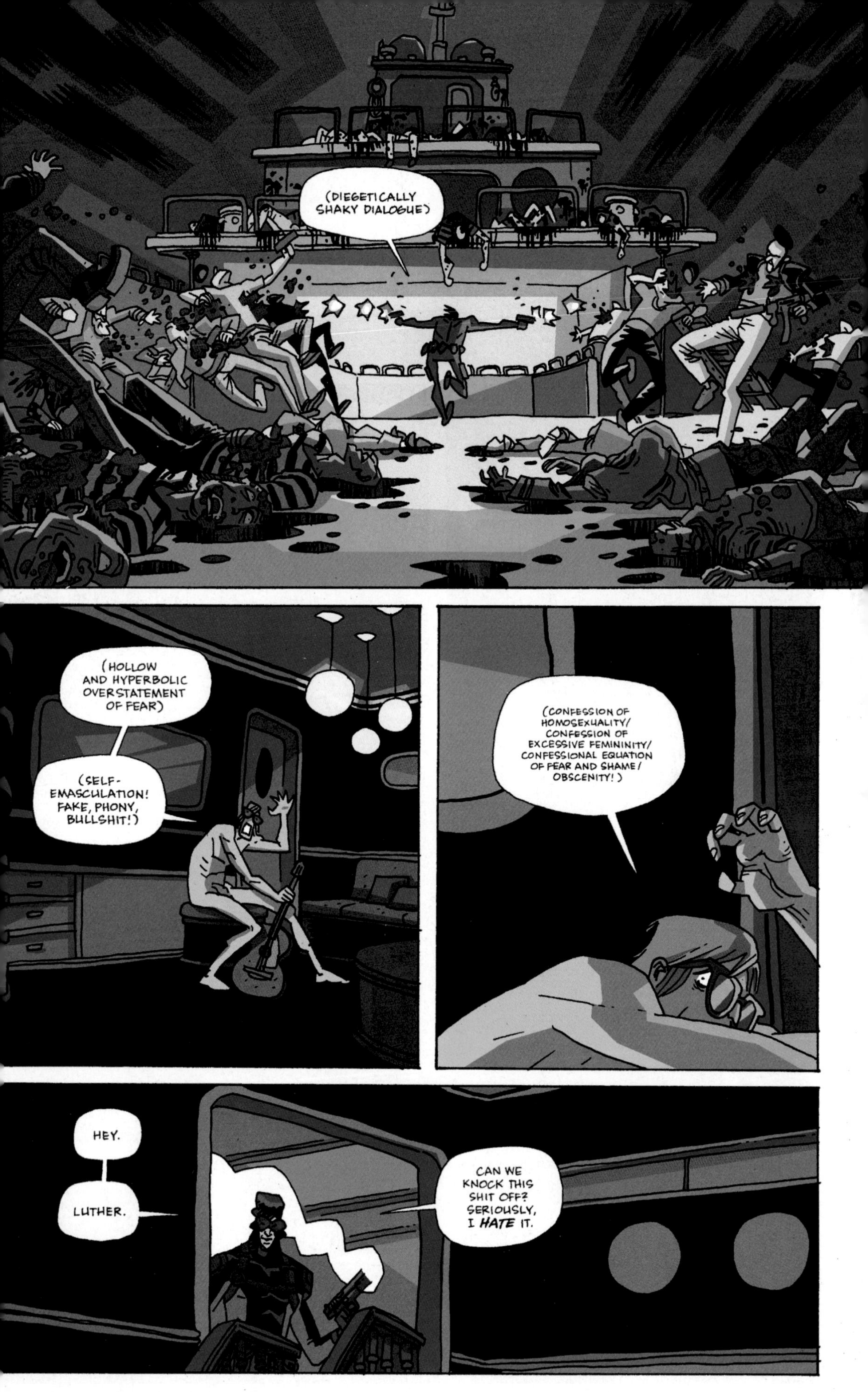
(DIEGETICALLY SHAKY DIALOGUE)
(HOLLOW AND HYPERBOLIC OVERSTATEMENT OF FEAR)
(SELF-EMASCULATION! FAKE, PHONY, BULLSHIT!)
(CONFESSION OF HOMOSEXUALITY/ CONFESSION OF EXCESSIVE FEMININITY/ CONFESSIONAL EQUATION OF FEAR AND SHAME/ OBSCENITY!)
HEY.
LUTHER.
CAN WE KNOCK THIS SHIT OFF? SERIOUSLY, I *HATE* IT.

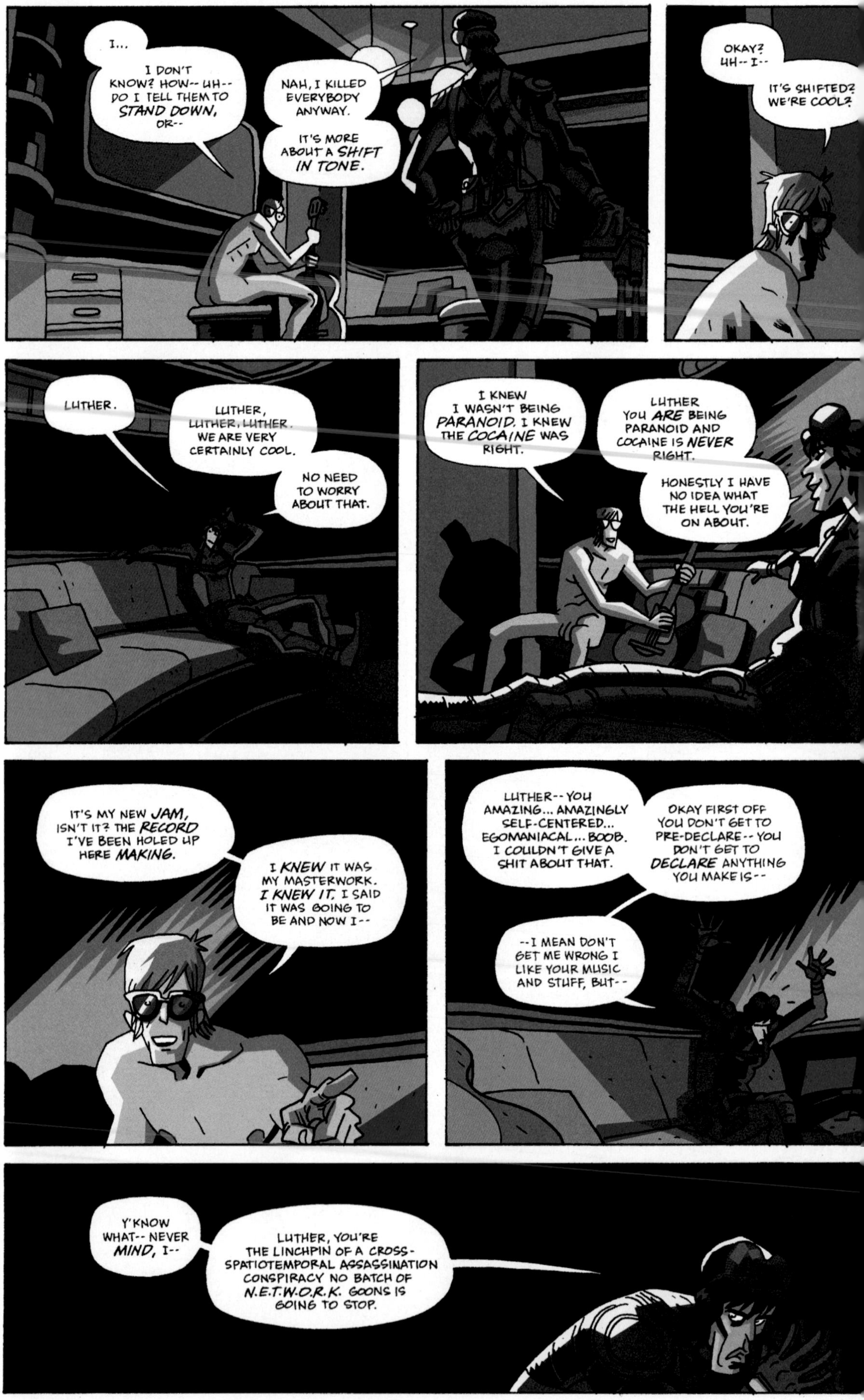
I...
I DON'T KNOW? HOW-- UH-- DO I TELL THEM TO STAND DOWN, OR--
NAH, I KILLED EVERYBODY ANYWAY.
IT'S MORE ABOUT A SHIFT IN TONE.
OKAY? UH-- I--
IT'S SHIFTED? WE'RE COOL?
LUTHER.
LUTHER, LUTHER, LUTHER. WE ARE VERY CERTAINLY COOL.
NO NEED TO WORRY ABOUT THAT.
I KNEW I WASN'T BEING PARANOID. I KNEW THE COCAINE WAS RIGHT.
LUTHER YOU ARE BEING PARANOID AND COCAINE IS NEVER RIGHT.
HONESTLY I HAVE NO IDEA WHAT THE HELL YOU'RE ON ABOUT.
IT'S MY NEW JAM, ISN'T IT? THE RECORD I'VE BEEN HOLED UP HERE MAKING.
I KNEW IT WAS MY MASTERWORK. I KNEW IT. I SAID IT WAS GOING TO BE AND NOW I--
LUTHER-- YOU AMAZING... AMAZINGLY SELF-CENTERED... EGOMANIACAL... BOOB. I COULDN'T GIVE A SHIT ABOUT THAT.
OKAY FIRST OFF YOU DON'T GET TO PRE-DECLARE-- YOU DON'T GET TO DECLARE ANYTHING YOU MAKE IS--
--I MEAN DON'T GET ME WRONG I LIKE YOUR MUSIC AND STUFF, BUT--
Y'KNOW WHAT-- NEVER MIND, I--
LUTHER, YOU'RE THE LINCHPIN OF A CROSS-SPATIOTEMPORAL ASSASSINATION CONSPIRACY NO BATCH OF N.E.T.W.O.R.K. GOONS IS GOING TO STOP.

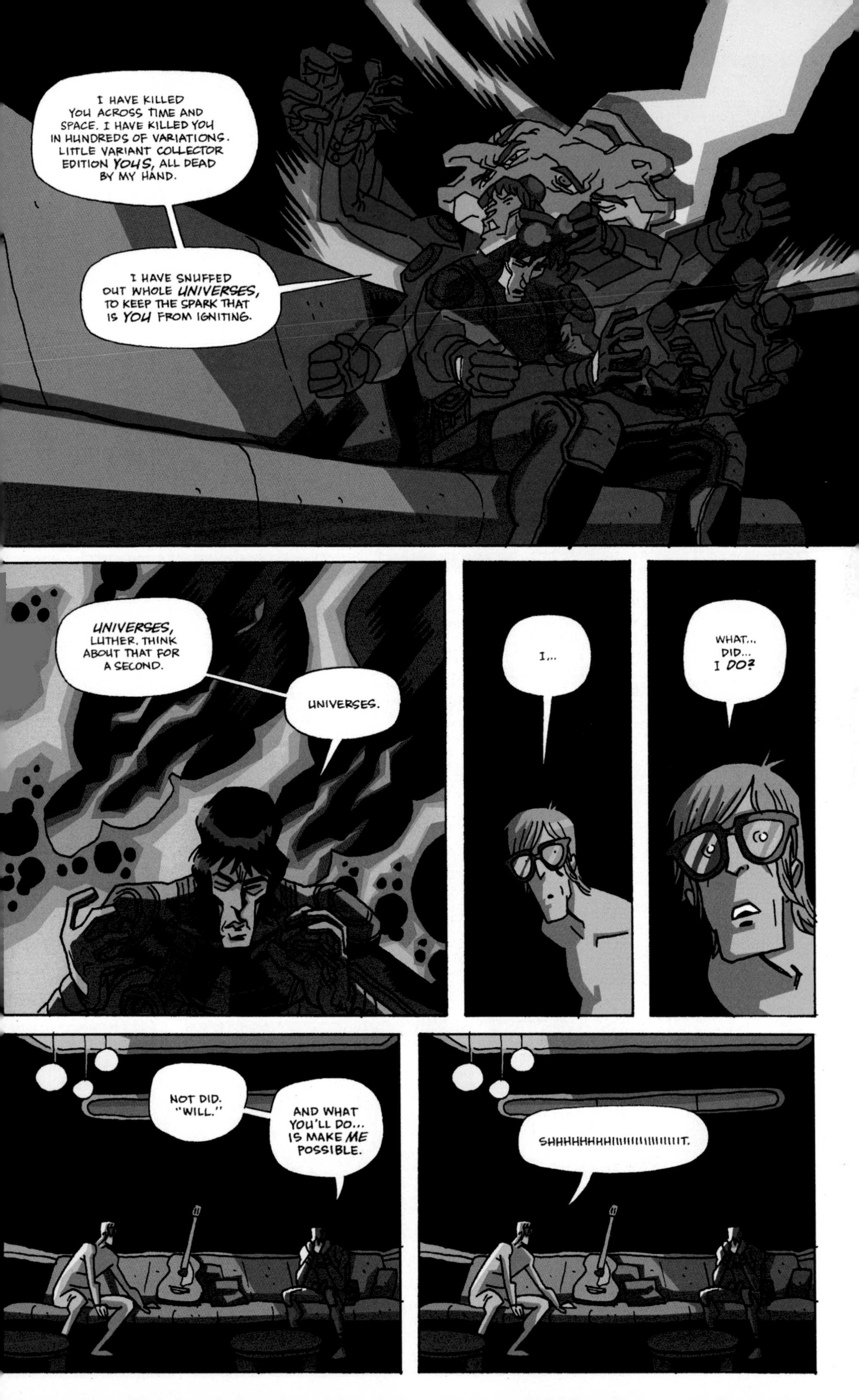
I HAVE KILLED YOU ACROSS TIME AND SPACE. I HAVE KILLED YOU IN HUNDREDS OF VARIATIONS. LITTLE VARIANT COLLECTOR EDITION YOUS, ALL DEAD BY MY HAND.
I HAVE SNUFFED OUT WHOLE UNIVERSES, TO KEEP THE SPARK THAT IS YOU FROM IGNITING.
UNIVERSES, LUTHER. THINK ABOUT THAT FOR A SECOND.
UNIVERSES.
I...
WHAT... DID... I DO?
NOT DID. "WILL."
AND WHAT YOU'LL DO... IS MAKE ME POSSIBLE.
SHHHHHHHHIIIIIIIIIIIIIIIIIT.

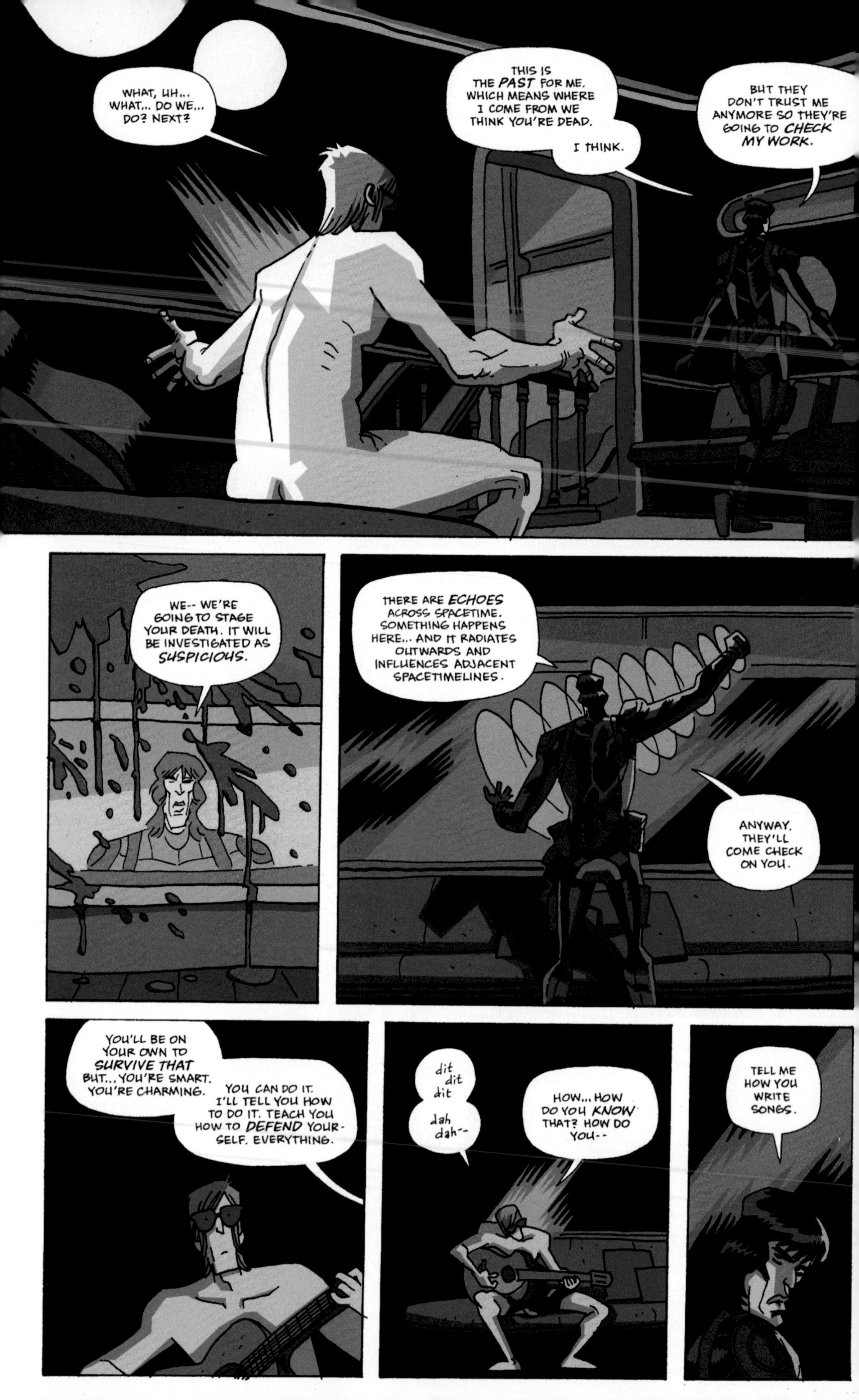
WHAT, UH... WHAT... DO WE... DO? NEXT?
THIS IS THE PAST FOR ME, WHICH MEANS WHERE I COME FROM WE THINK YOU'RE DEAD.
I THINK.
BUT THEY DON'T TRUST ME ANYMORE SO THEY'RE GOING TO CHECK MY WORK.
WE-- WE'RE GOING TO STAGE YOUR DEATH. IT WILL BE INVESTIGATED AS SUSPICIOUS.
THERE ARE ECHOES ACROSS SPACETIME. SOMETHING HAPPENS HERE... AND IT RADIATES OUTWARDS AND INFLUENCES ADJACENT SPACETIMELINES.
ANYWAY. THEY'LL COME CHECK ON YOU.
YOU'LL BE ON YOUR OWN TO SURVIVE THAT BUT... YOU'RE SMART. YOU'RE CHARMING.
YOU CAN DO IT. I'LL TELL YOU HOW TO DO IT. TEACH YOU HOW TO DEFEND YOURSELF. EVERYTHING.
dit dit dit
dah dah--
HOW... HOW DO YOU KNOW THAT? HOW DO YOU--
TELL ME HOW YOU WRITE SONGS.

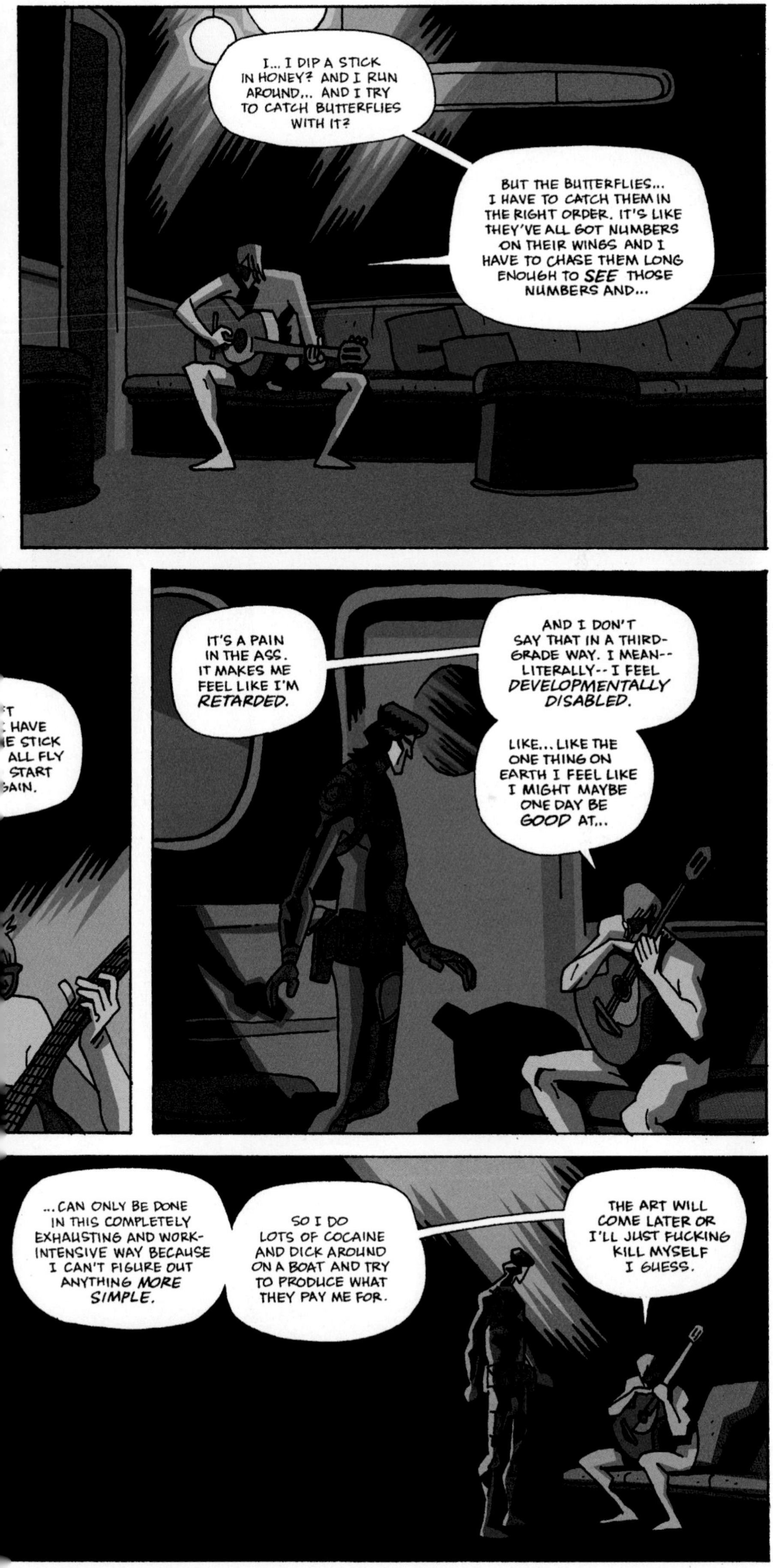
I... I DIP A STICK IN HONEY? AND I RUN AROUND... AND I TRY TO CATCH BUTTERFLIES WITH IT?
BUT THE BUTTERFLIES... I HAVE TO CATCH THEM IN THE RIGHT ORDER. IT'S LIKE THEY'VE ALL GOT NUMBERS ON THEIR WINGS AND I HAVE TO CHASE THEM LONG ENOUGH TO SEE THOSE NUMBERS AND...
IT'S A PAIN IN THE ASS. IT MAKES ME FEEL LIKE I'M RETARDED.
AND I DON'T SAY THAT IN A THIRD-GRADE WAY. I MEAN-- LITERALLY-- I FEEL DEVELOPMENTALLY DISABLED.
LIKE... LIKE THE ONE THING ON EARTH I FEEL LIKE I MIGHT MAYBE ONE DAY BE GOOD AT...
...CAN ONLY BE DONE IN THIS COMPLETELY EXHAUSTING AND WORK-INTENSIVE WAY BECAUSE I CAN'T FIGURE OUT ANYTHING MORE SIMPLE.
SO I DO LOTS OF COCAINE AND DICK AROUND ON A BOAT AND TRY TO PRODUCE WHAT THEY PAY ME FOR.
THE ART WILL COME LATER OR I'LL JUST FUCKING KILL MYSELF I GUESS.

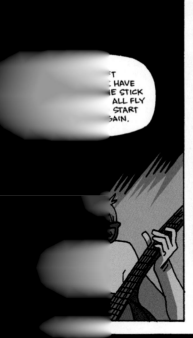

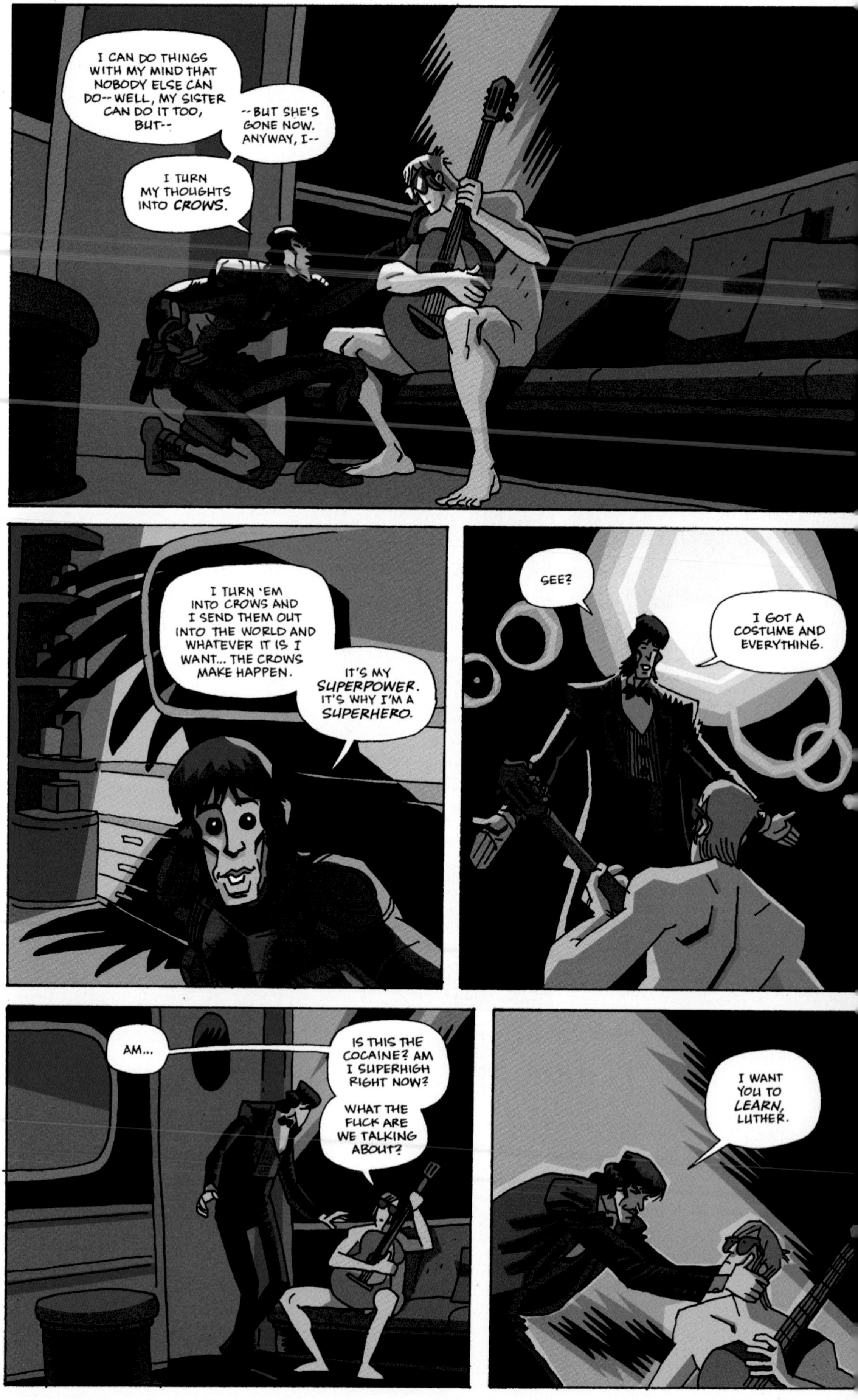
I CAN DO THINGS WITH MY MIND THAT NOBODY ELSE CAN DO-- WELL, MY SISTER CAN DO IT TOO, BUT--
--BUT SHE'S GONE NOW. ANYWAY, I--
I TURN MY THOUGHTS INTO CROWS.
I TURN 'EM INTO CROWS AND I SEND THEM OUT INTO THE WORLD AND WHATEVER IT IS I WANT... THE CROWS MAKE HAPPEN.
IT'S MY SUPERPOWER. IT'S WHY I'M A SUPERHERO.
SEE?
I GOT A COSTUME AND EVERYTHING.
AM...
IS THIS THE COCAINE? AM I SUPERHIGH RIGHT NOW?
WHAT THE FUCK ARE WE TALKING ABOUT?
I WANT YOU TO LEARN, LUTHER.

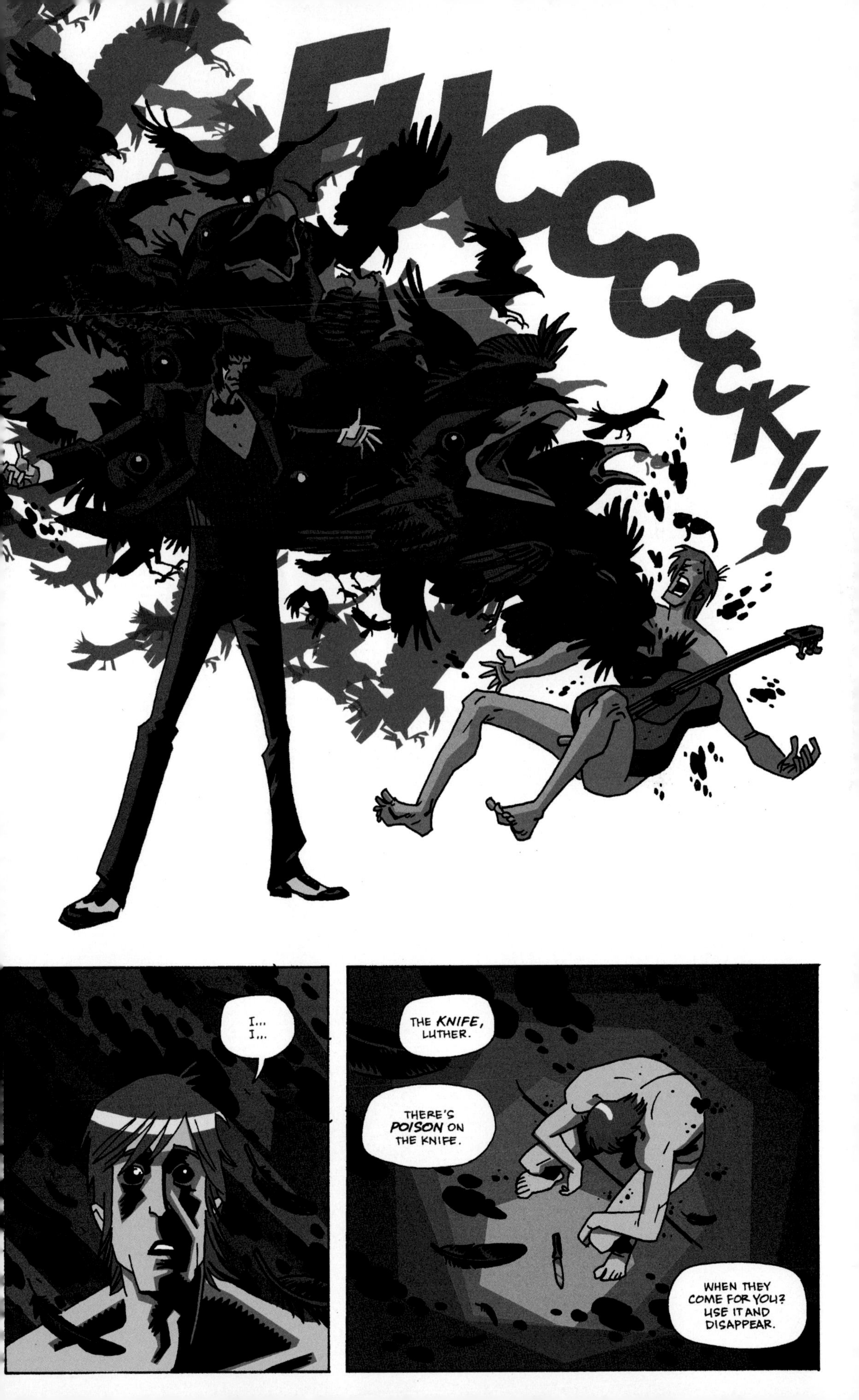
FUCCCCCKY!!
I...
I...
THE KNIFE, LUTHER.
THERE'S POISON ON THE KNIFE.
WHEN THEY COME FOR YOU? USE IT AND DISAPPEAR.

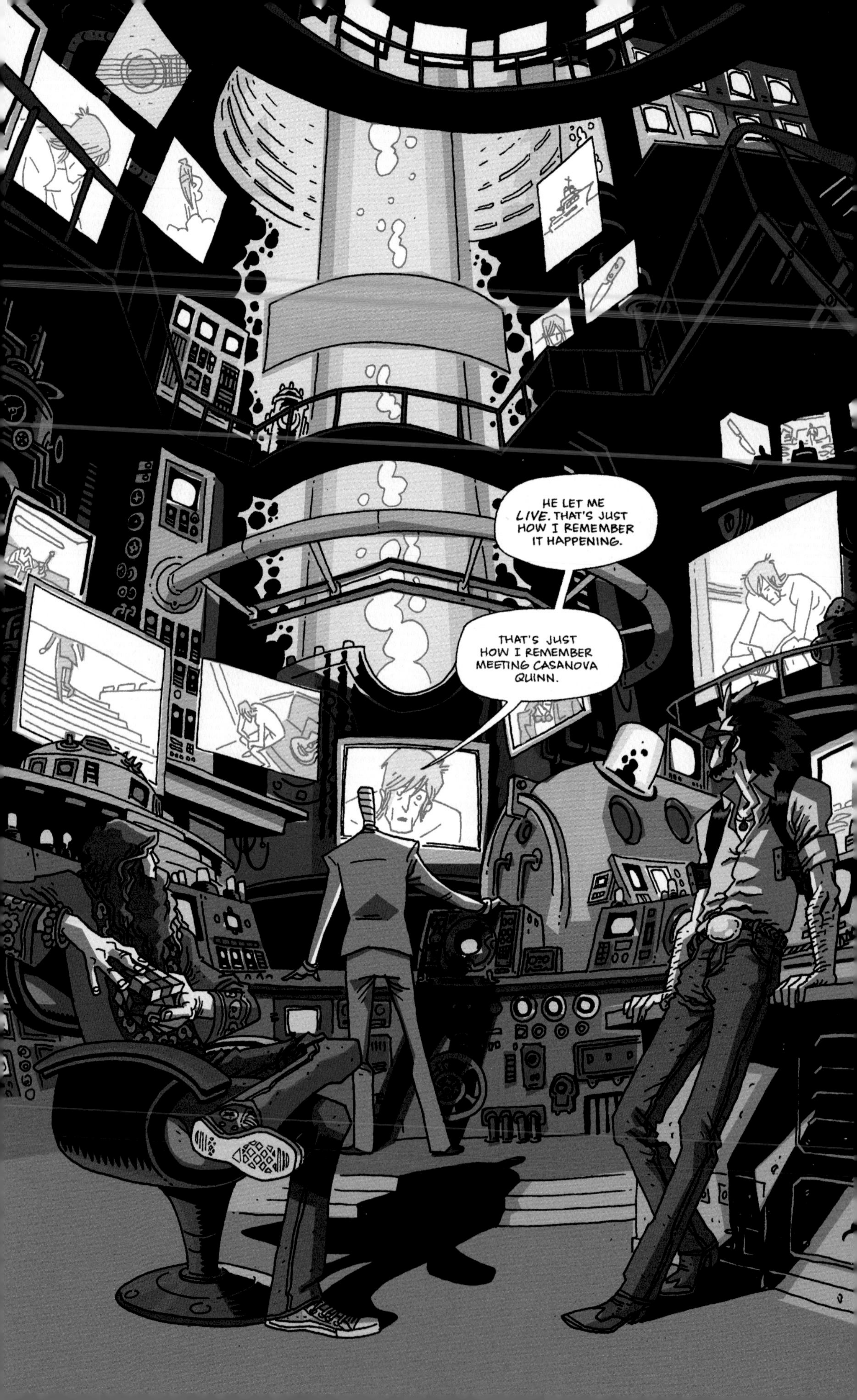
HE LET ME *LIVE*. THAT'S JUST HOW I REMEMBER IT HAPPENING.
THAT'S JUST HOW I REMEMBER MEETING CASANOVA QUINN.

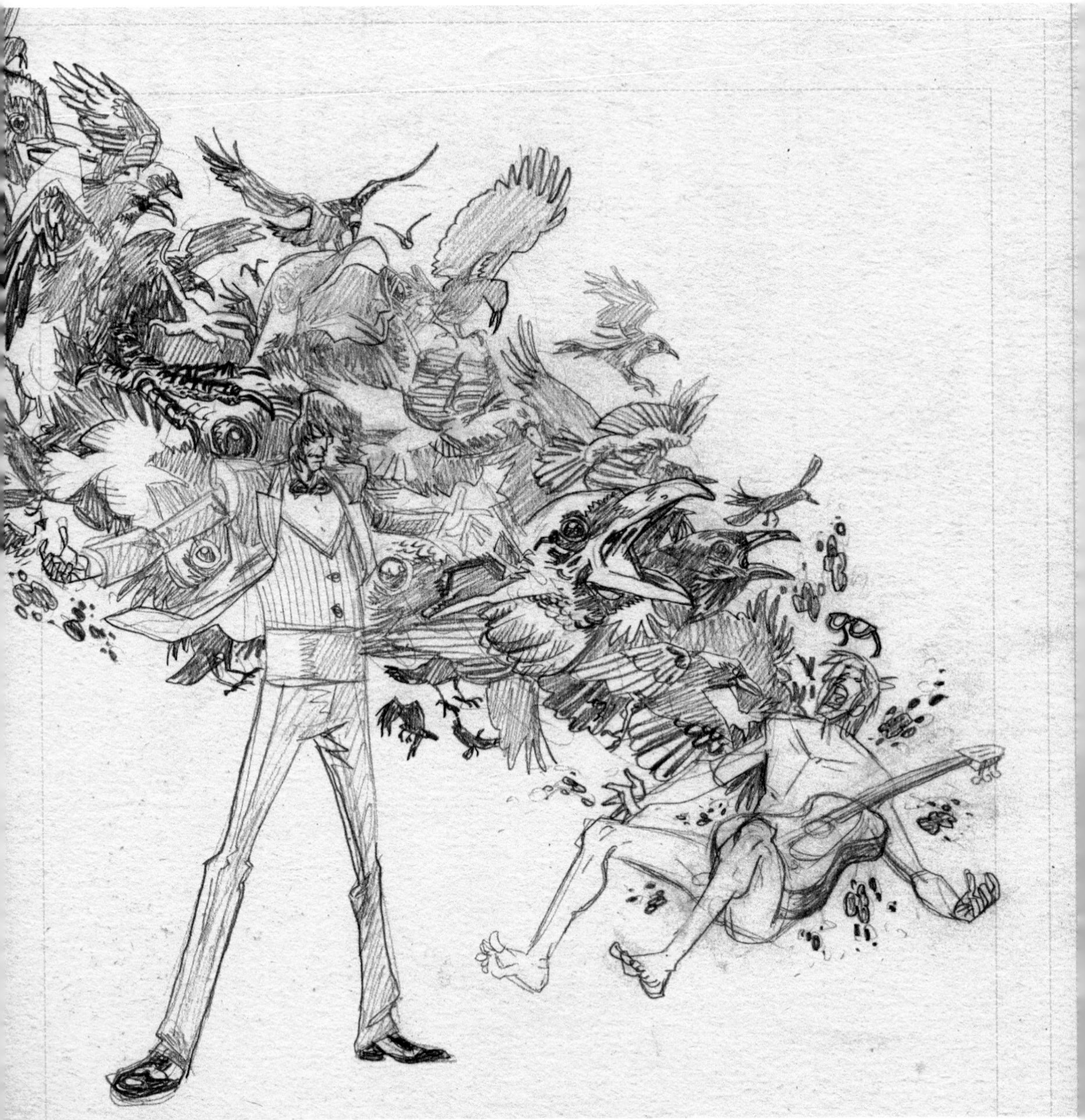

7. THE WIDTH OF A CIRCLE

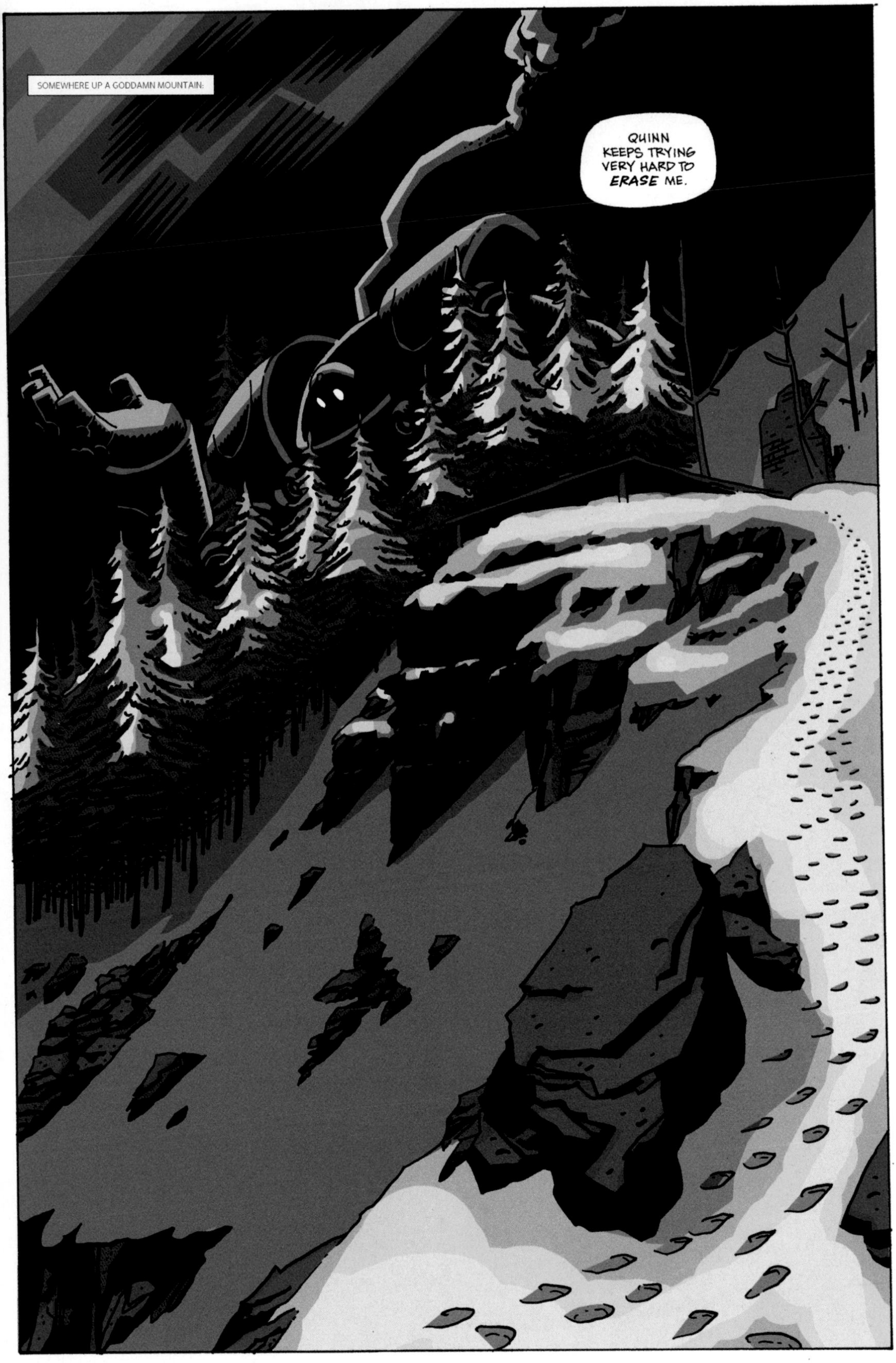

SOMEWHERE UP A GODDAMN MOUNTAIN:
QUINN KEEPS TRYING VERY HARD TO ERASE ME.

...THERE IS THE BOOT OF *E.M.P.I.R.E.* TO STOMP IT TO DEATH.

BUT *YOU'RE FAMILIAR* WITH THE QUINN FAMILY GOON-SQUAD DECIDING WHO GETS TO LIVE AND DIE, AREN'T YOU, KAITO?

HE -- AND *E.M.P.I.R.E.*-- DISCOVERED MY *NAME* BEFORE I BECAME THE MAN I AM TODAY.

THEY TRAIPSE ACROSS SPACETIME LIKE THEY OWN IT, *KILLING* ME BEFORE I HAVE A CHANCE TO *GROW UP.*

ANYWHERE IN THE MYRIAD FOLDS OF THE INFINITE WHERE MY SEED MAY FIND PURCHASE...

BEST. IT'S MR. *BEST* WHEN YOU'RE IN MY HOME. AND TREAD *CAREFULLY,* MR. XENO.

I KNOW WHAT YOU AND YOUR MEN ARE *CAPABLE OF* AND I ASSURE YOU ...

...I'M NOT SCARED.

YOU CAN'T TELL BUT I'M *SMILING* UNDER THESE BANDAGES, REALLY I AM.

XENO WHAT DO YOU *WANT* FROM ME?

I'M NOT A *PART* OF *E.M.P.I.R.E.* ANYMORE AND I DON'T KNOW ANYTHING ABOUT *ANYTHING.*

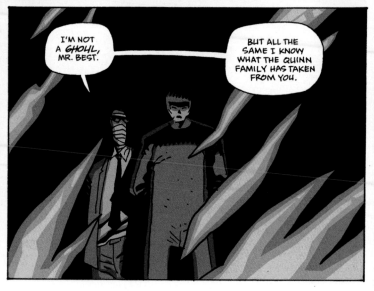

I'M NOT A *GHOUL,* MR. BEST.

BUT ALL THE SAME I KNOW WHAT THE QUINN FAMILY HAS TAKEN FROM YOU.

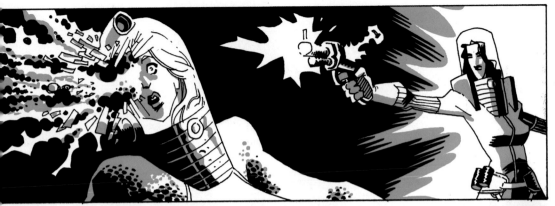

AND I KNOW YOU COULD KILL HIM AT ANY TIME, FOR *ANY* REASON.

LET ALONE THE VERY *SPECIFIC* REASON YOU HAVE...

WHAT ARE YOU WAITING FOR?

SKYLABS ARE FALLING, MR. BEST.

AREN'T YOU THE BEST KILLER IN THE WORLD?

HE IS.

HE'LL BE GONE SOON, KAITO. GONE-GONE. GONE.

DAVID, KUBARK, STAY HERE WITH MR. *BEST* AND SHINE HIS FUCKING SHOES FOR ALL I CARE.

WELCOME ABOARD. START TALKING EXECUTION.

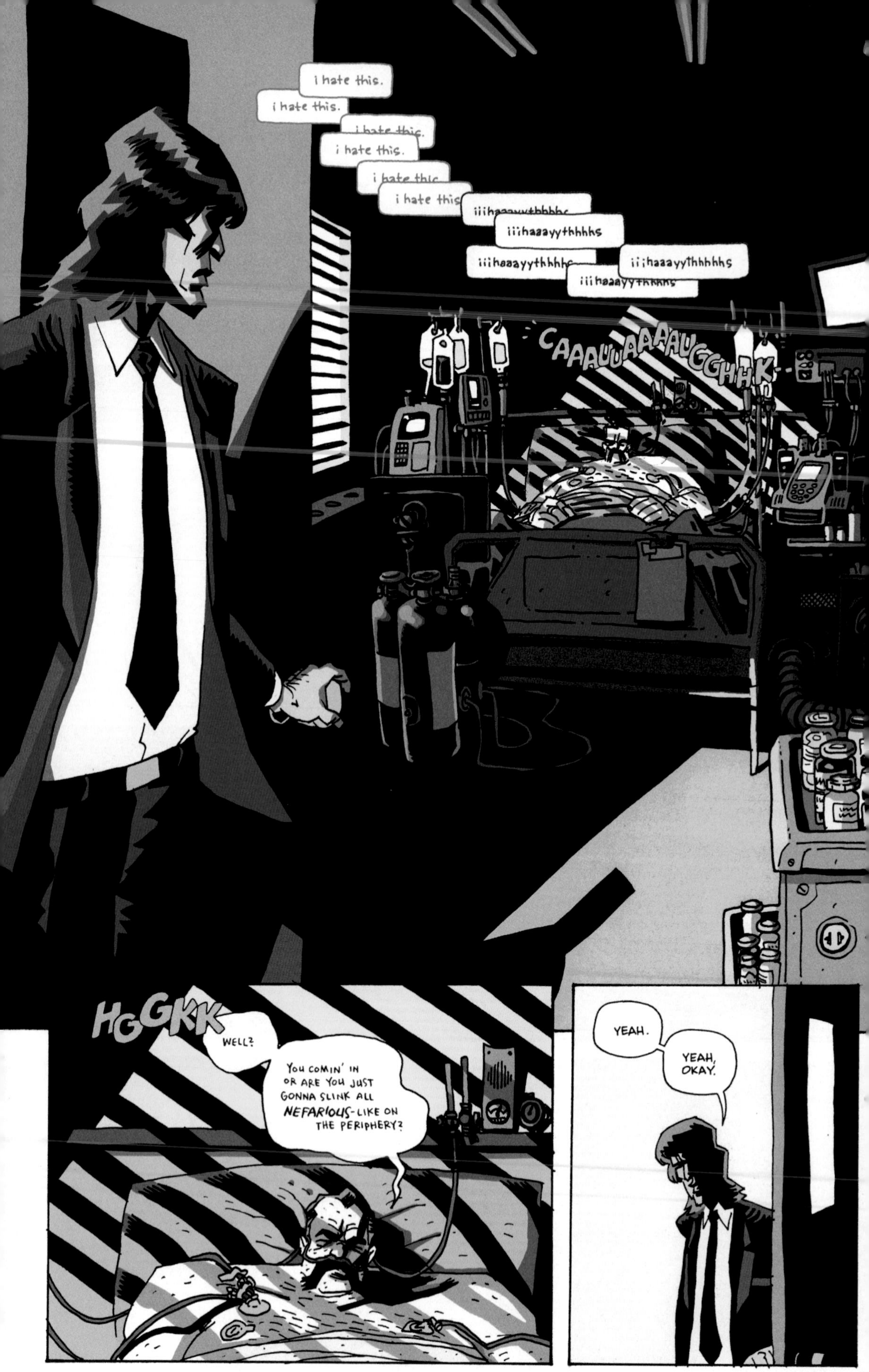
i hate this.
i hate this.
i hate this.
i hate this.
i hate this.
i hate this
iiihaaayythhhhs
iiihaaayythhhhs
iiihaaayythhhhs
iiihaaayythhhhhs
iiihaaayythhhhs
CAAAUUAAAAAUGGHHK
HGGKK
WELL?
YOU COMIN' IN OR ARE YOU JUST GONNA SLINK ALL *NEFARIOUS*-LIKE ON THE PERIPHERY?
YEAH.
YEAH, OKAY.

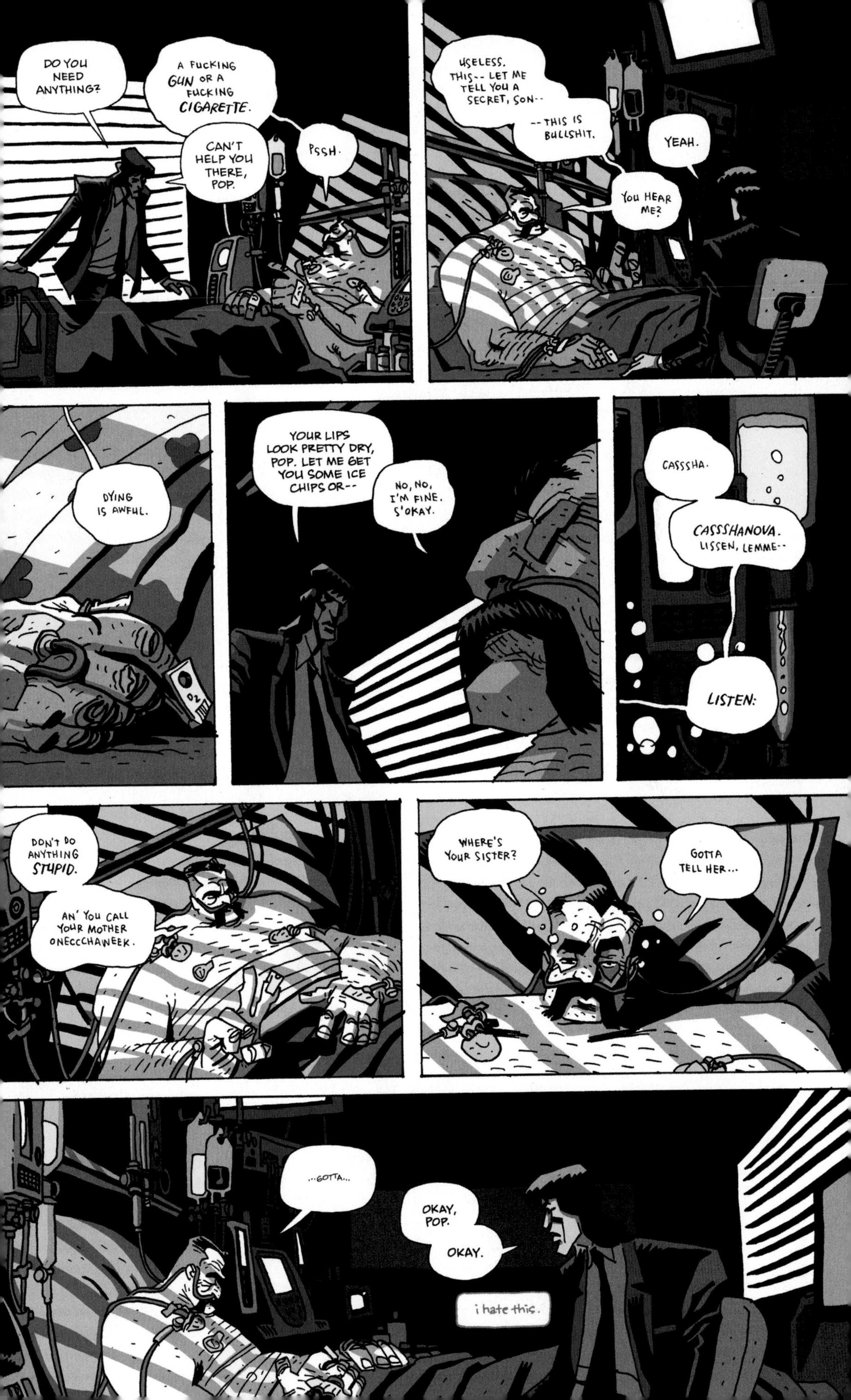
DO YOU NEED ANYTHING?
A FUCKING GUN OR A FUCKING CIGARETTE.
CAN'T HELP YOU THERE, POP.
PSSH.
USELESS. THIS-- LET ME TELL YOU A SECRET, SON--
--THIS IS BULLSHIT.
YEAH.
YOU HEAR ME?
DYING IS AWFUL.
O2
YOUR LIPS LOOK PRETTY DRY, POP. LET ME GET YOU SOME ICE CHIPS OR--
NO, NO, I'M FINE. S'OKAY.
CASSSHA.
CASSSHANOVA. LISSEN, LEMME--
LISTEN:
DON'T DO ANYTHING STUPID.
AN' YOU CALL YOUR MOTHER ONECCCHAWEEK.
WHERE'S YOUR SISTER?
GOTTA TELL HER...
...GOTTA...
OKAY, POP.
OKAY.
i hate this.

THE REPUBLIC OF SINGAPORE
N.E.T.W.O.R.K. HEADQUARTERS:

QUITE FRANKLY THIS IS *UNACCEPTABLE.*

E.M.P.I.R.E. HAS SENT ME *THROUGH GODDAMN TIME* TO CLEAN UP THE *MESS* BACK HERE, PEOPLE. AND WHAT'S *MORE...*

E.M.P.I.R.E. OUTSOURCED THIS JOB TO *N.E.T.W.O.R.K.* FOR ONE REASON AND ONE REASON ALONE:

WE NEEDED LUTHER DESMOND DIAMOND TO DIE AND COULDN'T RELY ON OUR OWN AGENT TO EXECUTE.

DID I SHOOT HIM MYSELF? NO.

I LEFT HIM COVERED IN BLISTERS, SITTING ON A BURNING, SINKING BOAT, DICKING AROUND ON HIS GUITAR.

HE DIDN'T GET AWAY. HE DIED ON THAT BOAT.

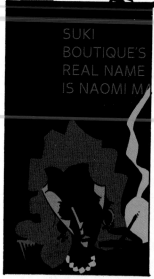

SUKI BOUTIQUE'S REAL NAME IS NAOMI MA

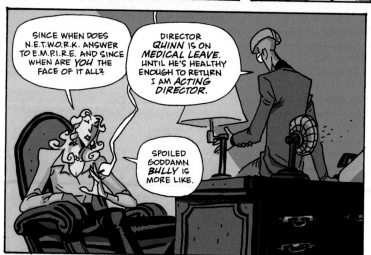

SINCE WHEN DOES N.E.T.W.O.R.K. ANSWER TO E.M.P.I.R.E. AND SINCE WHEN ARE *YOU* THE FACE OF IT ALL?

DIRECTOR *QUINN* IS ON *MEDICAL LEAVE.* UNTIL HE'S HEALTHY ENOUGH TO RETURN I AM *ACTING DIRECTOR.*

SPOILED *GODDAMN BULLY* IS MORE LIKE.

SUKI.

FINE. *ACTING DIRECTOR* GODDAMN BULLY.

LUTHER DESMOND DIAMOND DIED ON THAT BOAT.

MS. BOUTIQUE.

FOLLOW ME, PLEASE.

SABINE SEYCHELLE. THE VILLAIN.

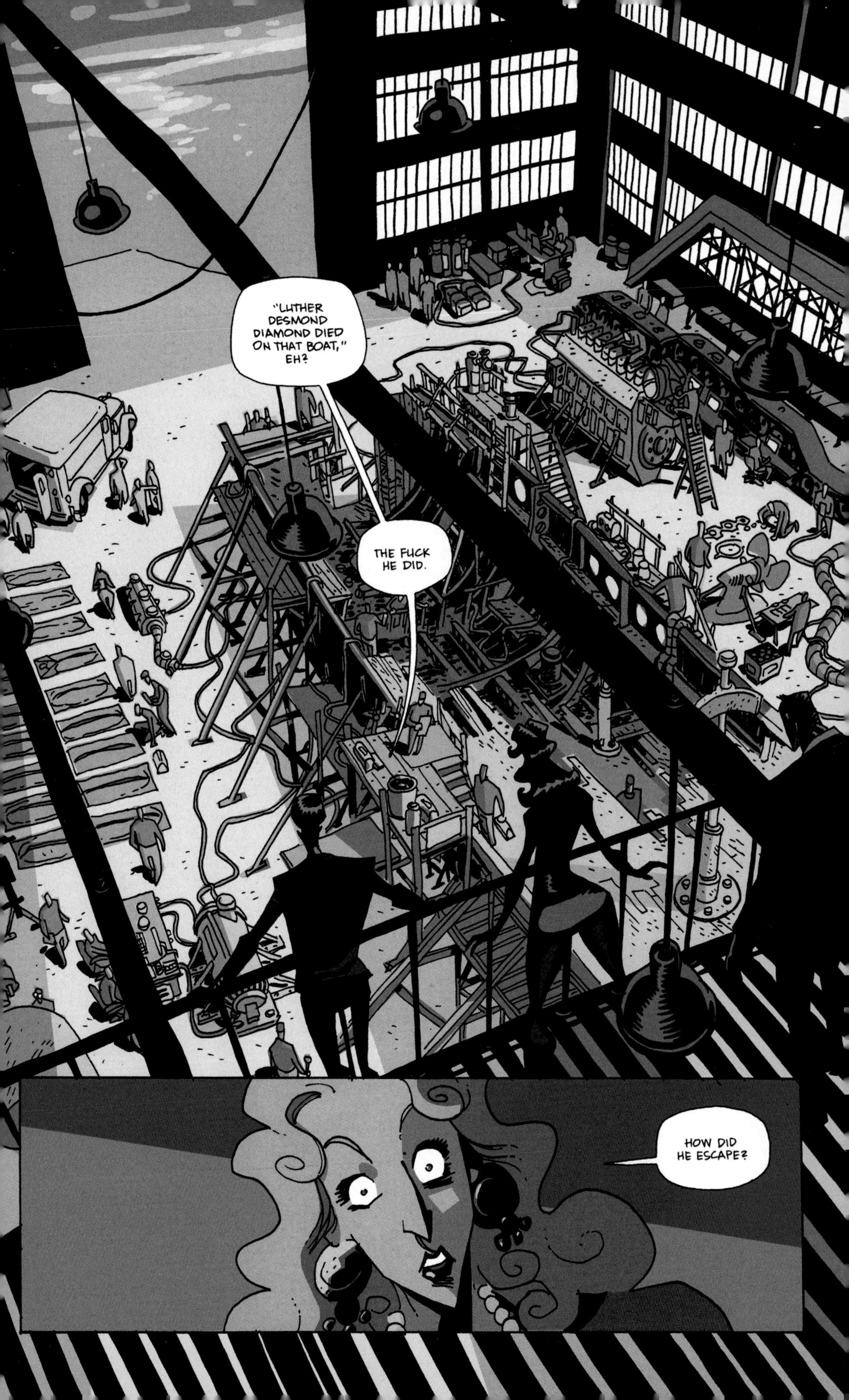
"LUTHER DESMOND DIAMOND DIED ON THAT BOAT," EH?
THE FUCK HE DID.
HOW DID HE ESCAPE?

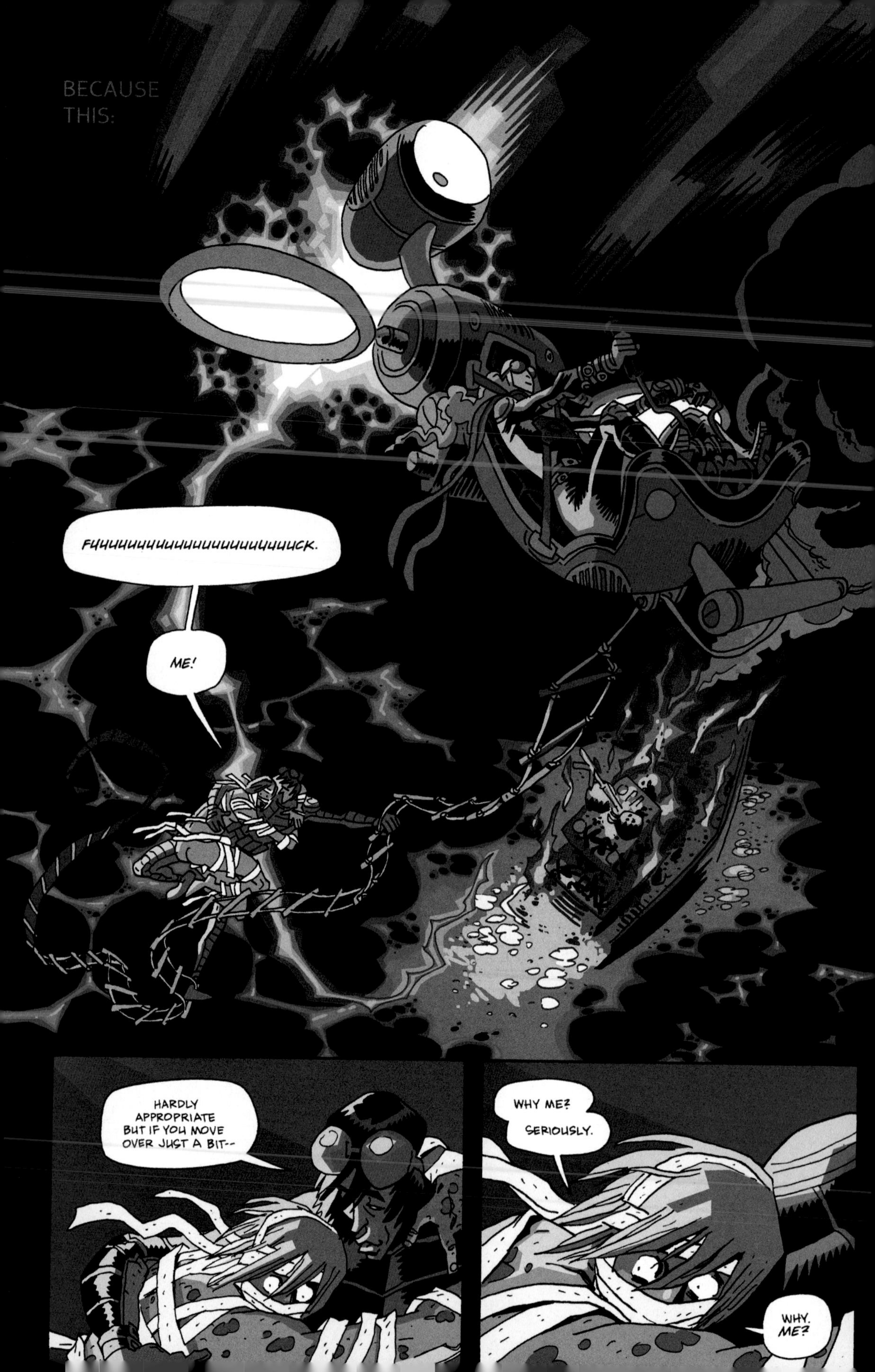
BECAUSE THIS:
FUUUUUUUUUUUUUUUUUUUUUUUUCK.
ME!
HARDLY APPROPRIATE BUT IF YOU MOVE OVER JUST A BIT--
WHY ME?
SERIOUSLY.
WHY. ME?

BECAUSE LATER:

BUT THE THING IS:

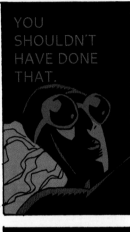

YOU SHOULDN'T HAVE DONE THAT.

I DIDN'T DO THAT.

BUT YOU WILL.

AND I'LL HELP YOU DO IT.

WHY WOULD YOU DO THAT?

BECAUSE YOU NEEDED ME TO.

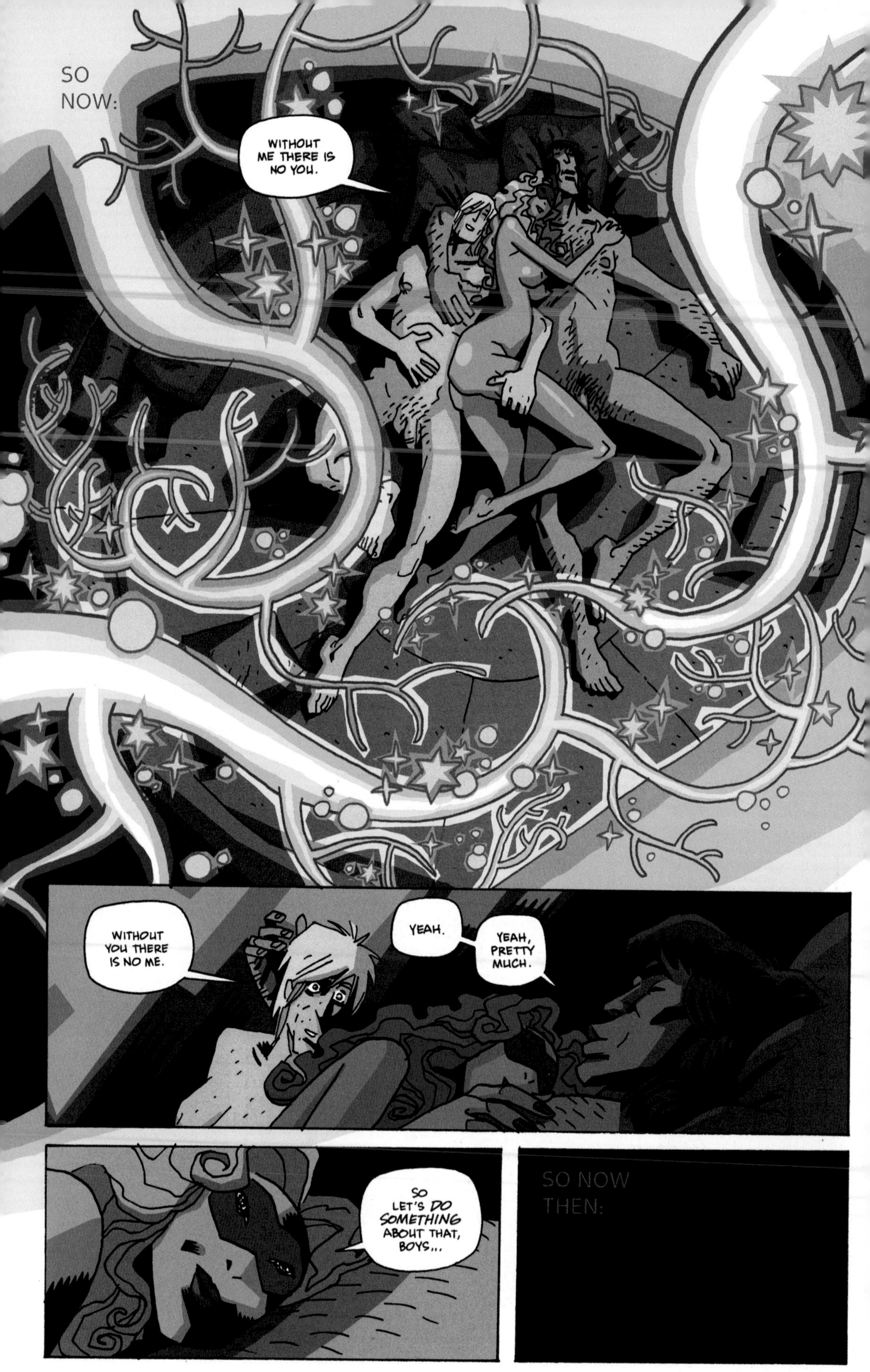
SO NOW:
WITHOUT ME THERE IS NO YOU.
WITHOUT YOU THERE IS NO ME.
YEAH.
YEAH, PRETTY MUCH.
SO LET'S *DO SOMETHING* ABOUT THAT, BOYS...
SO NOW THEN:

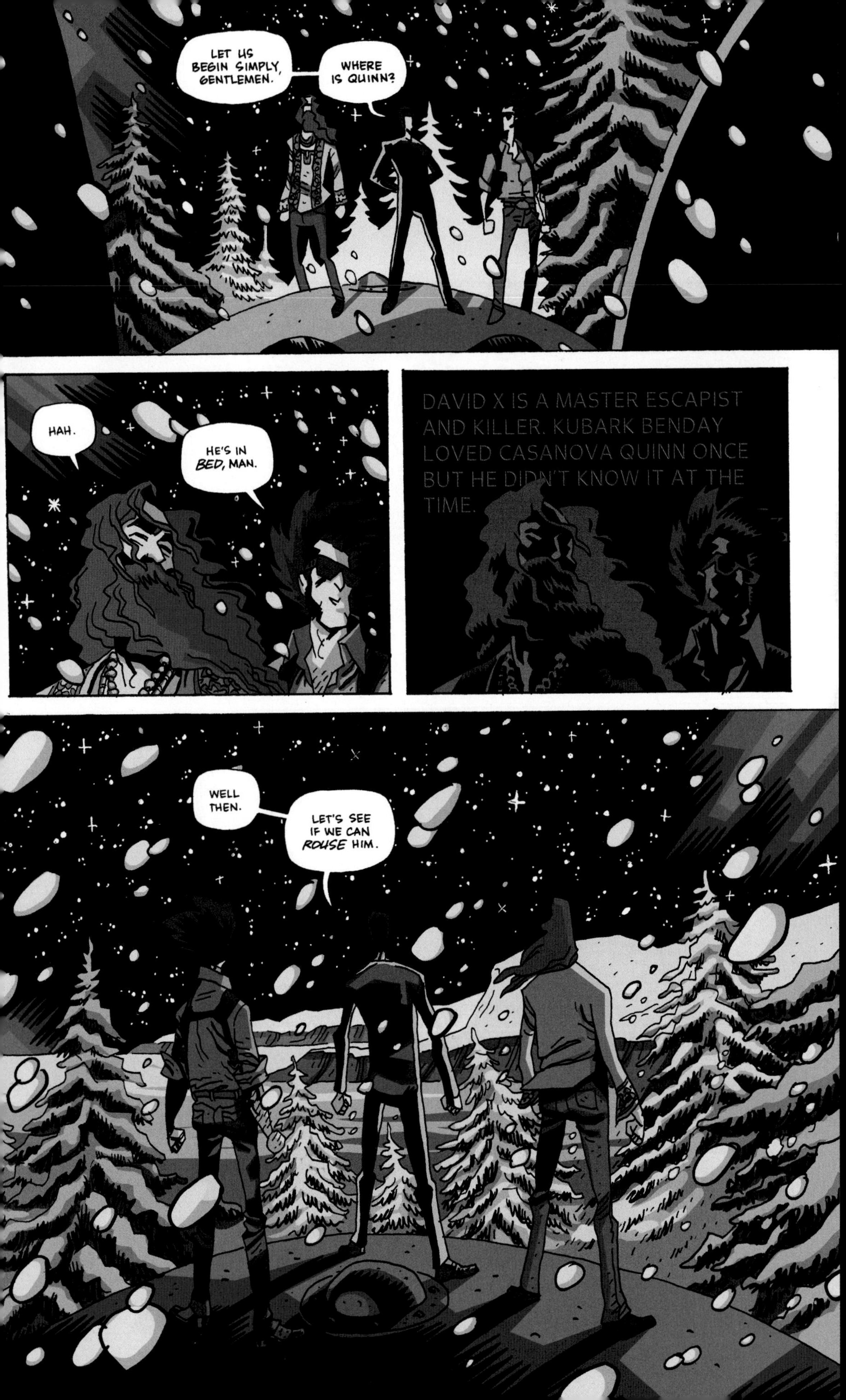
LET US BEGIN SIMPLY, GENTLEMEN.
WHERE IS QUINN?
HAH.
HE'S IN BED, MAN.
DAVID X IS A MASTER ESCAPIST AND KILLER. KUBARK BENDAY LOVED CASANOVA QUINN ONCE BUT HE DIDN'T KNOW IT AT THE TIME.
WELL THEN.
LET'S SEE IF WE CAN ROUSE HIM.

8. LA RITOURNELLE

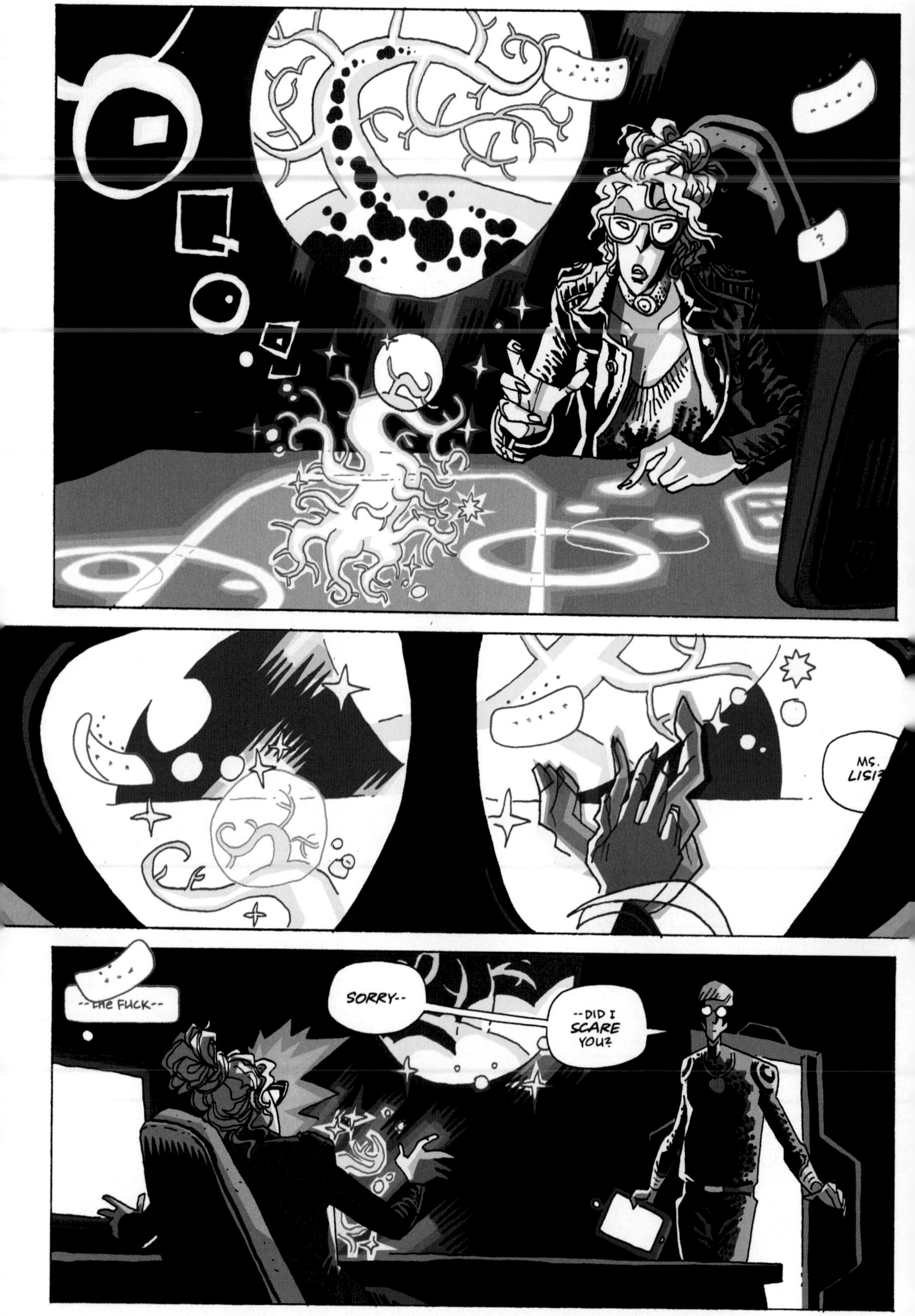

MS. LISI?
--the FUCK--
SORRY--
--DID I SCARE YOU?

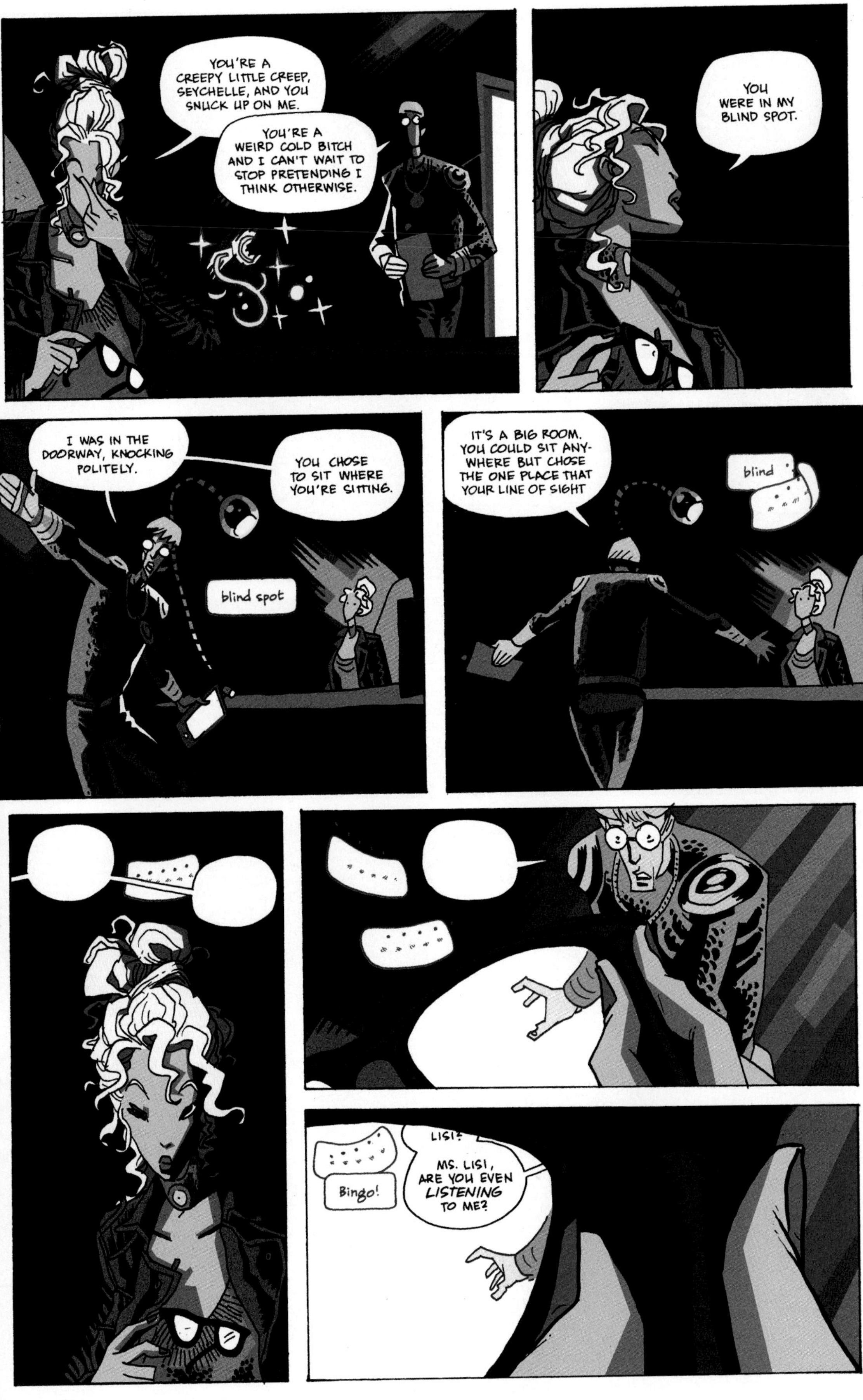
YOU'RE A CREEPY LITTLE CREEP, SEYCHELLE, AND YOU SNUCK UP ON ME.
YOU'RE A WEIRD COLD BITCH AND I CAN'T WAIT TO STOP PRETENDING I THINK OTHERWISE.
YOU WERE IN MY BLIND SPOT.
I WAS IN THE DOORWAY, KNOCKING POLITELY.
YOU CHOSE TO SIT WHERE YOU'RE SITTING.
blind spot
IT'S A BIG ROOM. YOU COULD SIT ANY-WHERE BUT CHOSE THE ONE PLACE THAT YOUR LINE OF SIGHT
blind
LISI?
MS. LISI, ARE YOU EVEN LISTENING TO ME?
Bingo!

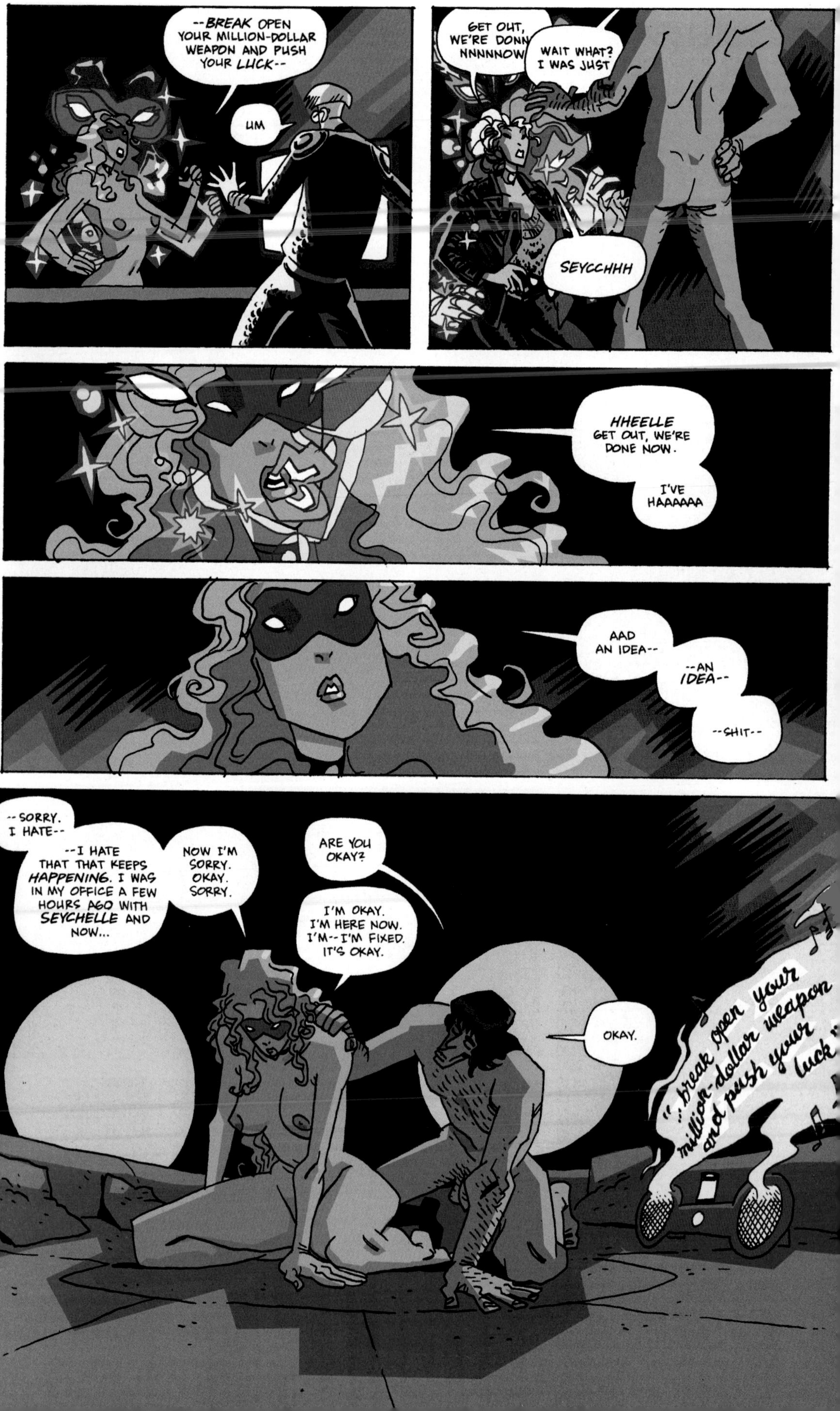
--BREAK OPEN YOUR MILLION-DOLLAR WEAPON AND PUSH YOUR LUCK--
UM
GET OUT, WE'RE DONN NNNNNOW
WAIT WHAT? I WAS JUST
SEYCCHHH
HHEELLE GET OUT, WE'RE DONE NOW.
I'VE HAAAAAA
AAD AN IDEA--
--AN IDEA--
--SHIT--
--SORRY. I HATE--
--I HATE THAT THAT KEEPS HAPPENING. I WAS IN MY OFFICE A FEW HOURS AGO WITH SEYCHELLE AND NOW...
NOW I'M SORRY. OKAY. SORRY.
ARE YOU OKAY?
I'M OKAY. I'M HERE NOW. I'M--I'M FIXED. IT'S OKAY.
OKAY.
"...break open your million-dollar weapon and push your luck"

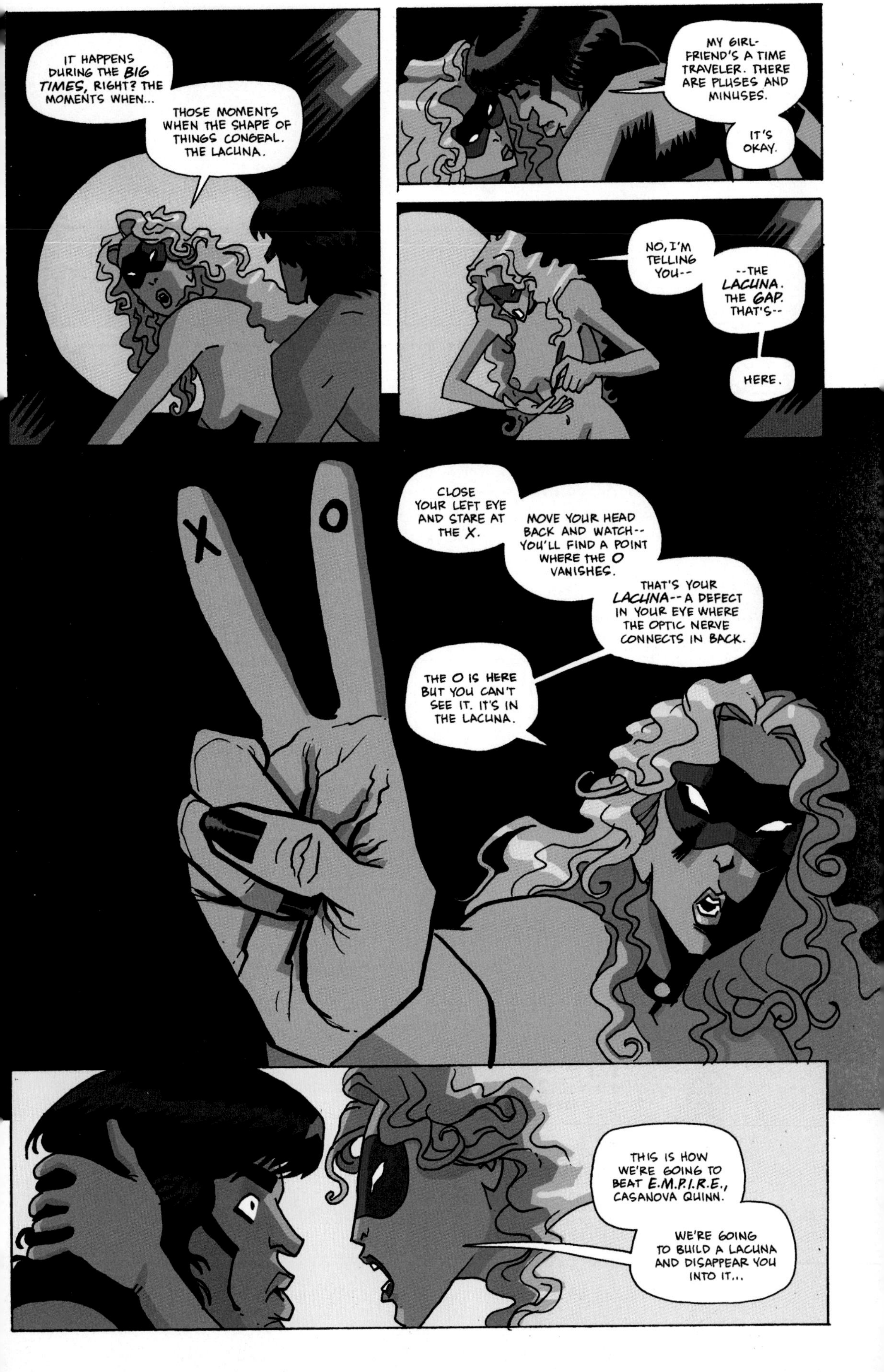
IT HAPPENS DURING THE BIG TIMES, RIGHT? THE MOMENTS WHEN...
THOSE MOMENTS WHEN THE SHAPE OF THINGS CONGEAL. THE LACUNA.
MY GIRL-FRIEND'S A TIME TRAVELER. THERE ARE PLUSES AND MINUSES.
IT'S OKAY.
NO, I'M TELLING YOU--
--THE LACUNA. THE GAP. THAT'S--
HERE.
X
O
CLOSE YOUR LEFT EYE AND STARE AT THE X.
MOVE YOUR HEAD BACK AND WATCH-- YOU'LL FIND A POINT WHERE THE O VANISHES.
THAT'S YOUR LACUNA-- A DEFECT IN YOUR EYE WHERE THE OPTIC NERVE CONNECTS IN BACK.
THE O IS HERE BUT YOU CAN'T SEE IT. IT'S IN THE LACUNA.
THIS IS HOW WE'RE GOING TO BEAT E.M.P.I.R.E., CASANOVA QUINN.
WE'RE GOING TO BUILD A LACUNA AND DISAPPEAR YOU INTO IT...

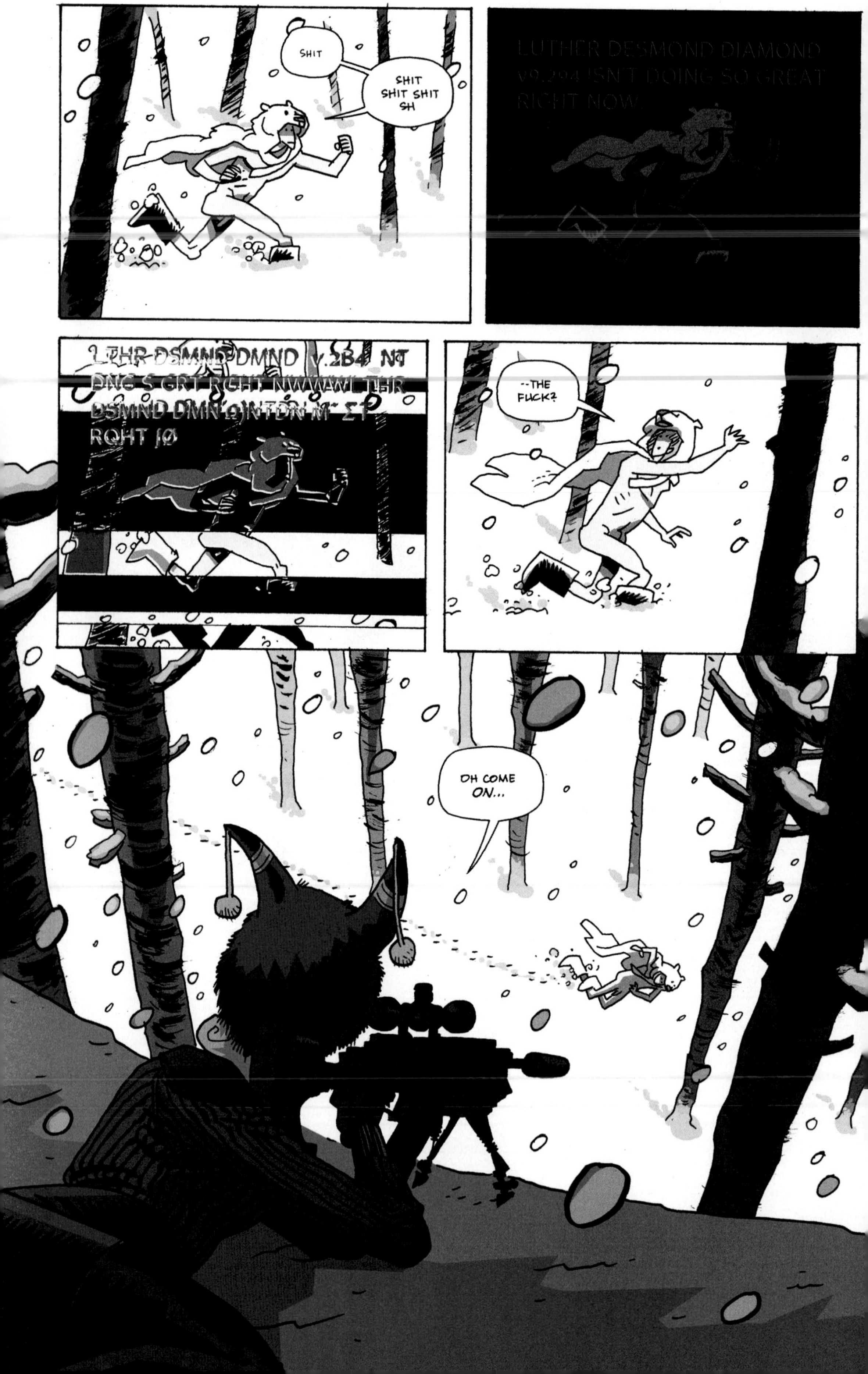
SHIT
SHIT SHIT SHIT SH
LUTHER DESMOND DIAMOND v9.294 ISN'T DOING SO GREAT RIGHT NOW.
LTHR DSMND DMND v.2B4 NT DNG S GRT RGHT NWWWL THR DSMND DMN
RQHT
--THE FUCK?
OH COME ON...

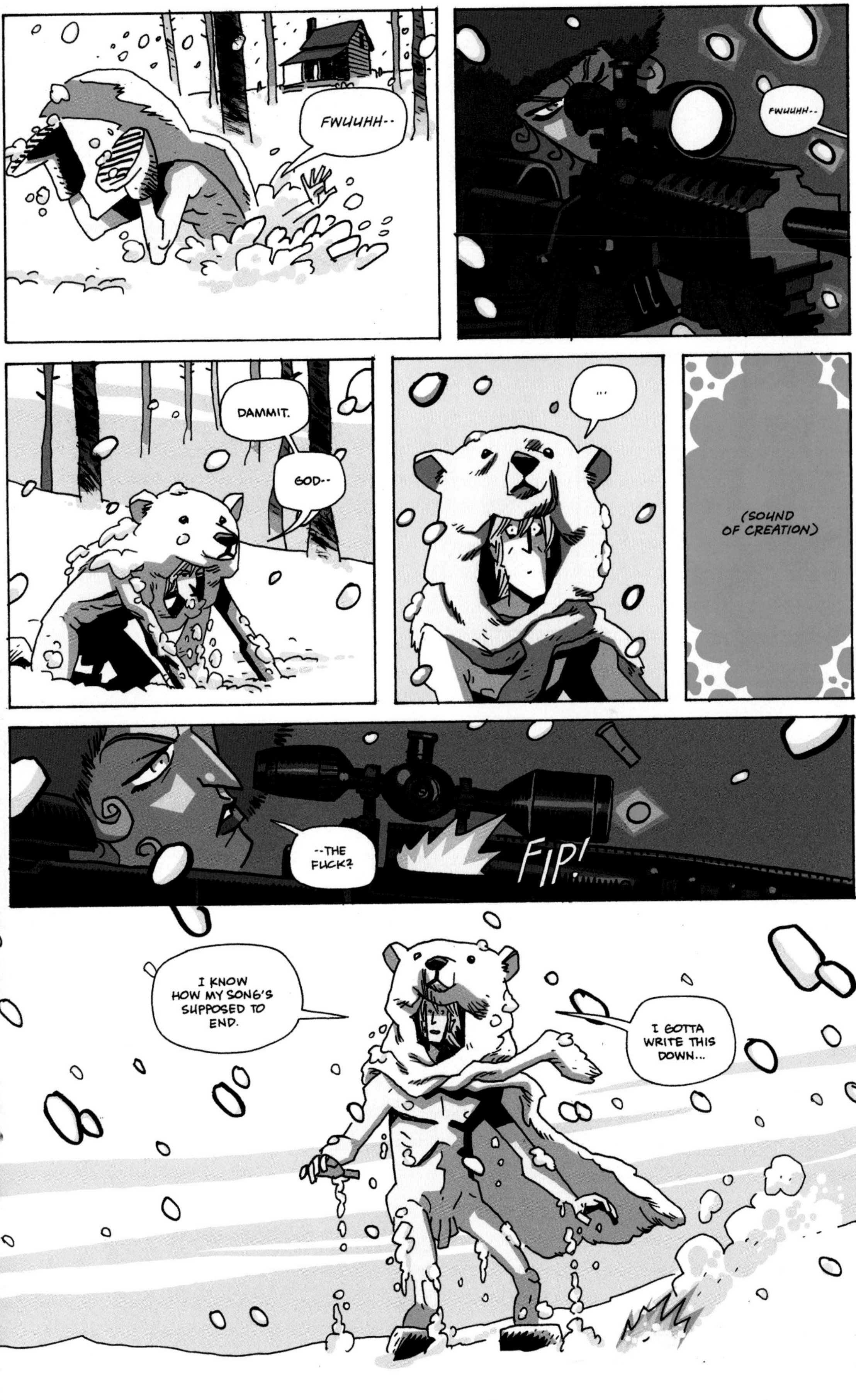
FWUUHH--
FWUUHH--
DAMMIT.
GOD--
...
(SOUND OF CREATION)
--THE FUCK?
FIP!
I KNOW HOW MY SONG'S SUPPOSED TO END.
I GOTTA WRITE THIS DOWN...

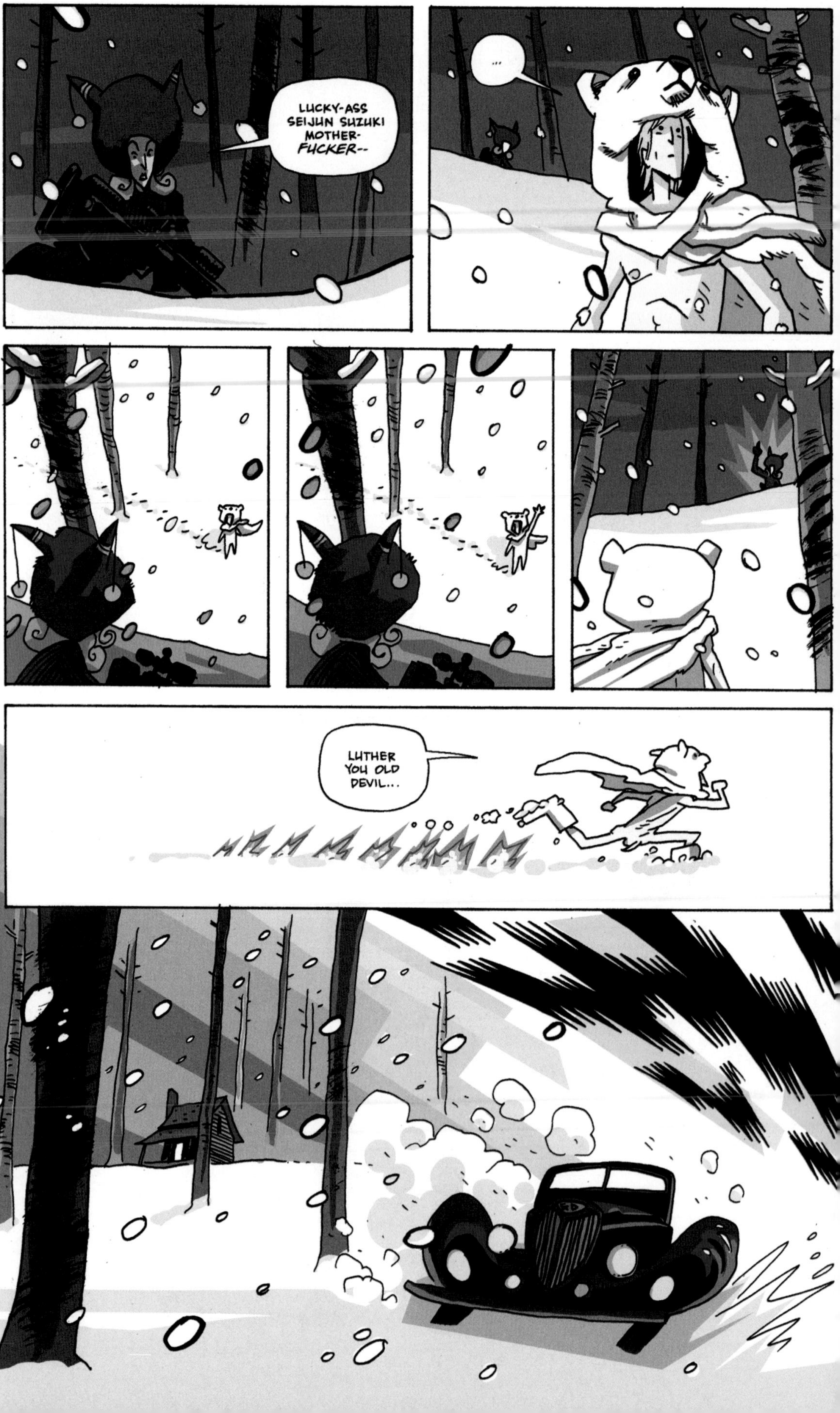
LUCKY-ASS SEIJUN SUZUKI MOTHER-FUCKER--
...
LUTHER YOU OLD DEVIL...

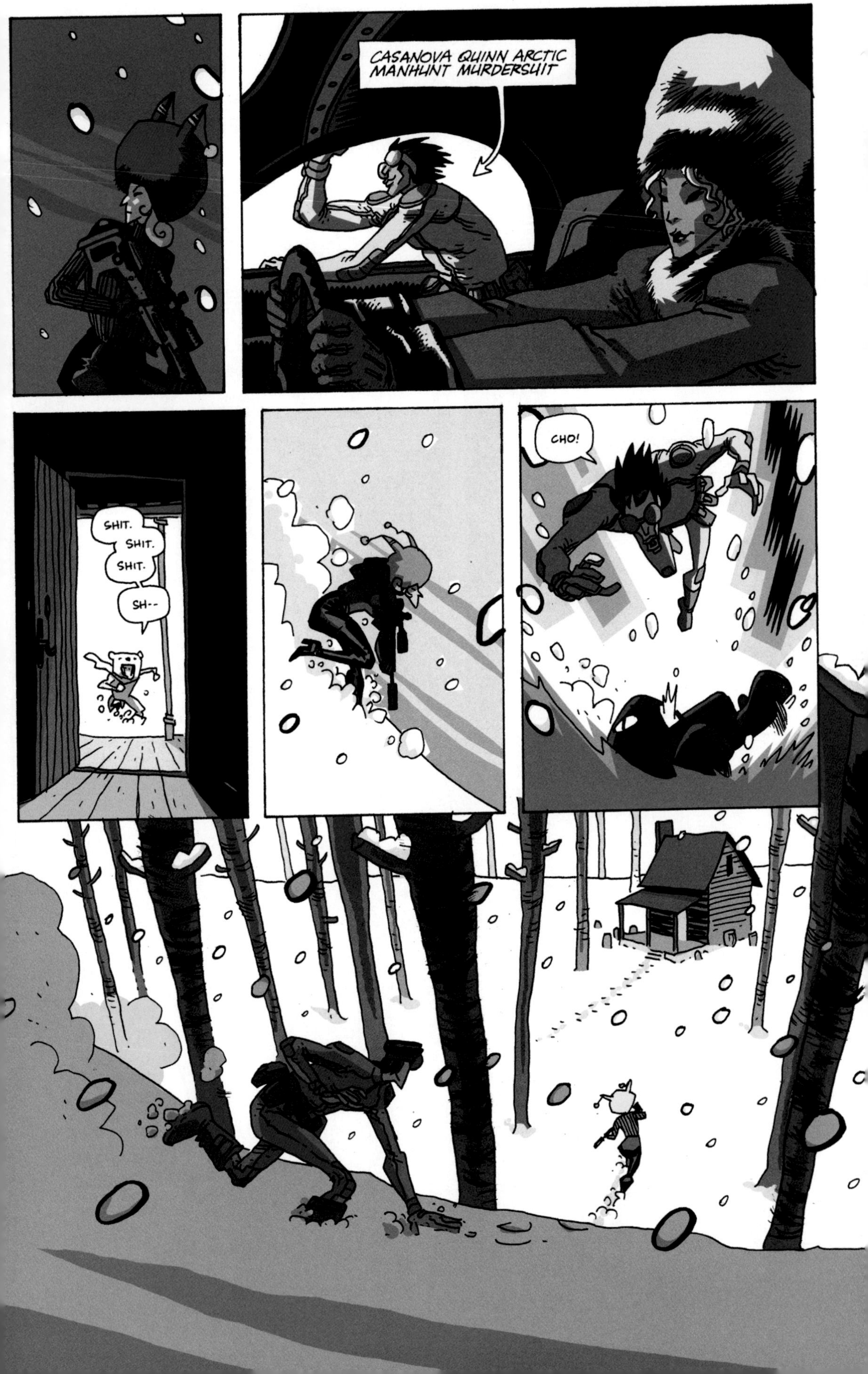
CASANOVA QUINN ARCTIC MANHUNT MURDERSUIT
SHIT.
SHIT.
SHIT.
SH--
CHO!

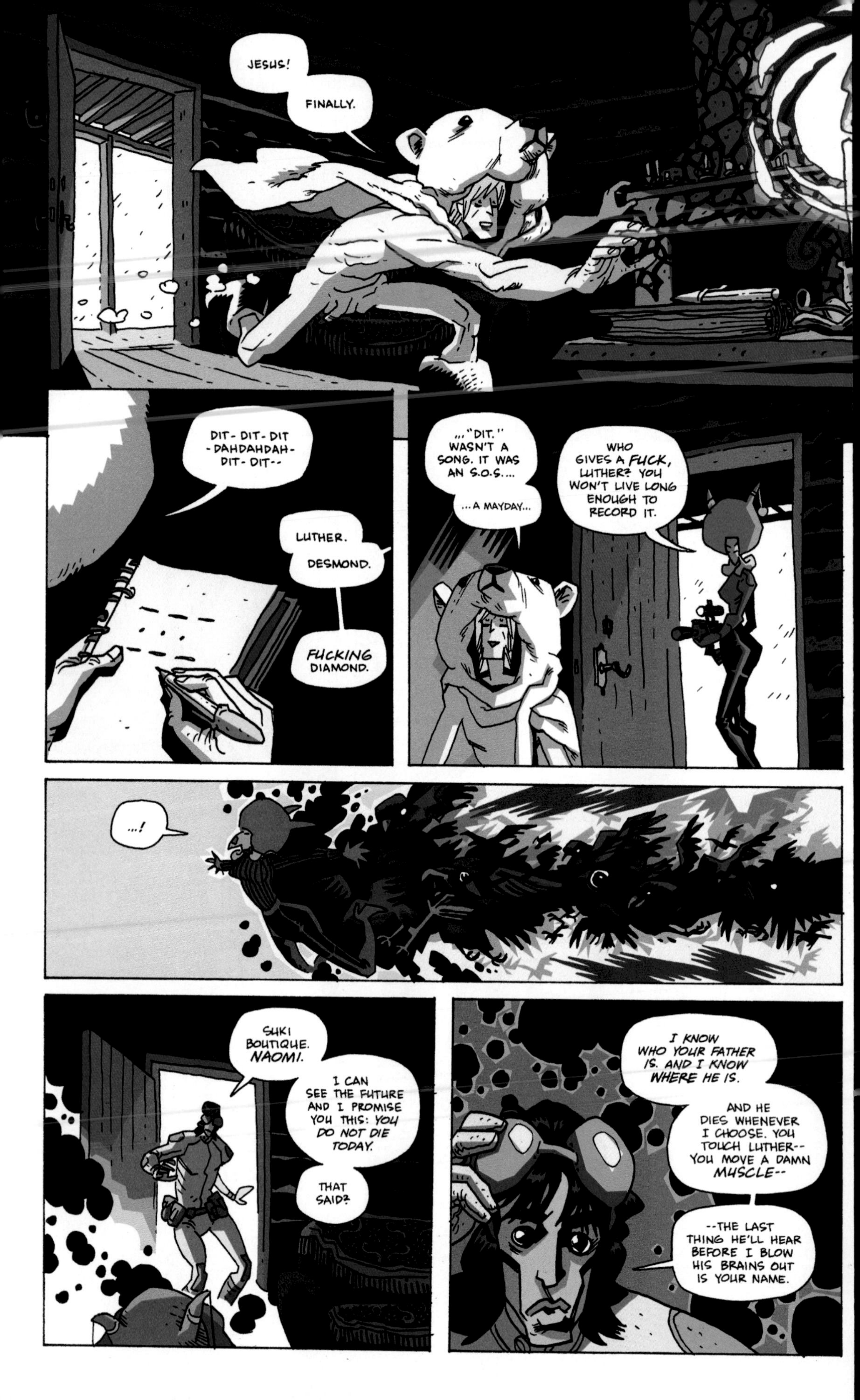
JESUS!
FINALLY.
DIT- DIT- DIT -DAHDAHDAH- DIT- DIT--
LUTHER.
DESMOND.
FUCKING DIAMOND.
..."DIT." WASN'T A SONG. IT WAS AN S.O.S....
...A MAYDAY...
WHO GIVES A FUCK, LUTHER? YOU WON'T LIVE LONG ENOUGH TO RECORD IT.
...!
SUKI BOUTIQUE. NAOMI.
I CAN SEE THE FUTURE AND I PROMISE YOU THIS: YOU DO NOT DIE TODAY.
THAT SAID?
I KNOW WHO YOUR FATHER IS. AND I KNOW WHERE HE IS.
AND HE DIES WHENEVER I CHOOSE. YOU TOUCH LUTHER-- YOU MOVE A DAMN MUSCLE--
--THE LAST THING HE'LL HEAR BEFORE I BLOW HIS BRAINS OUT IS YOUR NAME.

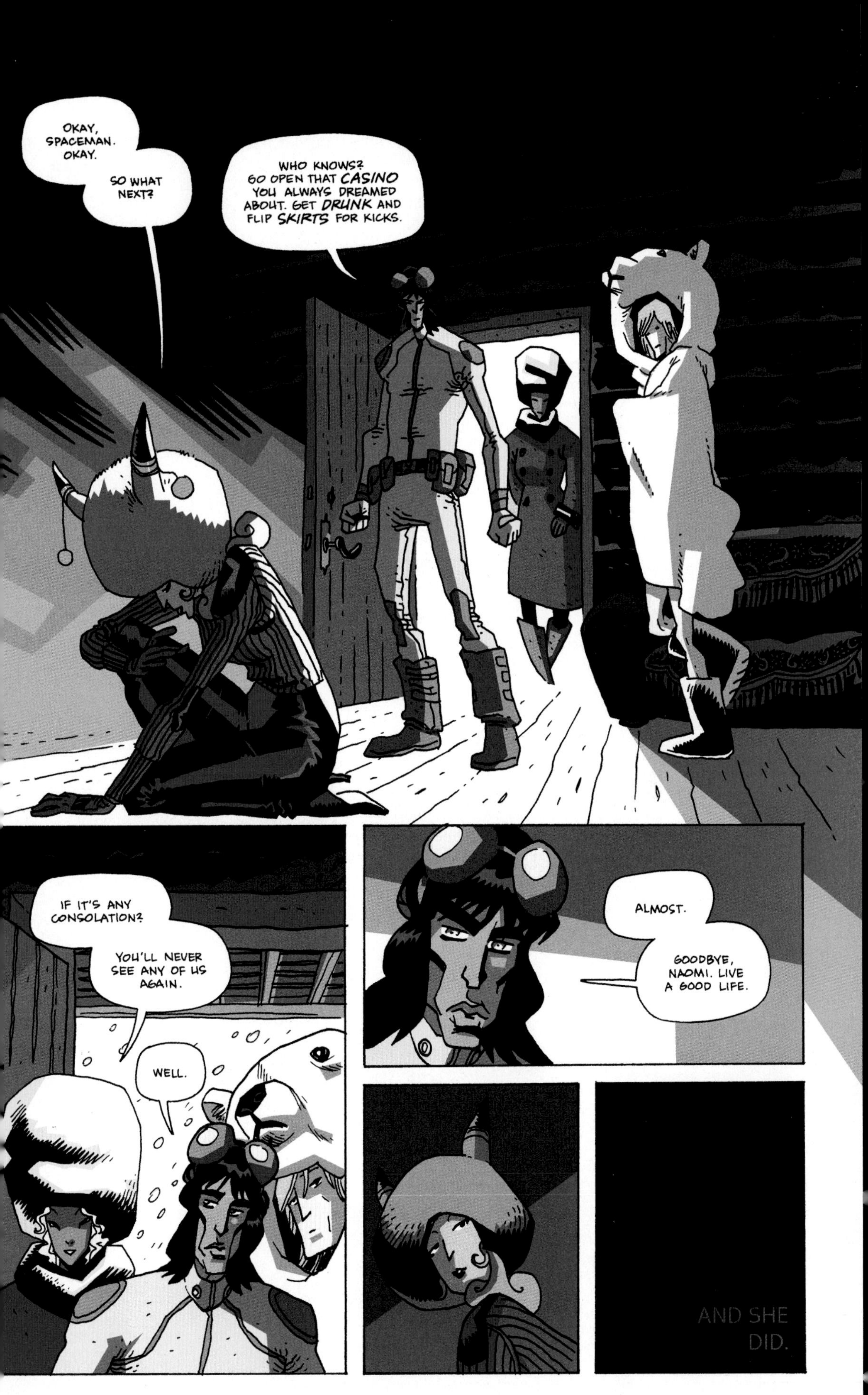
OKAY, SPACEMAN. OKAY.
SO WHAT NEXT?
WHO KNOWS? GO OPEN THAT CASINO YOU ALWAYS DREAMED ABOUT. GET DRUNK AND FLIP SKIRTS FOR KICKS.
IF IT'S ANY CONSOLATION?
YOU'LL NEVER SEE ANY OF US AGAIN.
WELL.
ALMOST.
GOODBYE, NAOMI. LIVE A GOOD LIFE.
AND SHE DID.

9. YOU'RE JUST A PRODUCT OF THE TIMES

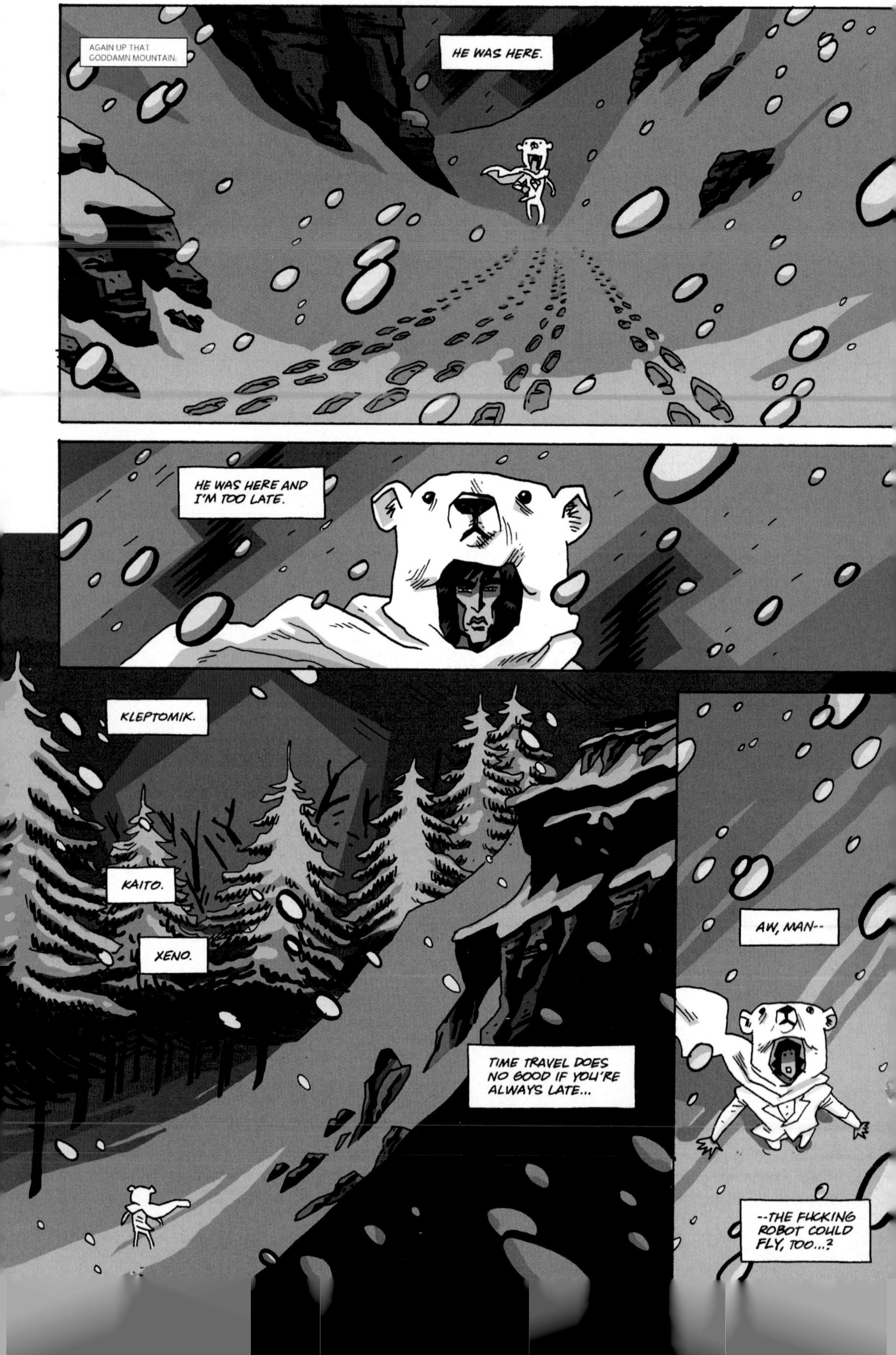

AGAIN UP THAT GODDAMN MOUNTAIN:
HE WAS HERE.
HE WAS HERE AND I'M TOO LATE.
KLEPTOMIK.
KAITO.
XENO.
TIME TRAVEL DOES NO GOOD IF YOU'RE ALWAYS LATE...
AW, MAN--
--THE FUCKING ROBOT COULD FLY, TOO...?

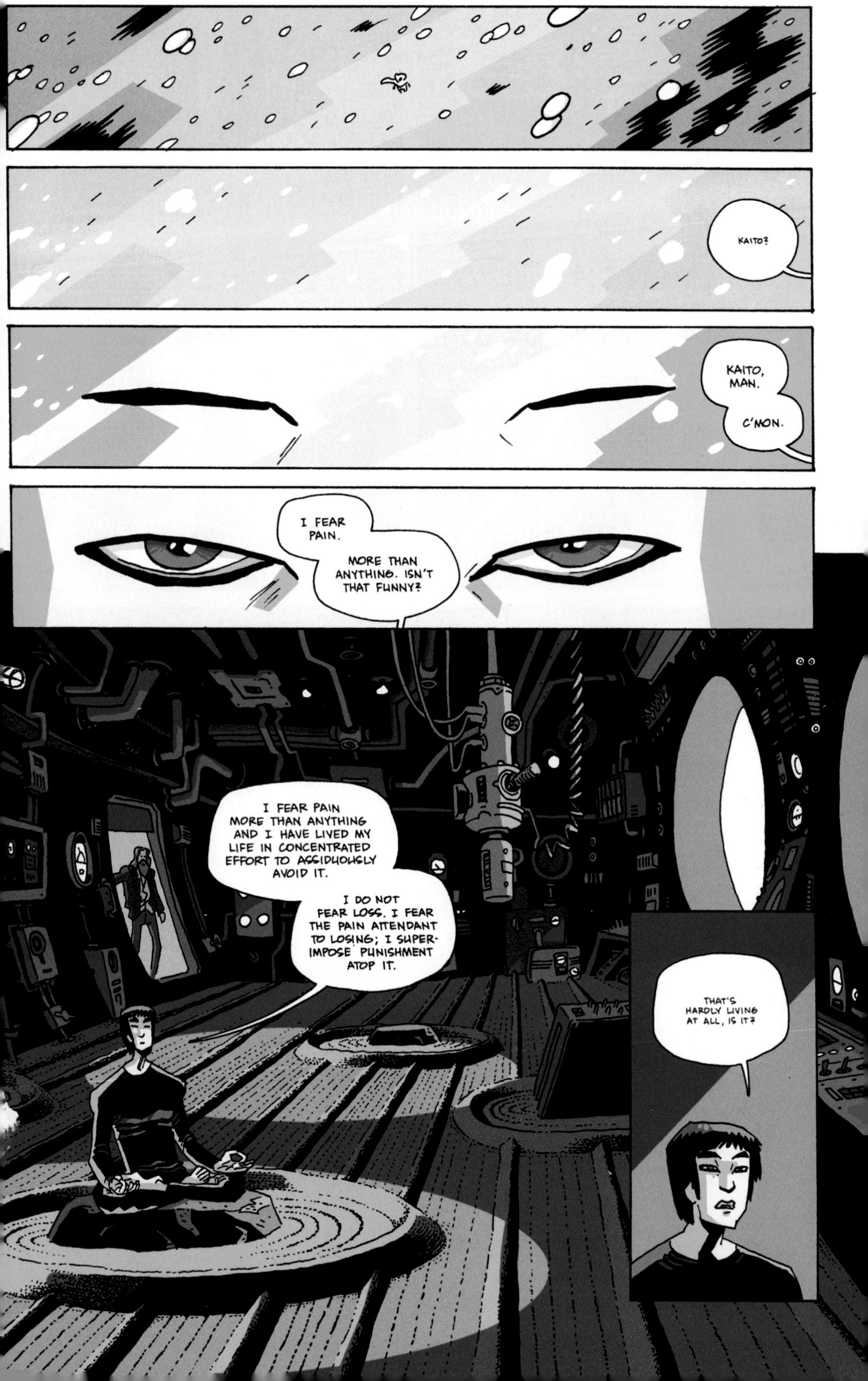
KAITO?
KAITO, MAN.
C'MON.
I FEAR PAIN.
MORE THAN ANYTHING. ISN'T THAT FUNNY?
I FEAR PAIN MORE THAN ANYTHING AND I HAVE LIVED MY LIFE IN CONCENTRATED EFFORT TO ASSIDUOUSLY AVOID IT.
I DO NOT FEAR LOSS. I FEAR THE PAIN ATTENDANT TO LOSING; I SUPER-IMPOSE PUNISHMENT ATOP IT.
THAT'S HARDLY LIVING AT ALL, IS IT?

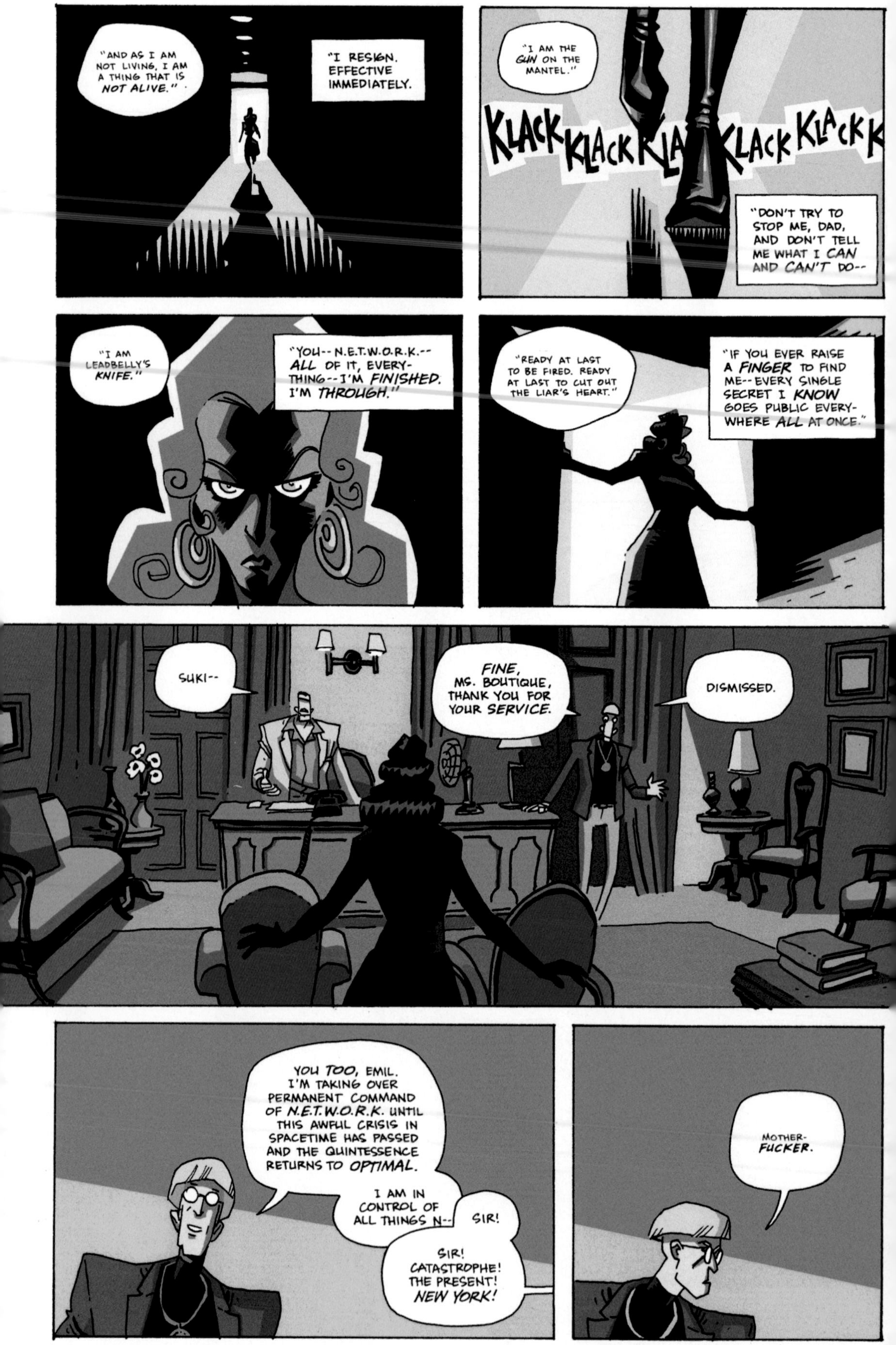
"AND AS I AM NOT LIVING, I AM A THING THAT IS NOT ALIVE."
"I RESIGN. EFFECTIVE IMMEDIATELY.
"I AM THE GUN ON THE MANTEL."
KLACK KLACK KLA KLACK KLACKK
"DON'T TRY TO STOP ME, DAD, AND DON'T TELL ME WHAT I CAN AND CAN'T DO--
"I AM LEADBELLY'S KNIFE."
"YOU-- N.E.T.W.O.R.K.-- ALL OF IT, EVERYTHING-- I'M FINISHED. I'M THROUGH."
"READY AT LAST TO BE FIRED. READY AT LAST TO CUT OUT THE LIAR'S HEART."
"IF YOU EVER RAISE A FINGER TO FIND ME-- EVERY SINGLE SECRET I KNOW GOES PUBLIC EVERYWHERE ALL AT ONCE."
SUKI--
FINE, MS. BOUTIQUE, THANK YOU FOR YOUR SERVICE.
DISMISSED.
YOU TOO, EMIL. I'M TAKING OVER PERMANENT COMMAND OF N.E.T.W.O.R.K. UNTIL THIS AWFUL CRISIS IN SPACETIME HAS PASSED AND THE QUINTESSENCE RETURNS TO OPTIMAL.
I AM IN CONTROL OF ALL THINGS N--
SIR!
SIR! CATASTROPHE! THE PRESENT! NEW YORK!
MOTHER-FUCKER.

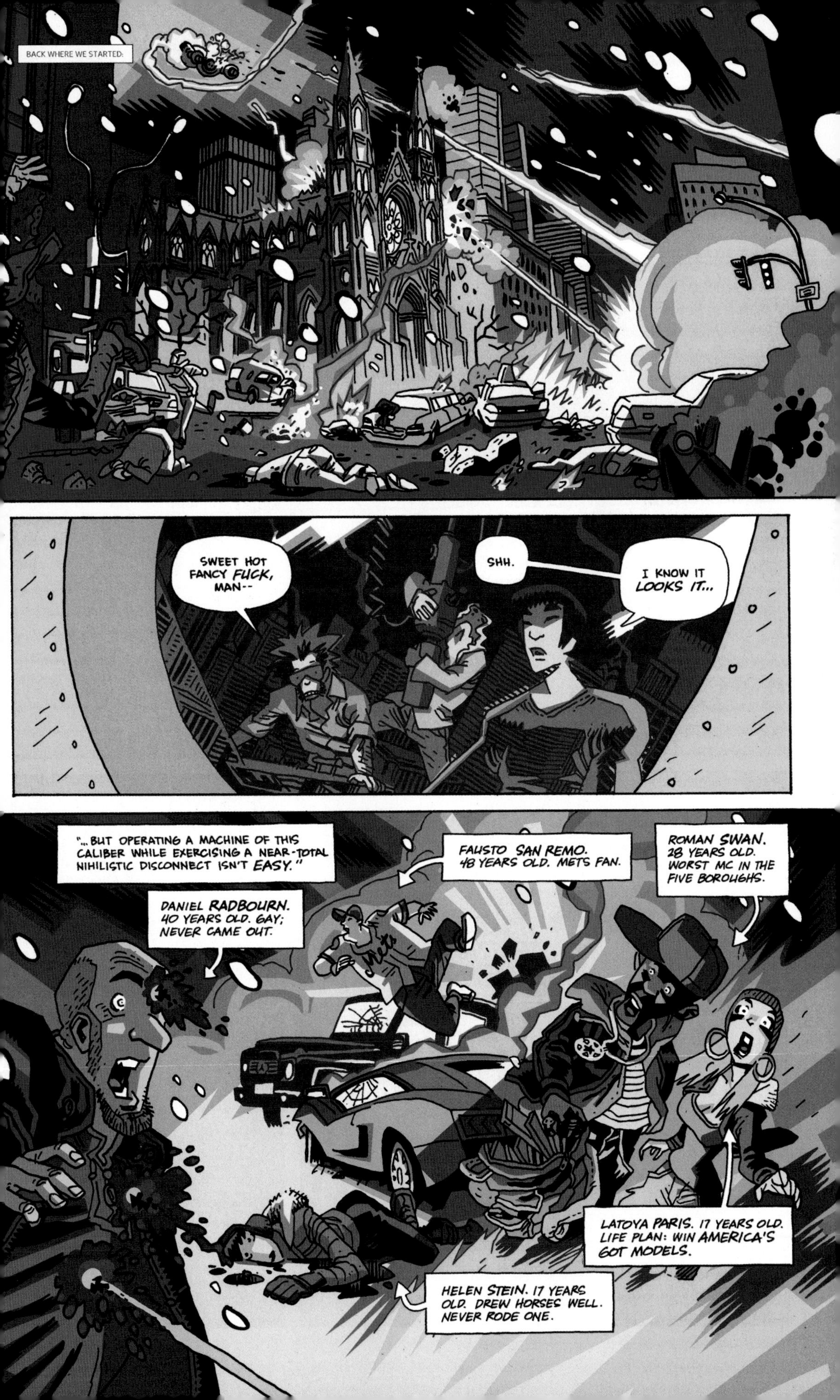
BACK WHERE WE STARTED:
SWEET HOT FANCY FUCK, MAN--
SHH.
I KNOW IT LOOKS IT...
"...BUT OPERATING A MACHINE OF THIS CALIBER WHILE EXERCISING A NEAR-TOTAL NIHILISTIC DISCONNECT ISN'T EASY."
FAUSTO SAN REMO. 48 YEARS OLD. METS FAN.
ROMAN SWAN. 28 YEARS OLD. WORST MC IN THE FIVE BOROUGHS.
DANIEL RADBOURN. 40 YEARS OLD. GAY; NEVER CAME OUT.
LATOYA PARIS. 17 YEARS OLD. LIFE PLAN: WIN AMERICA'S GOT MODELS.
HELEN STEIN. 17 YEARS OLD. DREW HORSES WELL. NEVER RODE ONE.

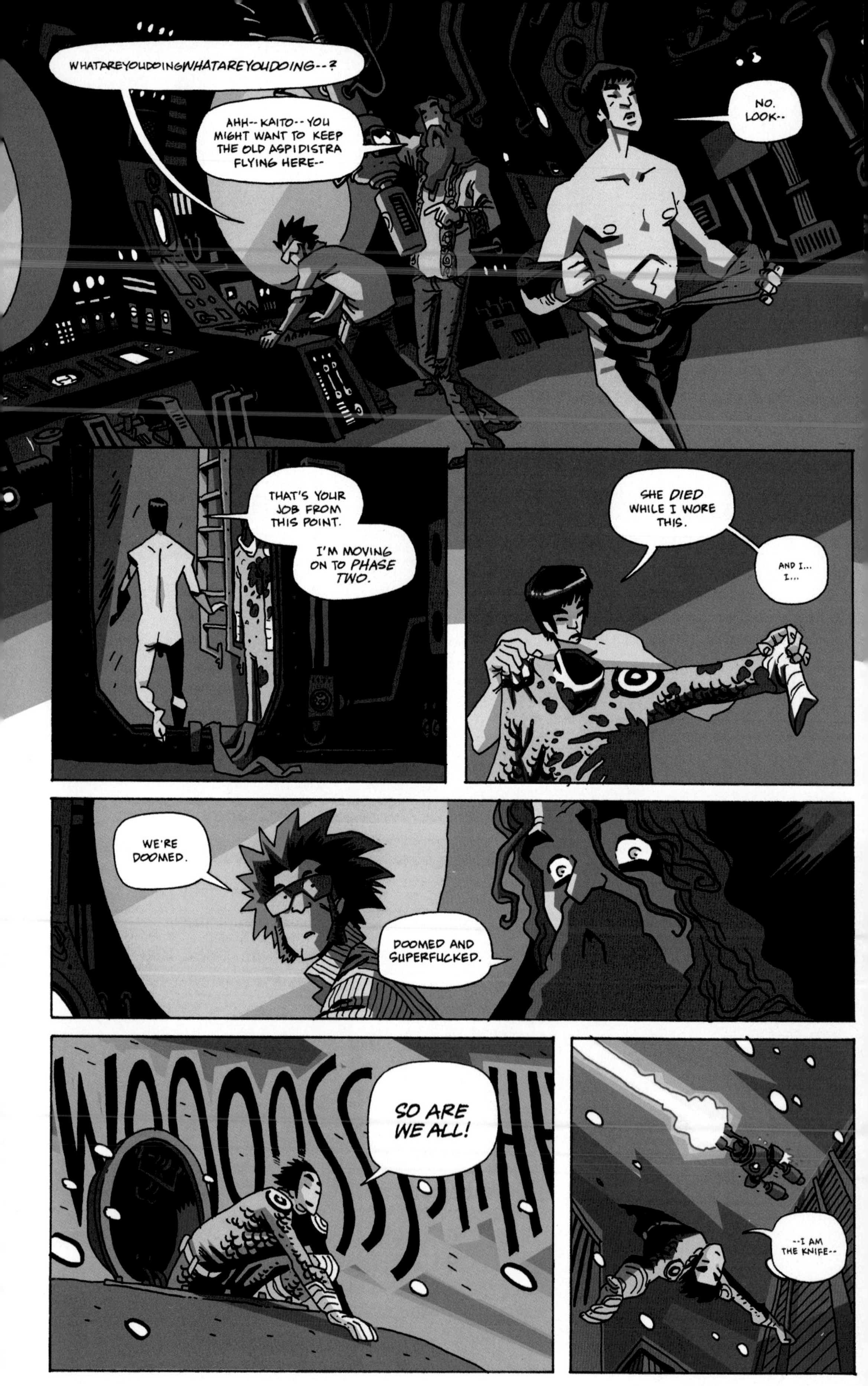
WHATAREYOUDOINGWHATAREYOUDOING--?
AHH--KAITO--YOU MIGHT WANT TO KEEP THE OLD ASPIDISTRA FLYING HERE--
NO. LOOK--
THAT'S YOUR JOB FROM THIS POINT.
I'M MOVING ON TO PHASE TWO.
SHE DIED WHILE I WORE THIS.
AND I... I...
WE'RE DOOMED.
DOOMED AND SUPERFUCKED.
WOOOOSSSHHH
SO ARE WE ALL!
--I AM THE KNIFE--

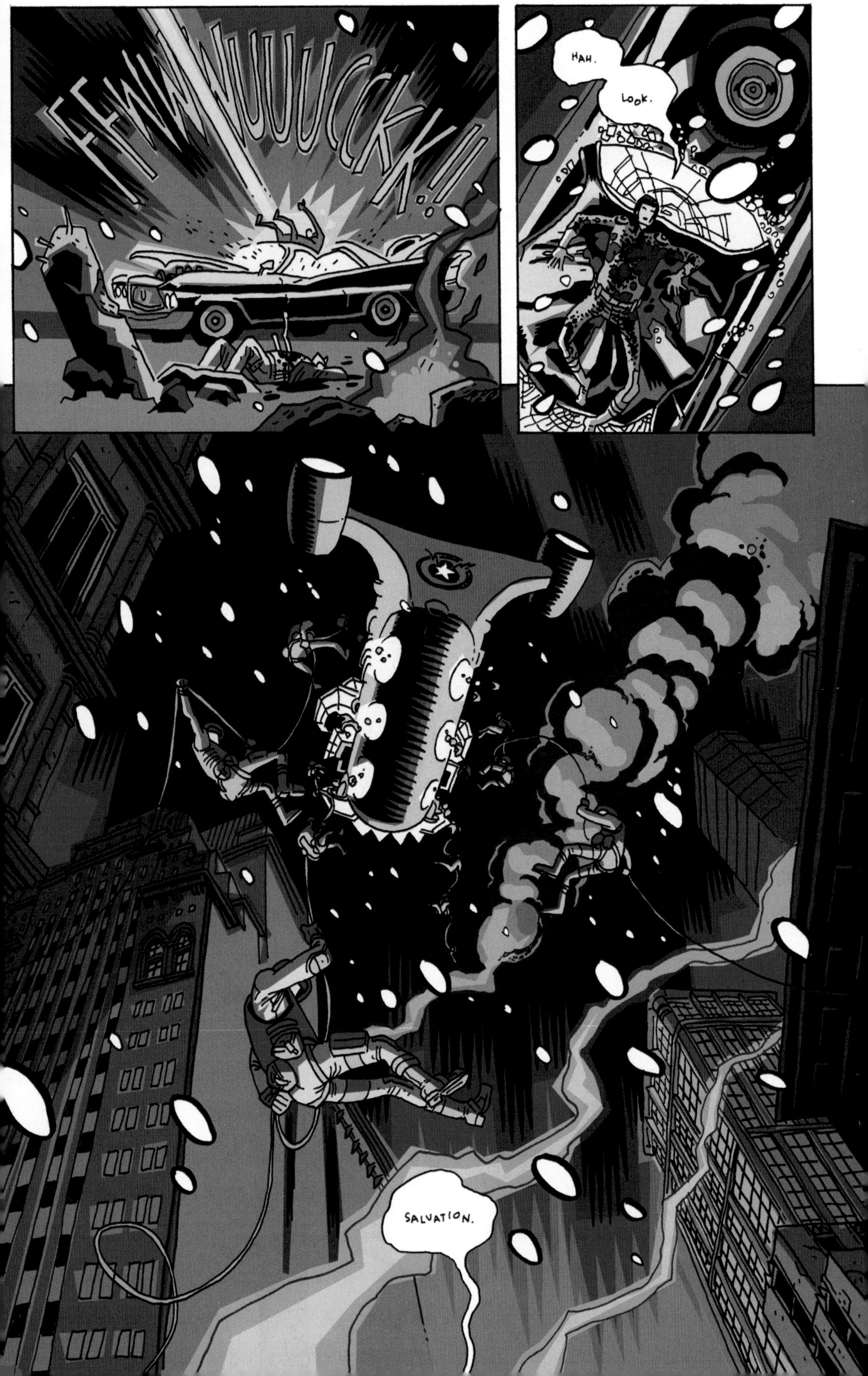
FFWWUUUCCK!!
HAH.
LOOK.
SALVATION.

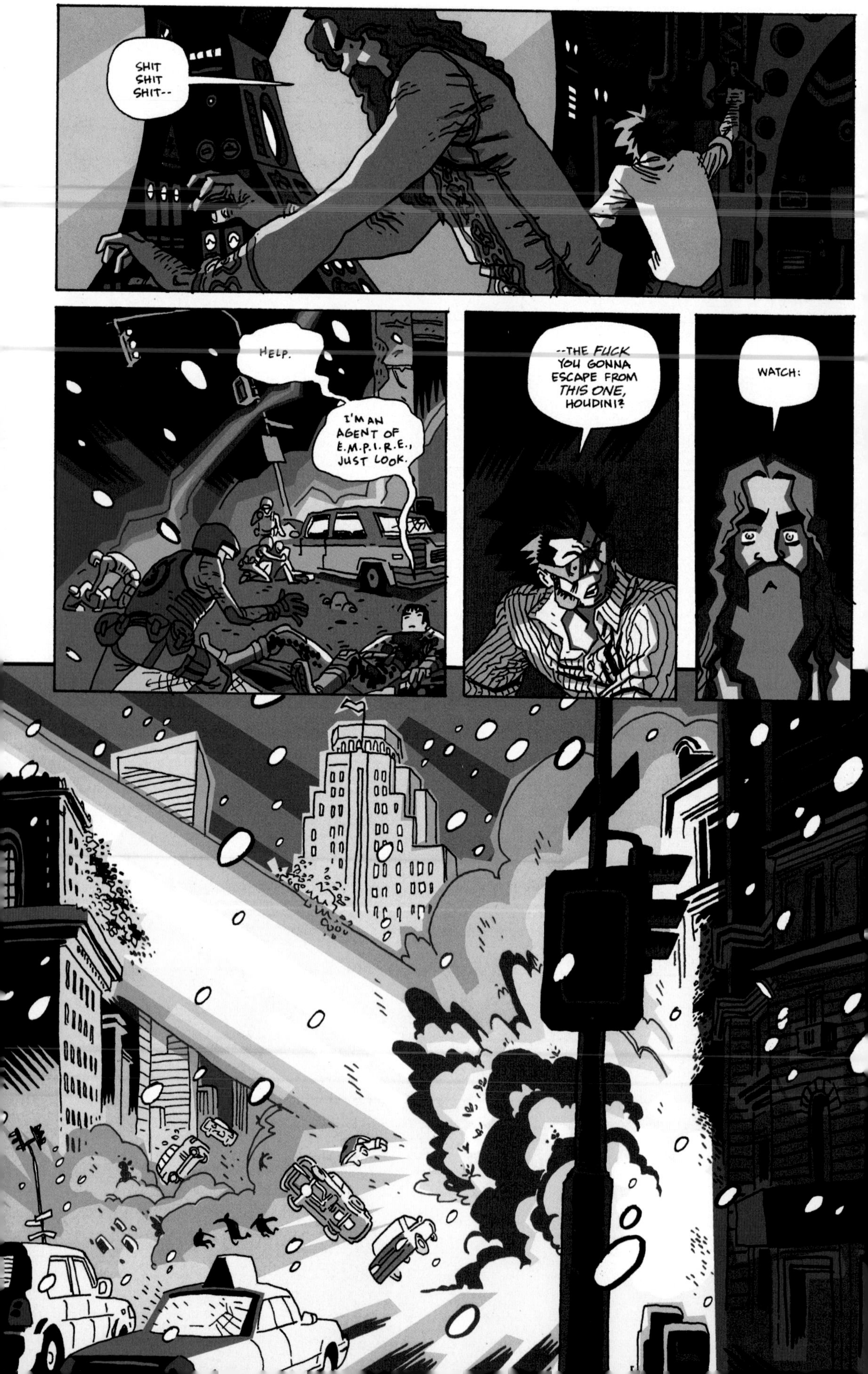
SHIT
SHIT
SHIT--
HELP.
I'M AN AGENT OF E.M.P.I.R.E., JUST LOOK.
--THE FUCK YOU GONNA ESCAPE FROM THIS ONE, HOUDINI?
WATCH:

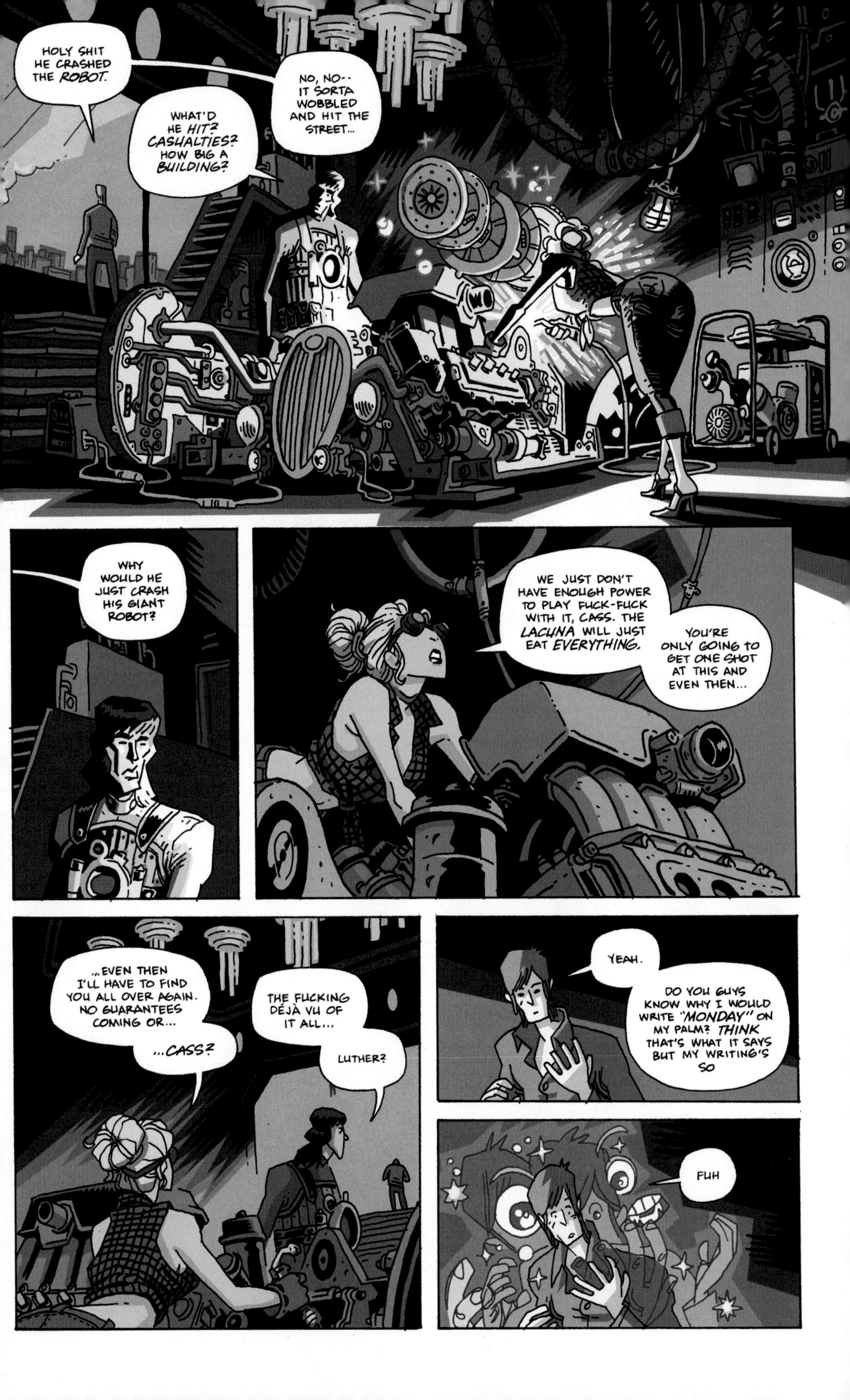
HOLY SHIT HE CRASHED THE ROBOT.
WHAT'D HE HIT? CASUALTIES? HOW BIG A BUILDING?
NO, NO-- IT SORTA WOBBLED AND HIT THE STREET...
WHY WOULD HE JUST CRASH HIS GIANT ROBOT?
WE JUST DON'T HAVE ENOUGH POWER TO PLAY FUCK-FUCK WITH IT, CASS. THE LACUNA WILL JUST EAT EVERYTHING.
YOU'RE ONLY GOING TO GET ONE SHOT AT THIS AND EVEN THEN...
...EVEN THEN I'LL HAVE TO FIND YOU ALL OVER AGAIN. NO GUARANTEES COMING OR...
...CASS?
THE FUCKING DÉJÀ VU OF IT ALL...
LUTHER?
YEAH.
DO YOU GUYS KNOW WHY I WOULD WRITE "MONDAY" ON MY PALM? THINK THAT'S WHAT IT SAYS BUT MY WRITING'S SO
FUH

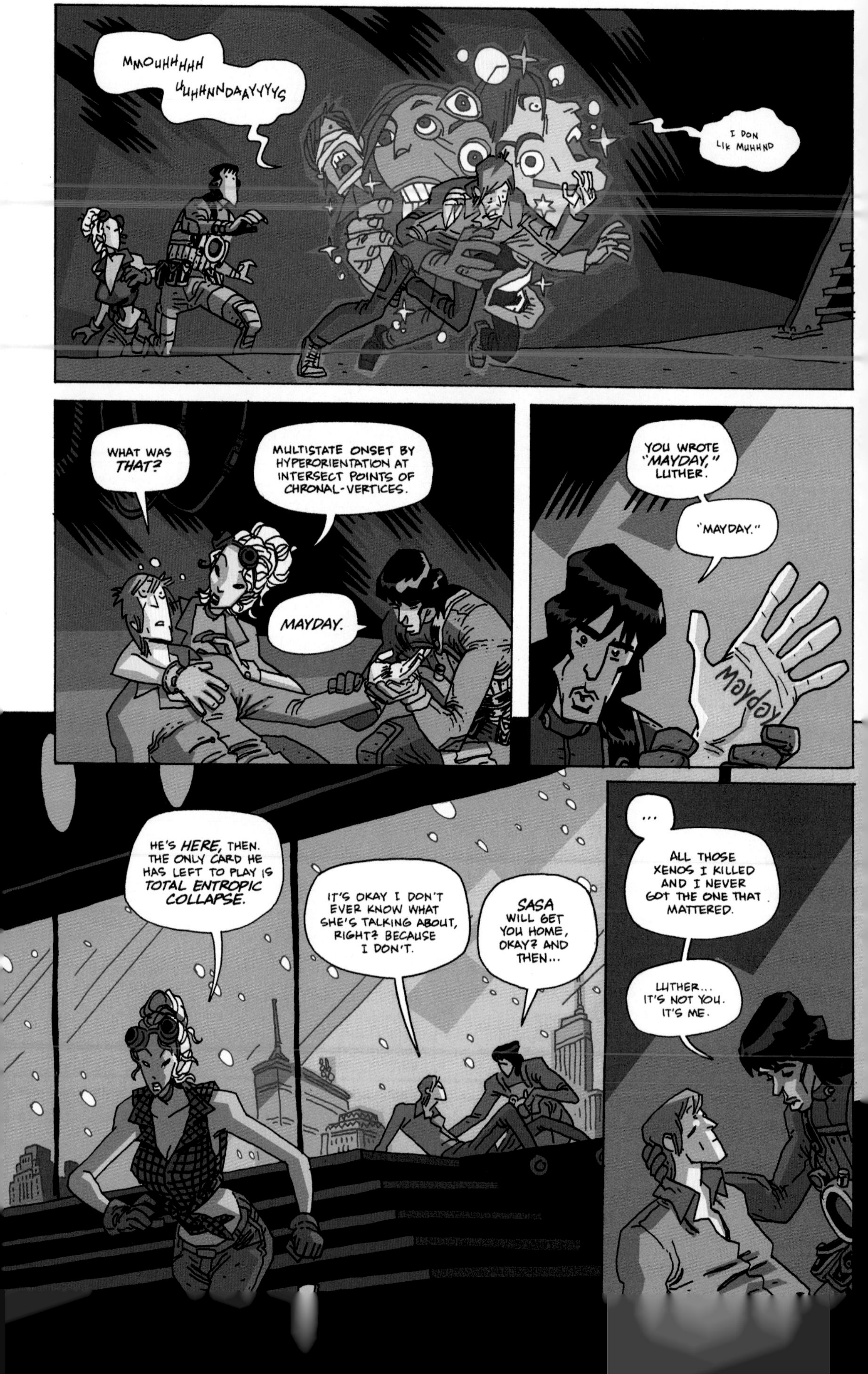
MMOUHHHHH UUHHNNDAAYYYYG
I DON LIK MUHHND
WHAT WAS THAT?
MULTISTATE ONSET BY HYPERORIENTATION AT INTERSECT POINTS OF CHRONAL-VERTICES.
MAYDAY.
YOU WROTE "MAYDAY," LUTHER.
"MAYDAY."
Mayday
HE'S HERE, THEN. THE ONLY CARD HE HAS LEFT TO PLAY IS TOTAL ENTROPIC COLLAPSE.
IT'S OKAY I DON'T EVER KNOW WHAT SHE'S TALKING ABOUT, RIGHT? BECAUSE I DON'T.
SASA WILL GET YOU HOME, OKAY? AND THEN...
...
ALL THOSE XENOS I KILLED AND I NEVER GOT THE ONE THAT MATTERED.
LUTHER... IT'S NOT YOU. IT'S ME.

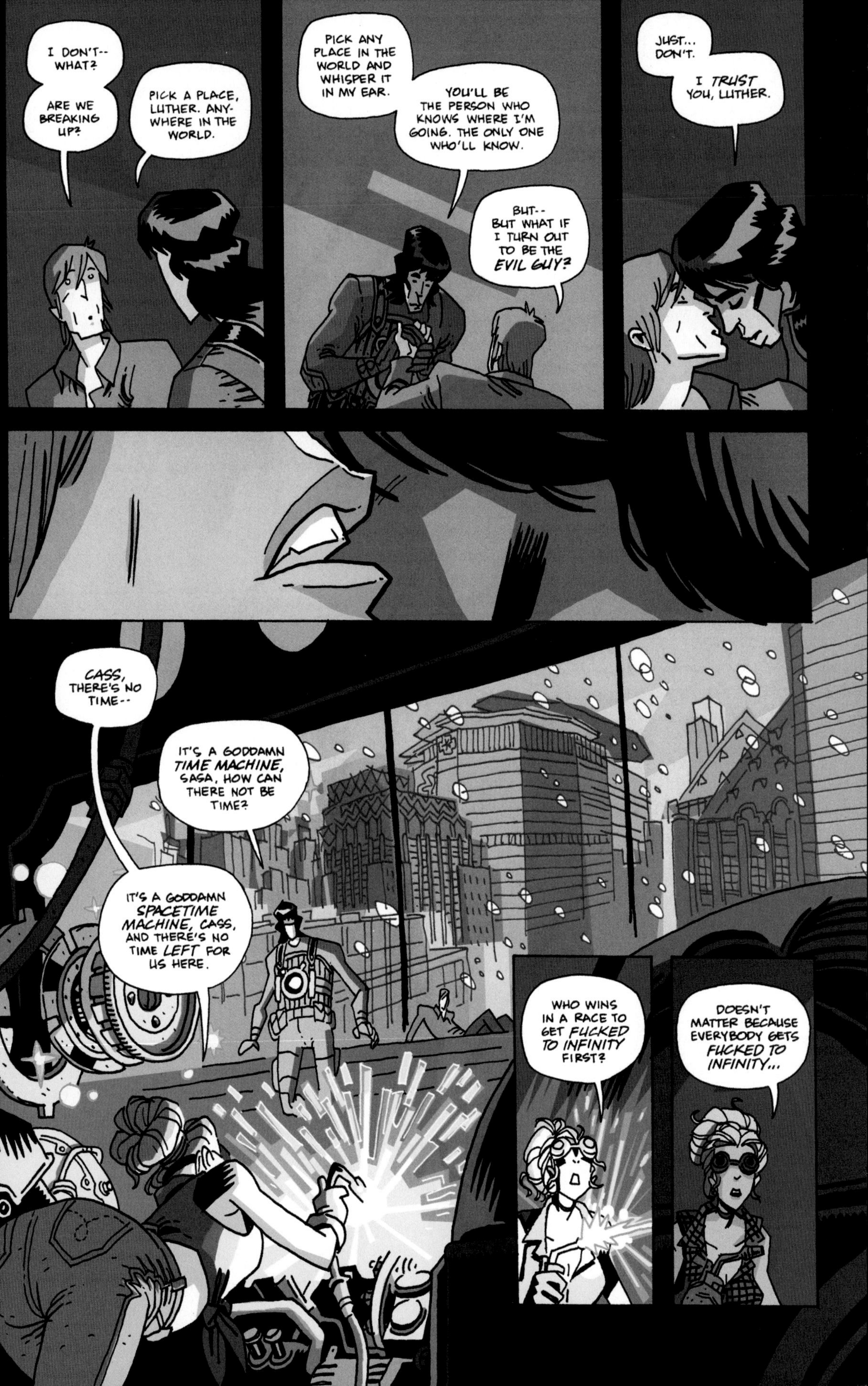
I DON'T-- WHAT?
ARE WE BREAKING UP?
PICK A PLACE, LUTHER. ANYWHERE IN THE WORLD.
PICK ANY PLACE IN THE WORLD AND WHISPER IT IN MY EAR.
YOU'LL BE THE PERSON WHO KNOWS WHERE I'M GOING. THE ONLY ONE WHO'LL KNOW.
BUT-- BUT WHAT IF I TURN OUT TO BE THE EVIL GUY?
JUST... DON'T.
I TRUST YOU, LUTHER.
CASS, THERE'S NO TIME--
IT'S A GODDAMN TIME MACHINE, SASA, HOW CAN THERE NOT BE TIME?
IT'S A GODDAMN SPACETIME MACHINE, CASS, AND THERE'S NO TIME LEFT FOR US HERE.
WHO WINS IN A RACE TO GET FUCKED TO INFINITY FIRST?
DOESN'T MATTER BECAUSE EVERYBODY GETS FUCKED TO INFINITY...

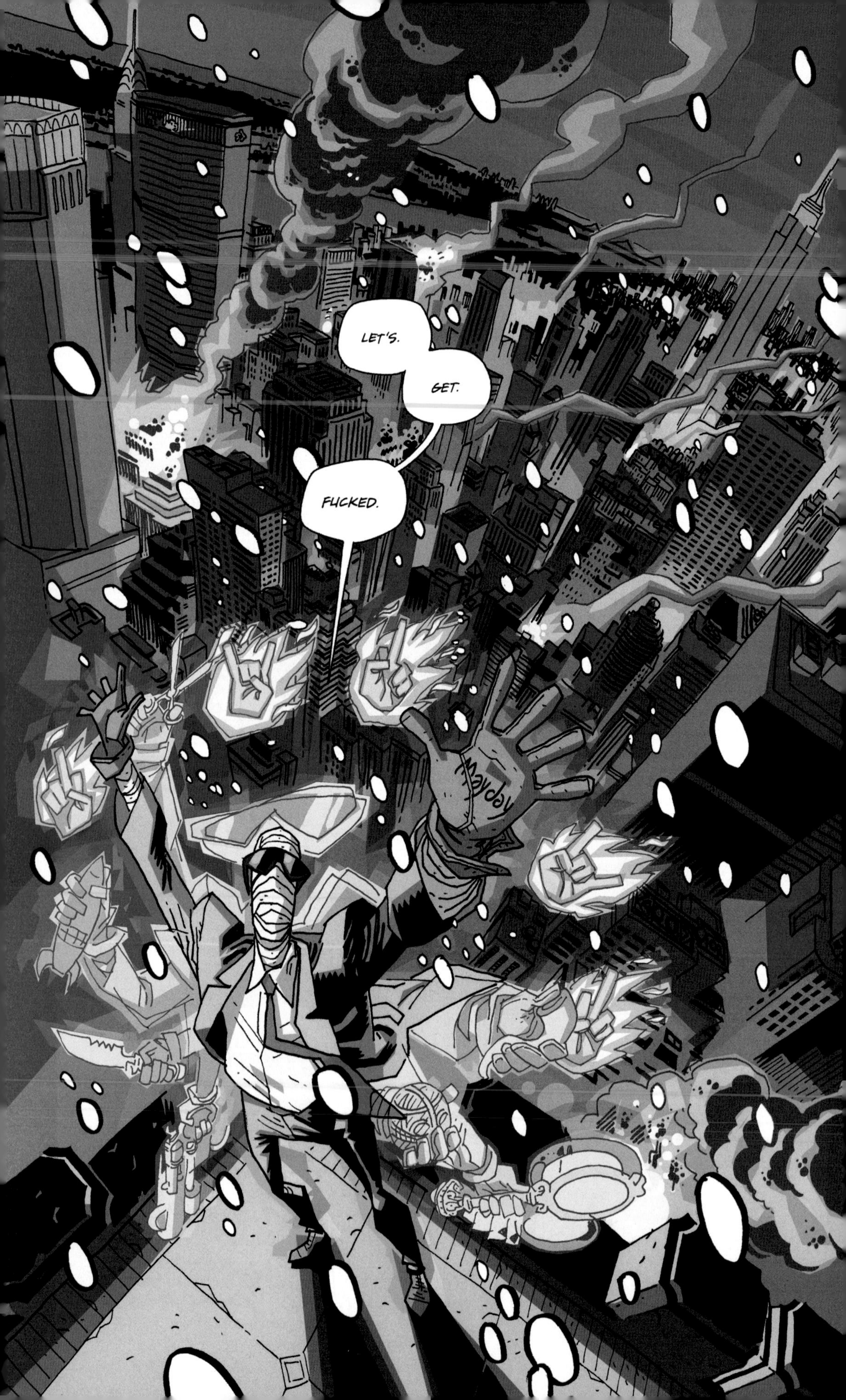
LET'S.
GET.
FUCKED.
Mayday

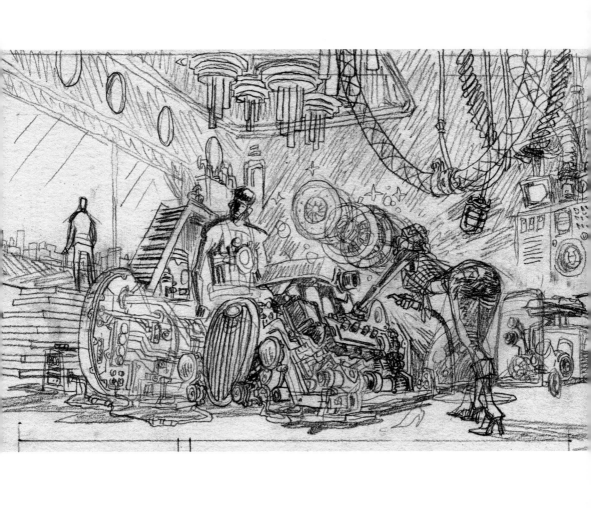

CHAPTER 4
RELAXED IN PERSON

10. CAMERAS IN BROOKLYN

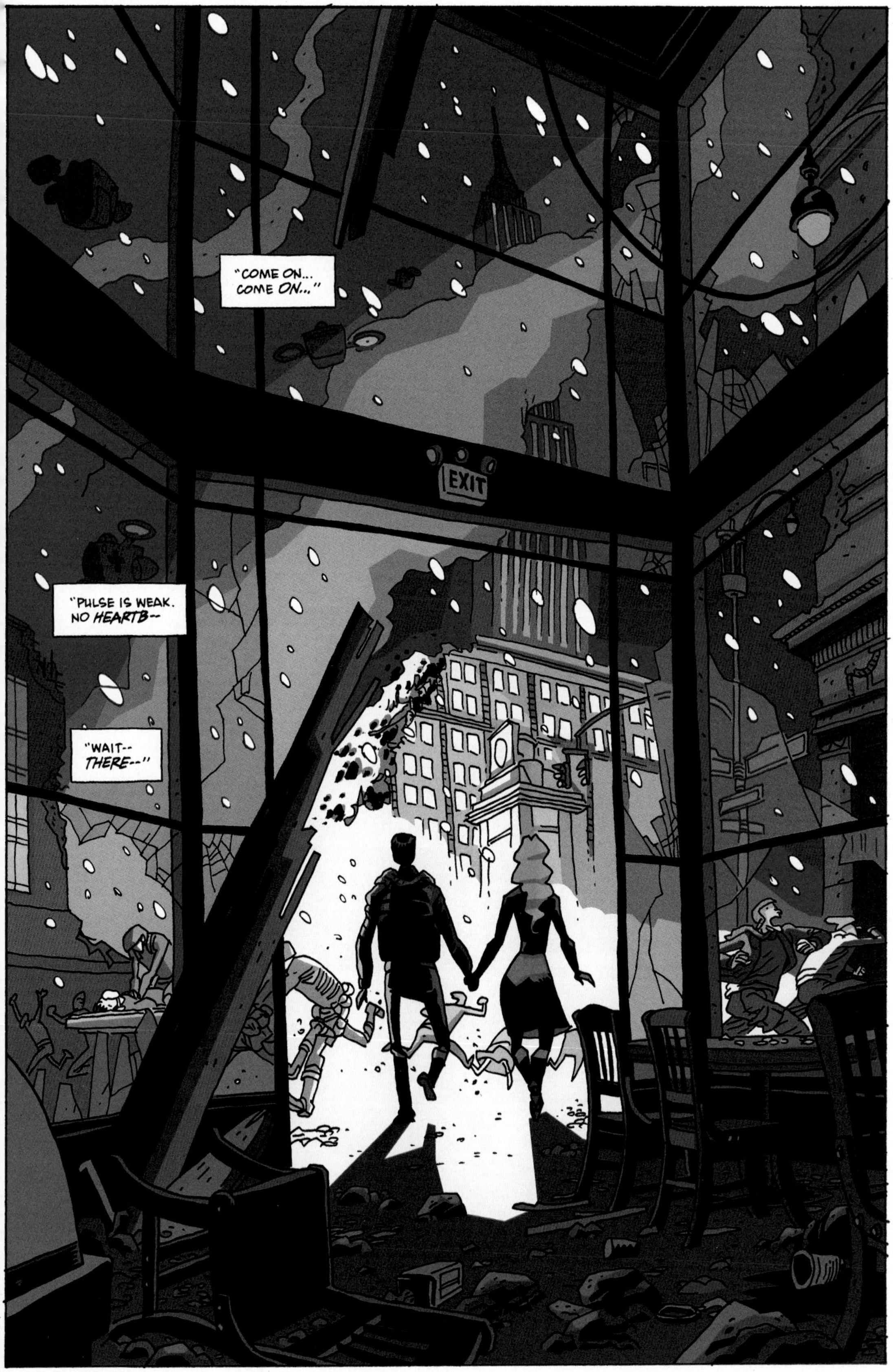
"COME ON...
COME ON..."
"PULSE IS WEAK.
NO HEARTB--
"WAIT--
THERE--"
EXIT

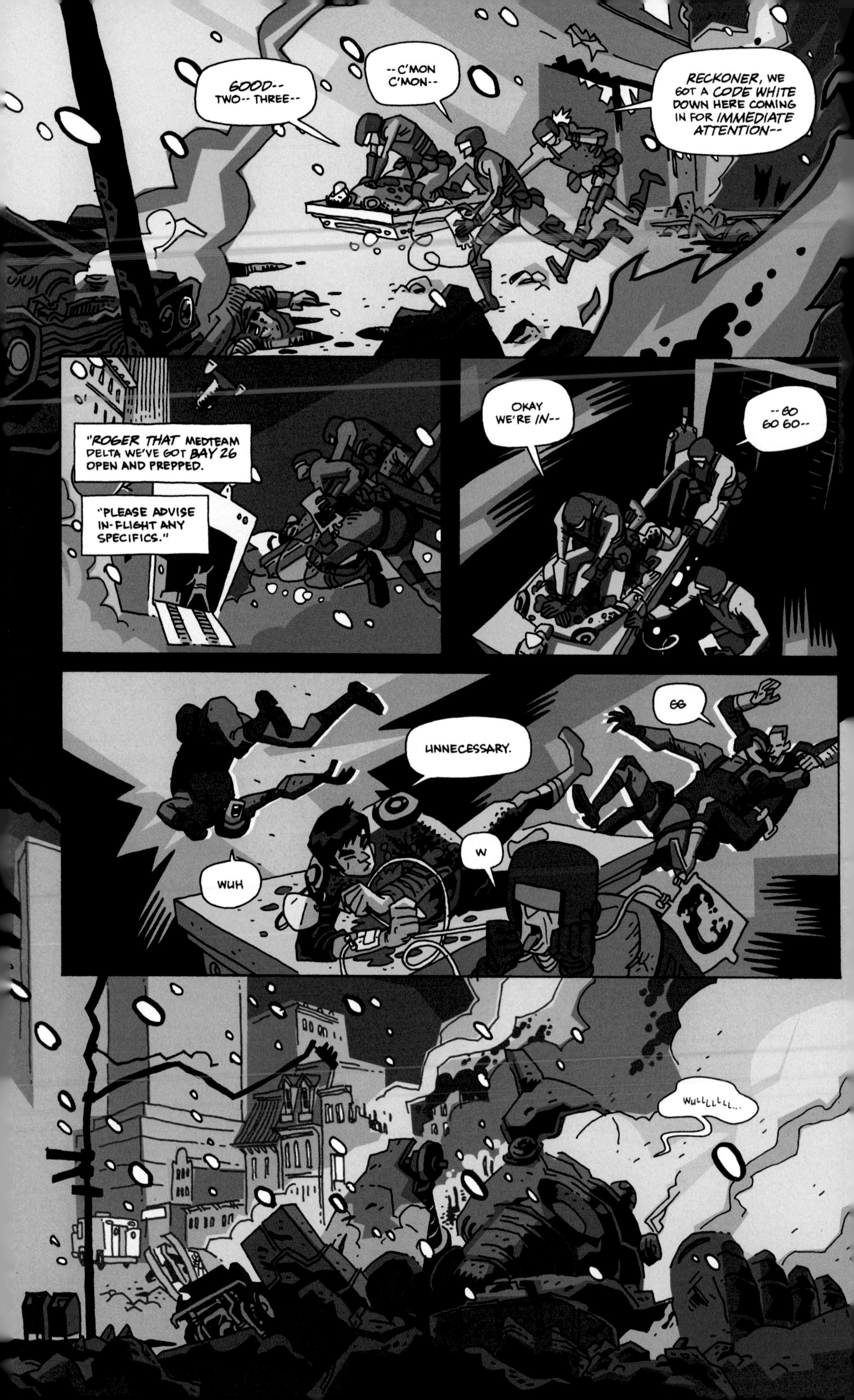
GOOD--
TWO-- THREE--
--C'MON
C'MON--
RECKONER, WE GOT A CODE WHITE DOWN HERE COMING IN FOR IMMEDIATE ATTENTION--
"ROGER THAT MEDTEAM DELTA WE'VE GOT BAY 26 OPEN AND PREPPED.
"PLEASE ADVISE IN-FLIGHT ANY SPECIFICS."
OKAY WE'RE IN--
--GO GO GO--
GG
UNNECESSARY.
WUH
W
WULLLLLL...

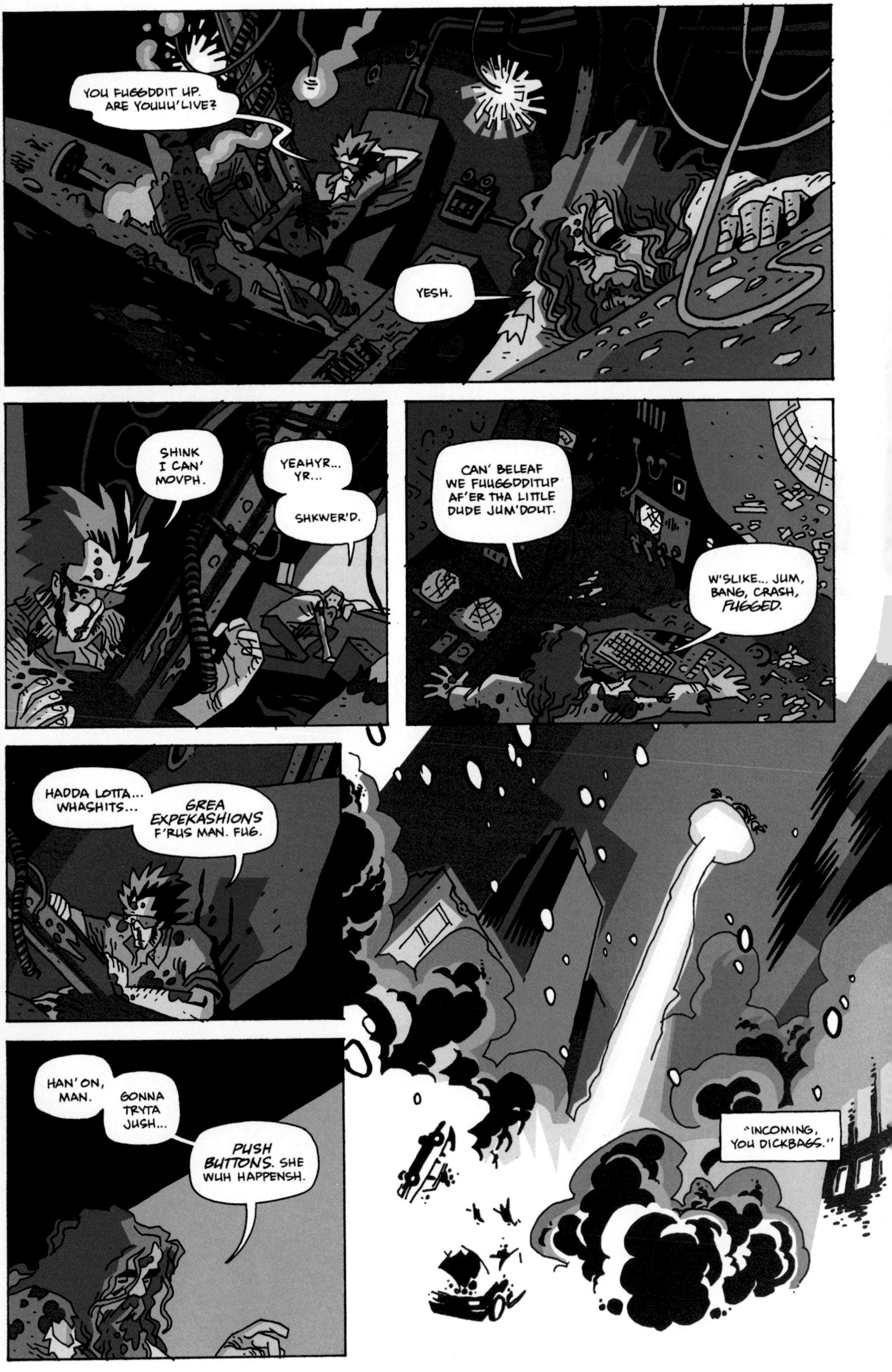

YOU FUGGDDIT UP. ARE YOUUU'LIVE?
YESH.
SHINK I CAN' MOVPH.
YEAHYR... YR...
SHKWER'D.
CAN' BELEAF WE FUUGGDDITUP AF'ER THA LITTLE DUDE JUM'DOUT.
W'SLIKE... JUM, BANG, CRASH, FUGGED.
HADDA LOTTA... WHASHITS...
GREA EXPEKASHIONS F'RUS MAN. FUG.
HAN' ON, MAN.
GONNA TRYTA JUSH...
PUSH BUTTONS. SHE WUH HAPPENSH.
"INCOMING, YOU DICKBAGS."

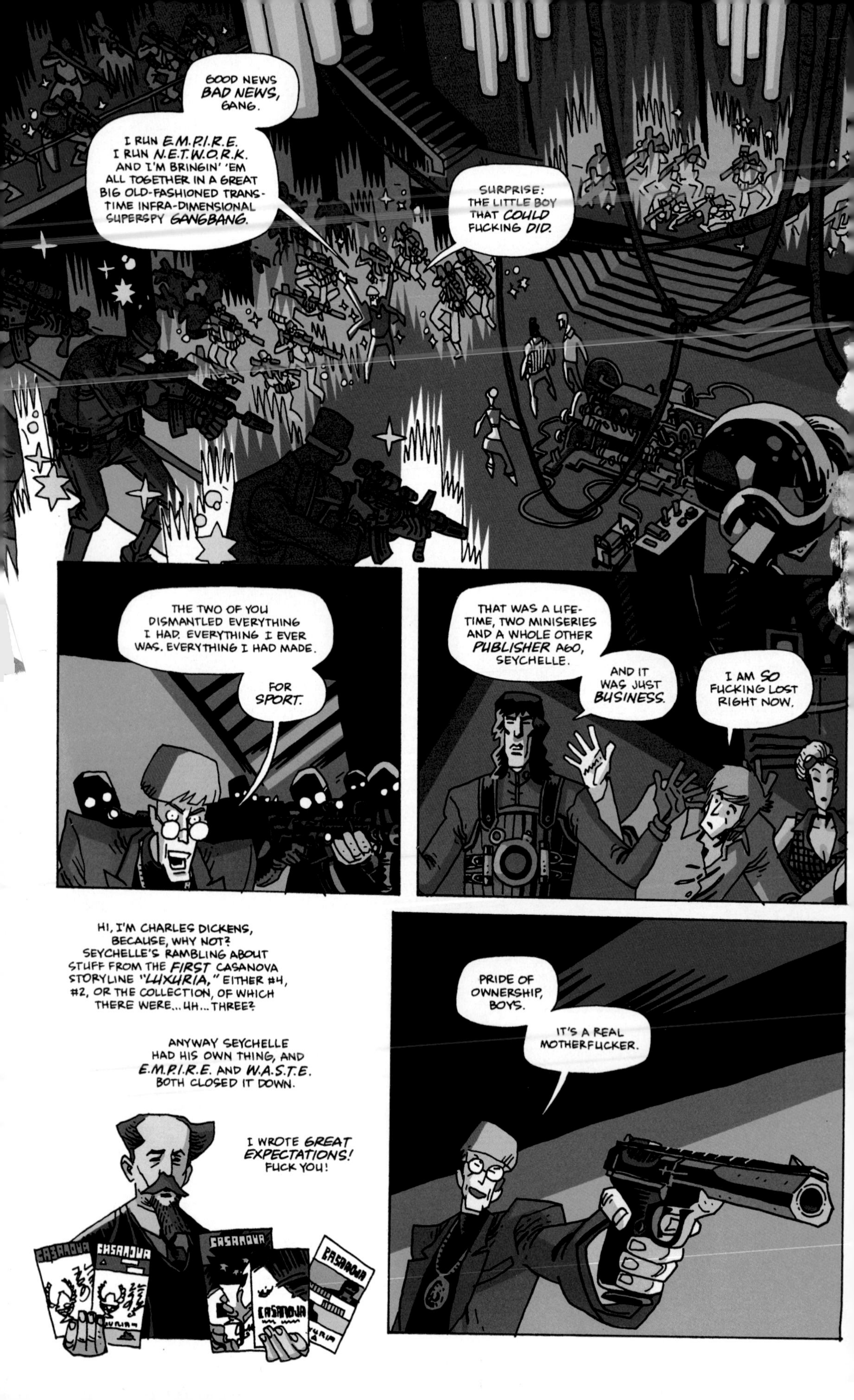
GOOD NEWS BAD NEWS, GANG.
I RUN E.M.P.I.R.E. I RUN N.E.T.W.O.R.K. AND I'M BRINGIN' 'EM ALL TOGETHER IN A GREAT BIG OLD-FASHIONED TRANS-TIME INFRA-DIMENSIONAL SUPERSPY GANGBANG.
SURPRISE: THE LITTLE BOY THAT COULD FUCKING DID.
THE TWO OF YOU DISMANTLED EVERYTHING I HAD. EVERYTHING I EVER WAS. EVERYTHING I HAD MADE.
FOR SPORT.
THAT WAS A LIFE-TIME, TWO MINISERIES AND A WHOLE OTHER PUBLISHER AGO, SEYCHELLE.
AND IT WAS JUST BUSINESS.
I AM SO FUCKING LOST RIGHT NOW.
HI, I'M CHARLES DICKENS, BECAUSE, WHY NOT? SEYCHELLE'S RAMBLING ABOUT STUFF FROM THE FIRST CASANOVA STORYLINE "LUXURIA," EITHER #4, #2, OR THE COLLECTION, OF WHICH THERE WERE... UH... THREE?
ANYWAY SEYCHELLE HAD HIS OWN THING, AND E.M.P.I.R.E. AND W.A.S.T.E. BOTH CLOSED IT DOWN.
I WROTE GREAT EXPECTATIONS! FUCK YOU!
PRIDE OF OWNERSHIP, BOYS.
IT'S A REAL MOTHERFUCKER.

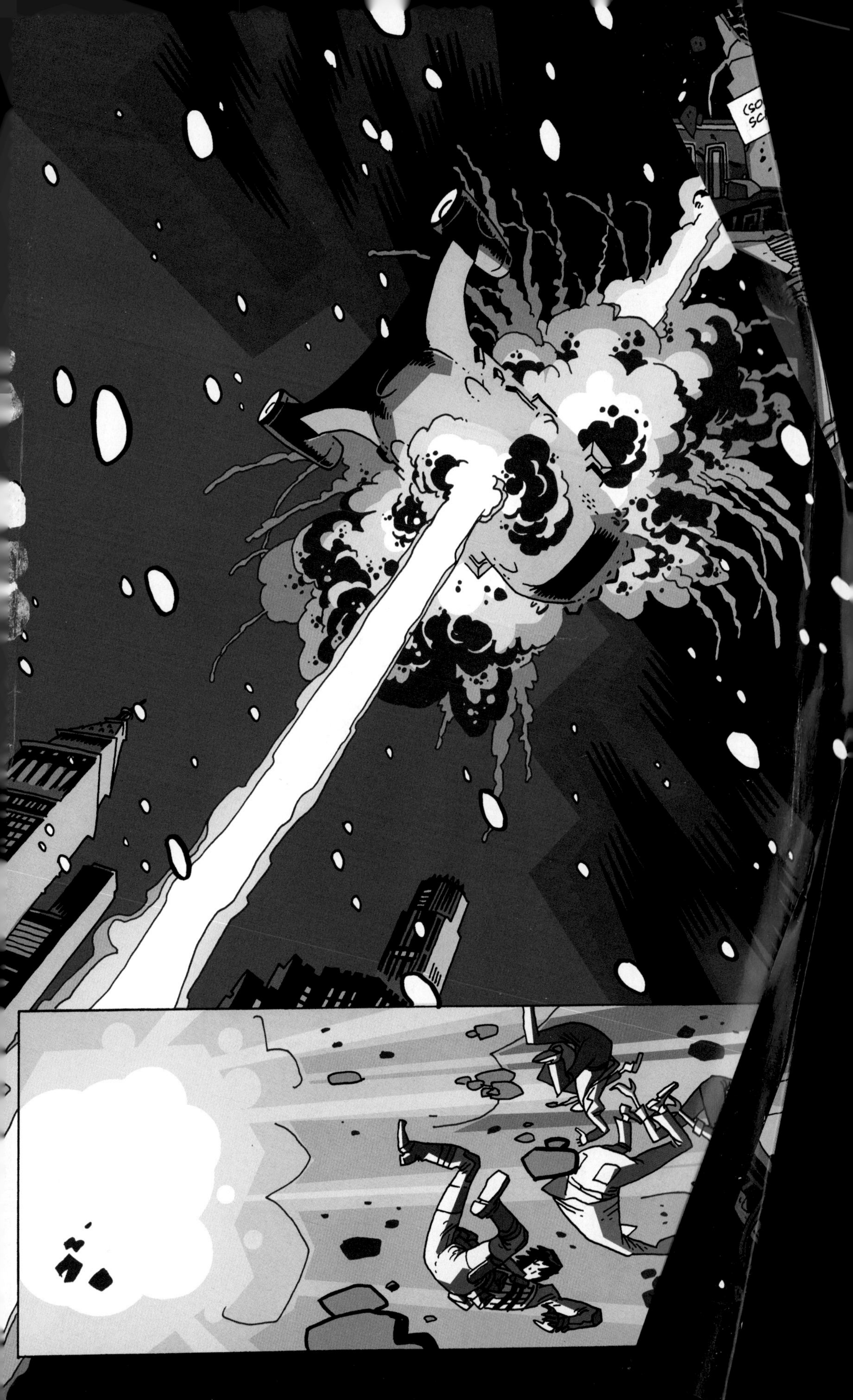

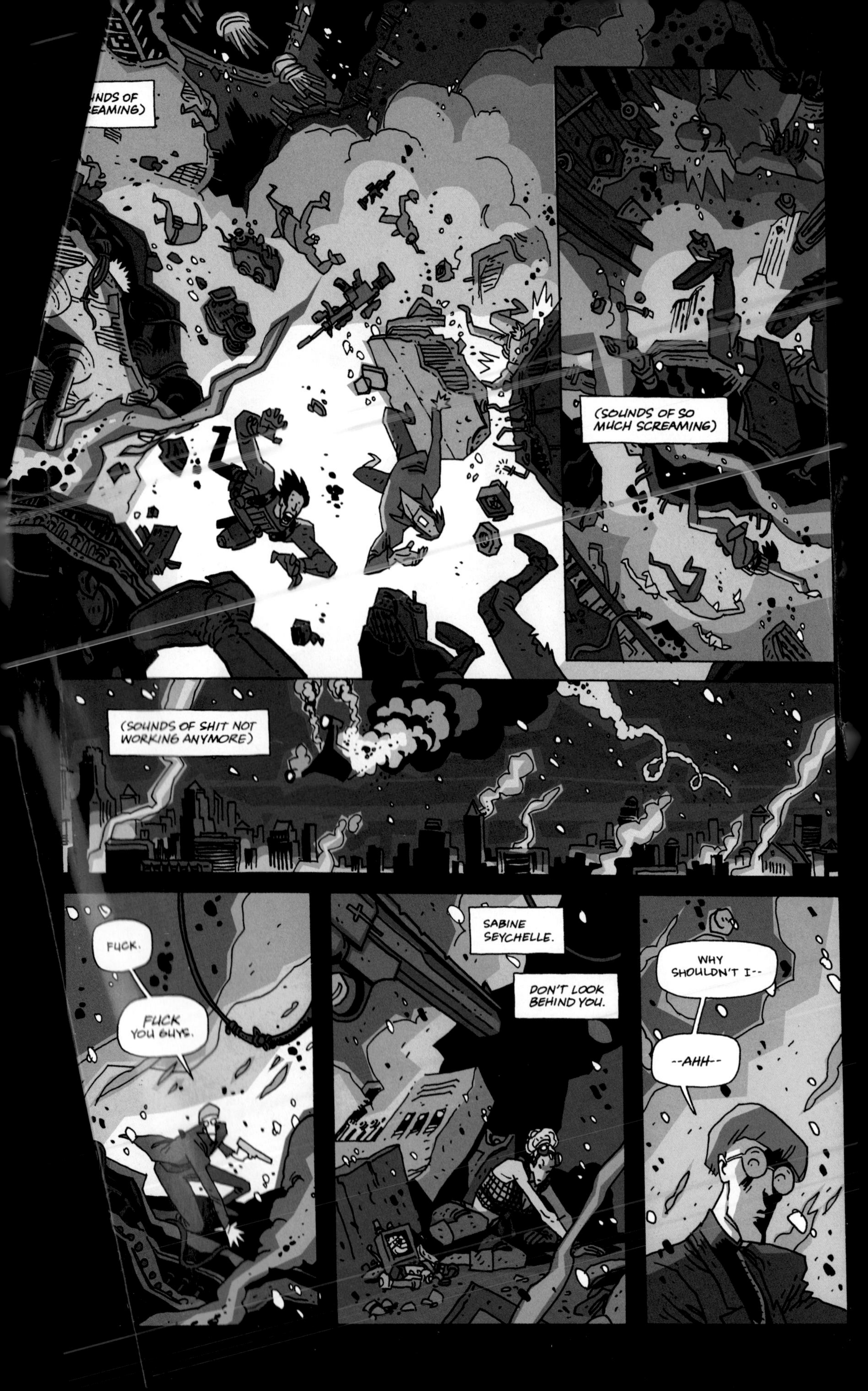
(SOUNDS OF SCREAMING)
(SOUNDS OF SO MUCH SCREAMING)
(SOUNDS OF SHIT NOT WORKING ANYMORE)
FUCK.
FUCK YOU GUYS.
SABINE SEYCHELLE.
DON'T LOOK BEHIND YOU.
WHY SHOULDN'T I--
--AHH--

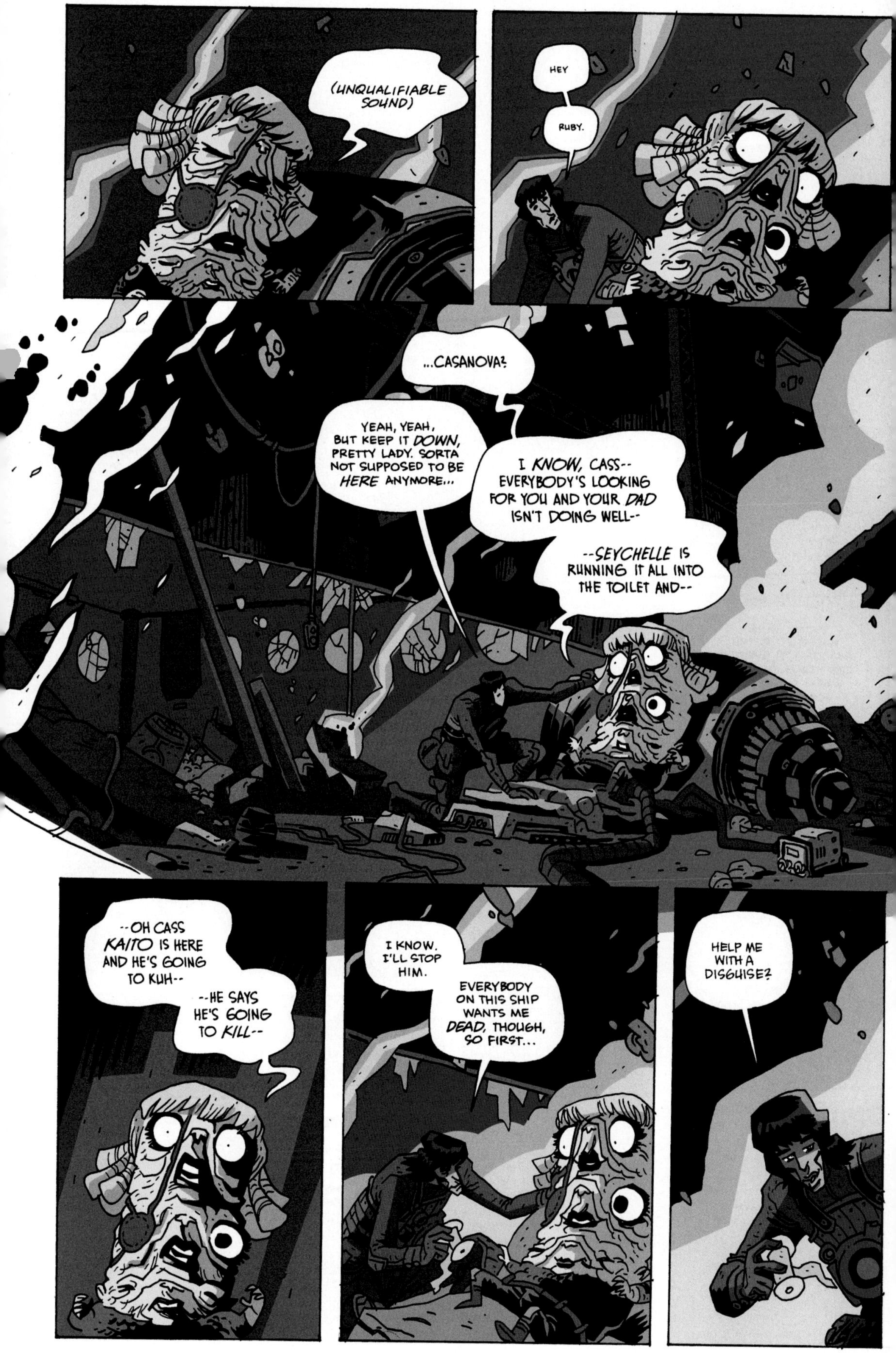
(UNQUALIFIABLE SOUND)
HEY
RUBY.
...CASANOVA?
YEAH, YEAH, BUT KEEP IT DOWN, PRETTY LADY. SORTA NOT SUPPOSED TO BE HERE ANYMORE...
I KNOW, CASS-- EVERYBODY'S LOOKING FOR YOU AND YOUR DAD ISN'T DOING WELL--
--SEYCHELLE IS RUNNING IT ALL INTO THE TOILET AND--
--OH CASS KAITO IS HERE AND HE'S GOING TO KUH--
--HE SAYS HE'S GOING TO KILL--
I KNOW. I'LL STOP HIM.
EVERYBODY ON THIS SHIP WANTS ME DEAD, THOUGH, SO FIRST...
HELP ME WITH A DISGUISE?

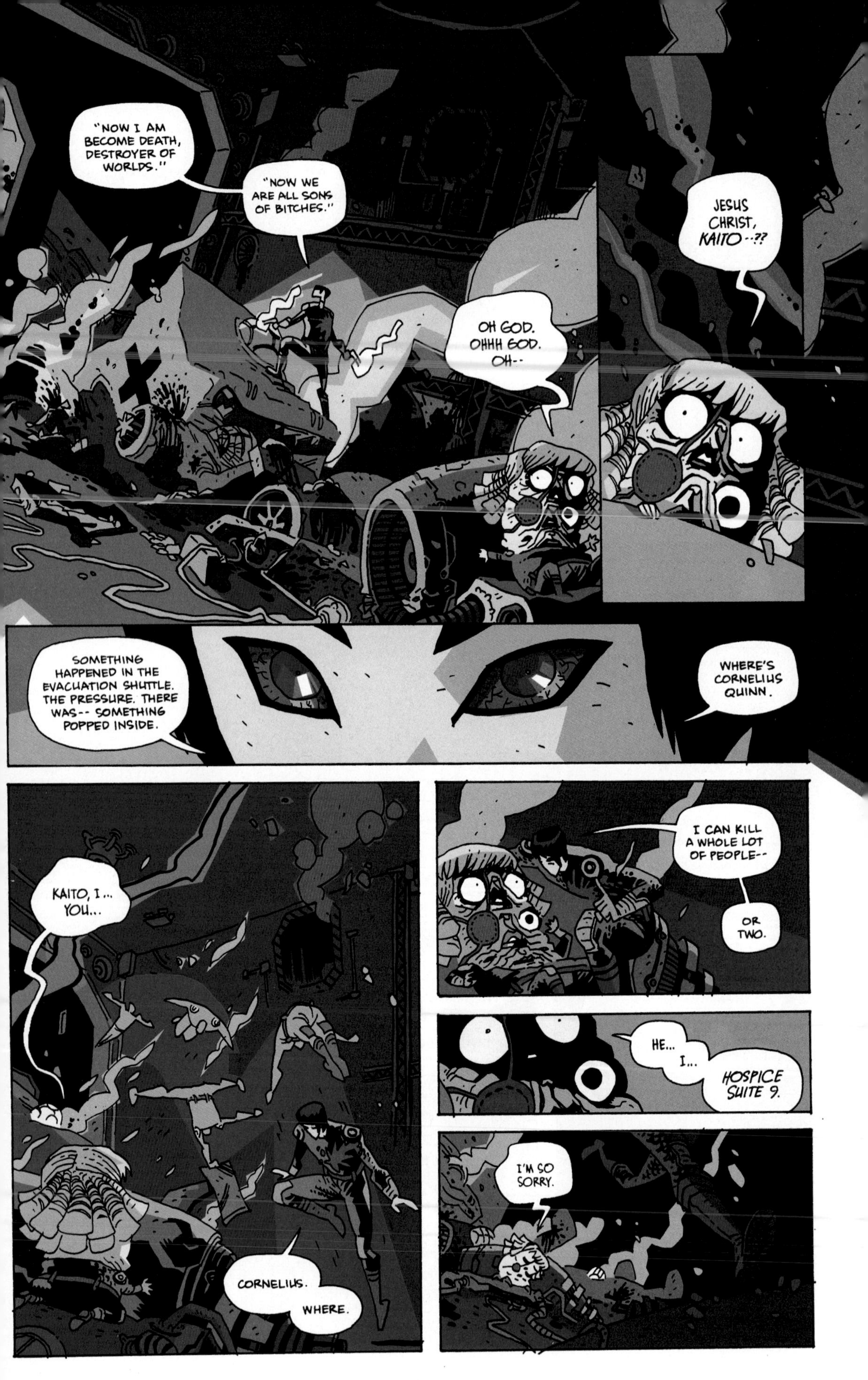
"NOW I AM BECOME DEATH, DESTROYER OF WORLDS."
"NOW WE ARE ALL SONS OF BITCHES."
OH GOD. OHHH GOD. OH--
JESUS CHRIST, KAITO--??
SOMETHING HAPPENED IN THE EVACUATION SHUTTLE. THE PRESSURE. THERE WAS-- SOMETHING POPPED INSIDE.
WHERE'S CORNELIUS QUINN.
KAITO, I... YOU...
CORNELIUS.
WHERE.
I CAN KILL A WHOLE LOT OF PEOPLE--
OR TWO.
HE...
I...
HOSPICE SUITE 9.
I'M SO SORRY.

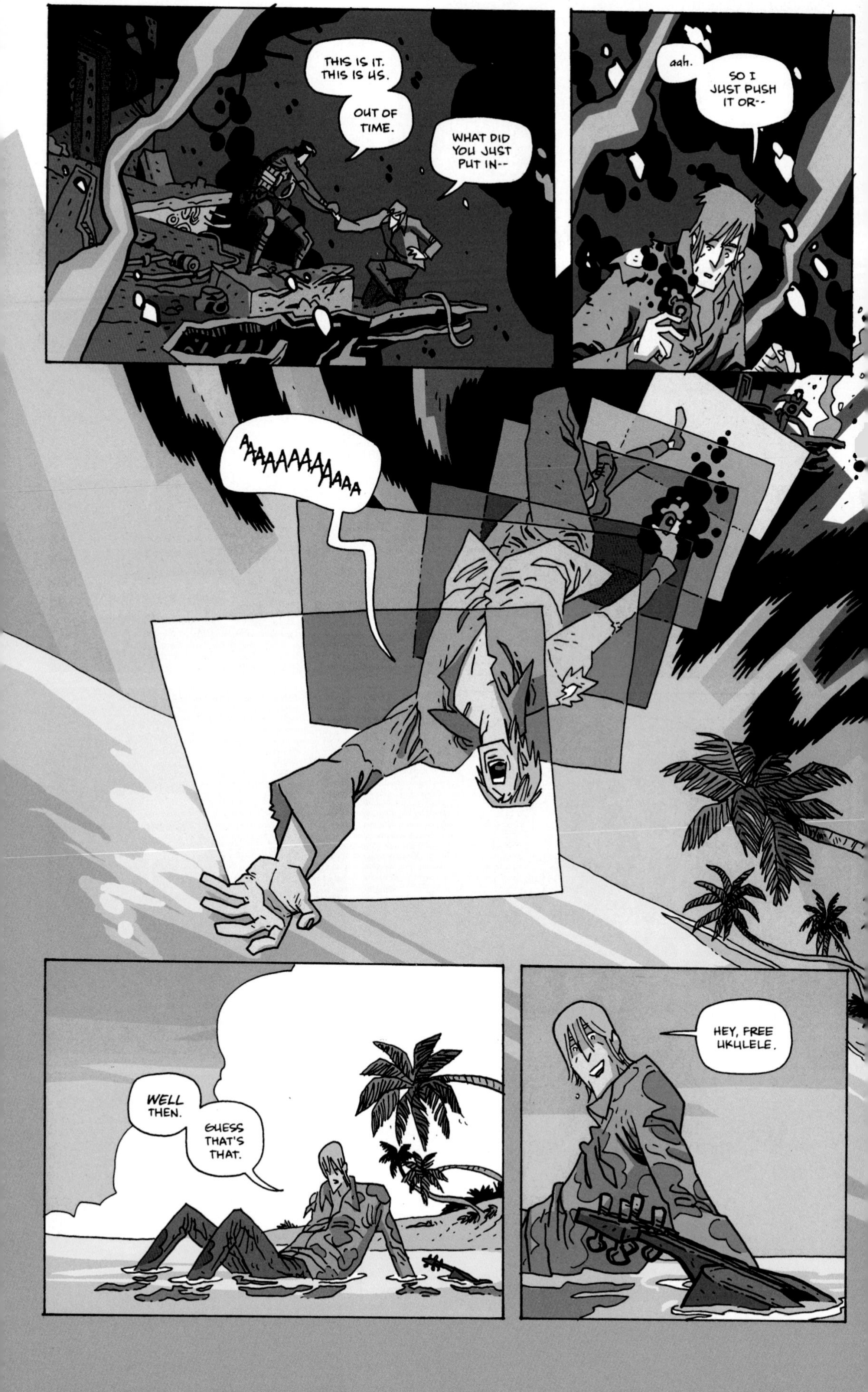
THIS IS IT. THIS IS US.
OUT OF TIME.
WHAT DID YOU JUST PUT IN--
aah.
SO I JUST PUSH IT OR--
AAAAAAAAAAAAA
WELL THEN.
GUESS THAT'S THAT.
HEY, FREE UKULELE.

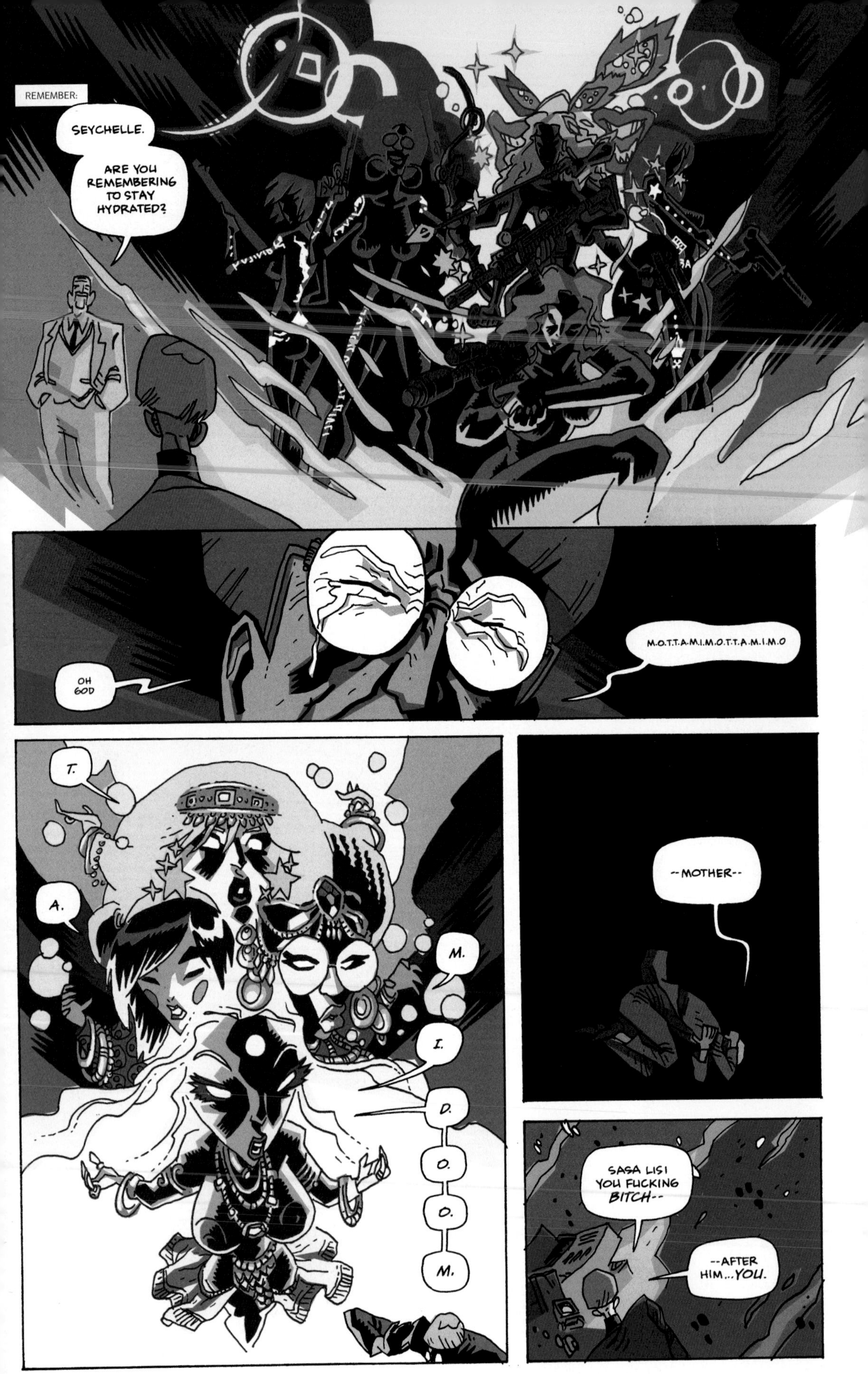
REMEMBER:
SEYCHELLE.
ARE YOU REMEMBERING TO STAY HYDRATED?
OH GOD
M.O.T.T.A.M.I.M.O.T.T.A.M.I.M.O
T.
A.
M.
I.
D.
O.
O.
M.
--MOTHER--
SASA LISI YOU FUCKING BITCH--
--AFTER HIM...YOU.

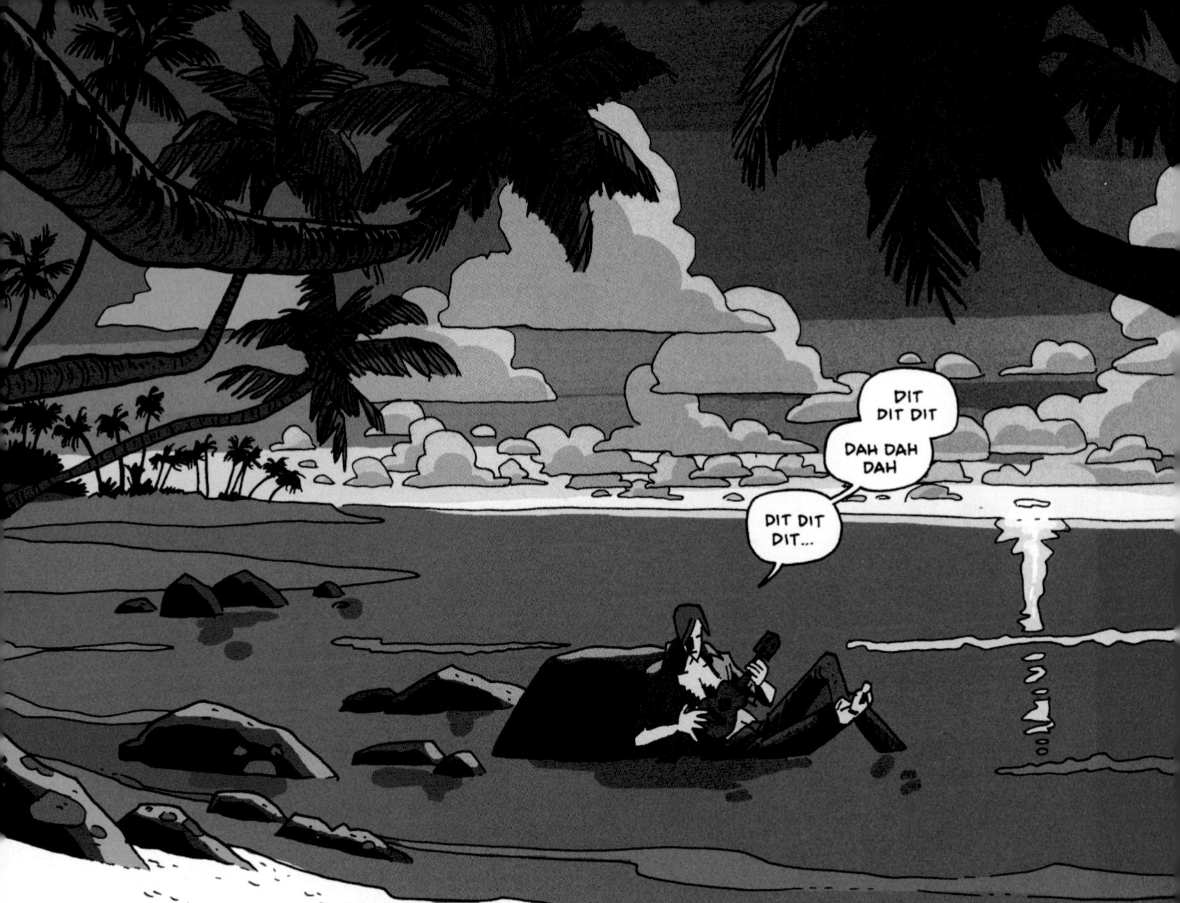
DIT
DIT DIT
DAH DAH
DAH
DIT DIT
DIT...

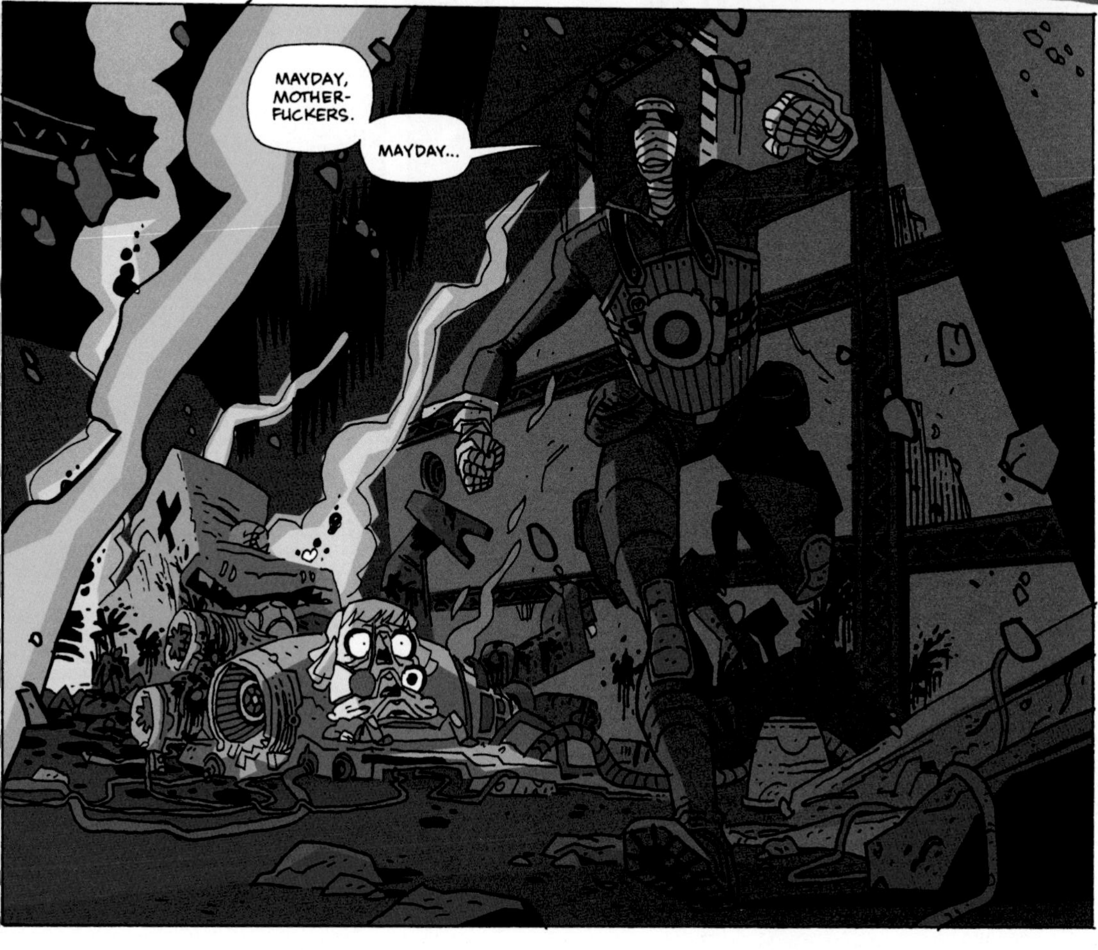
MAYDAY, MOTHER-FUCKERS.
MAYDAY...

11. PEOPLE ARE TURNING TO GOLD

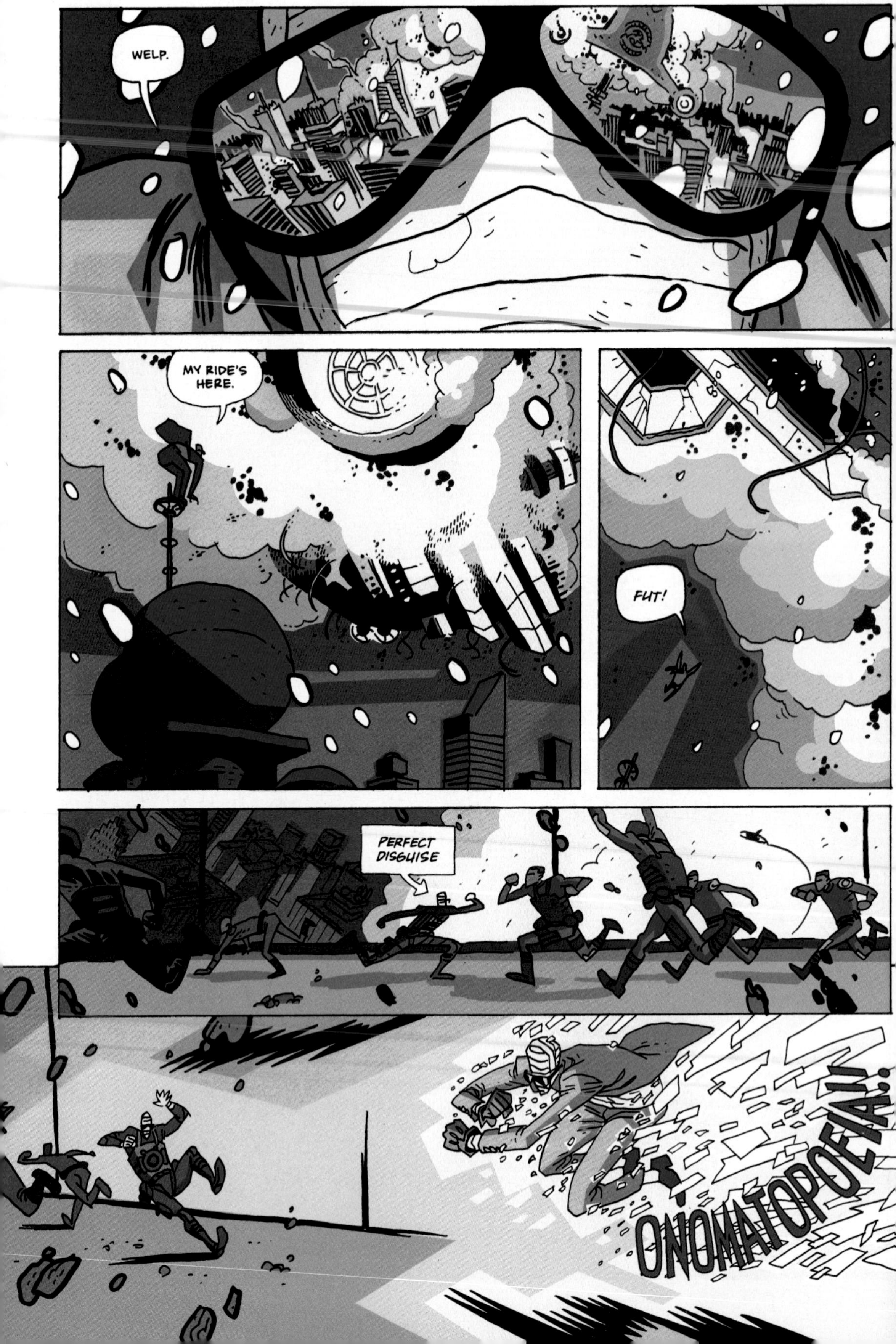
WELP.
MY RIDE'S HERE.
FUT!
PERFECT DISGUISE
ONOMATOPOEIA!!

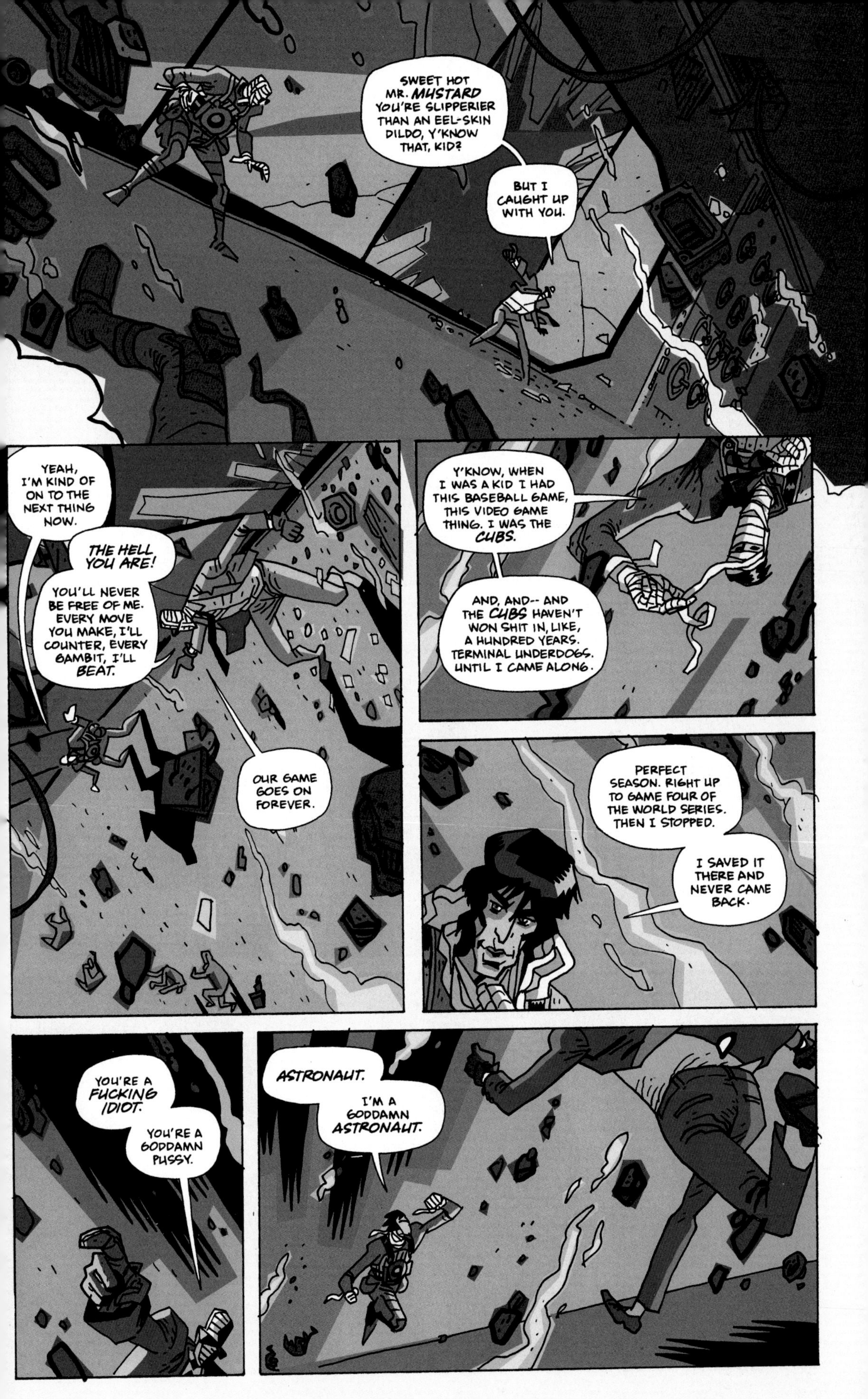
SWEET HOT MR. MUSTARD YOU'RE SLIPPERIER THAN AN EEL-SKIN DILDO, Y'KNOW THAT, KID?
BUT I CAUGHT UP WITH YOU.
YEAH, I'M KIND OF ON TO THE NEXT THING NOW.
THE HELL YOU ARE!
YOU'LL NEVER BE FREE OF ME. EVERY MOVE YOU MAKE, I'LL COUNTER, EVERY GAMBIT, I'LL BEAT.
OUR GAME GOES ON FOREVER.
Y'KNOW, WHEN I WAS A KID I HAD THIS BASEBALL GAME, THIS VIDEO GAME THING. I WAS THE CUBS.
AND, AND-- AND THE CUBS HAVEN'T WON SHIT IN, LIKE, A HUNDRED YEARS. TERMINAL UNDERDOGS. UNTIL I CAME ALONG.
PERFECT SEASON. RIGHT UP TO GAME FOUR OF THE WORLD SERIES. THEN I STOPPED.
I SAVED IT THERE AND NEVER CAME BACK.
YOU'RE A FUCKING IDIOT.
YOU'RE A GODDAMN PUSSY.
ASTRONAUT.
I'M A GODDAMN ASTRONAUT.

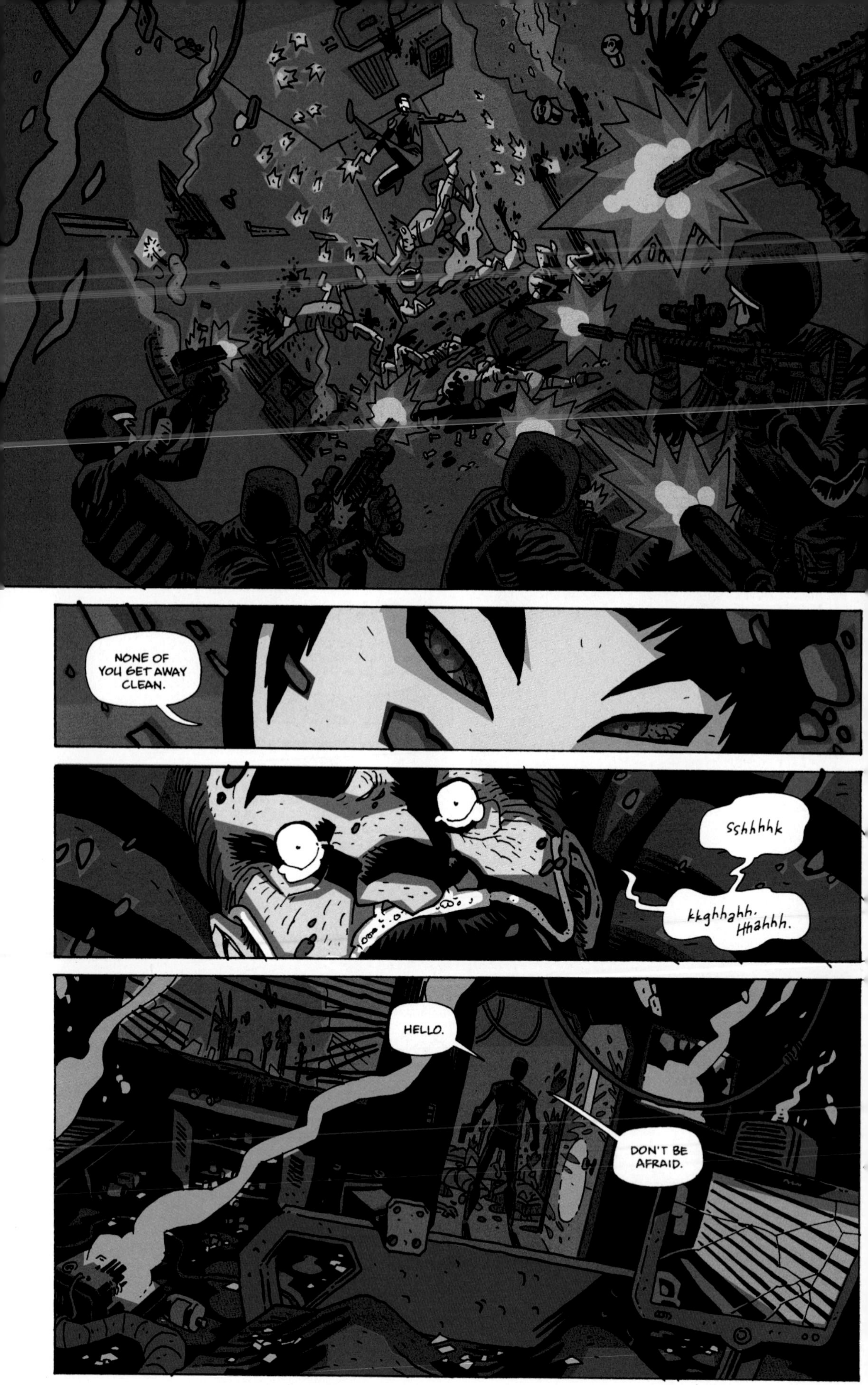
NONE OF YOU GET AWAY CLEAN.
sshhhhk
kkghhahh. Hhahhh.
HELLO.
DON'T BE AFRAID.

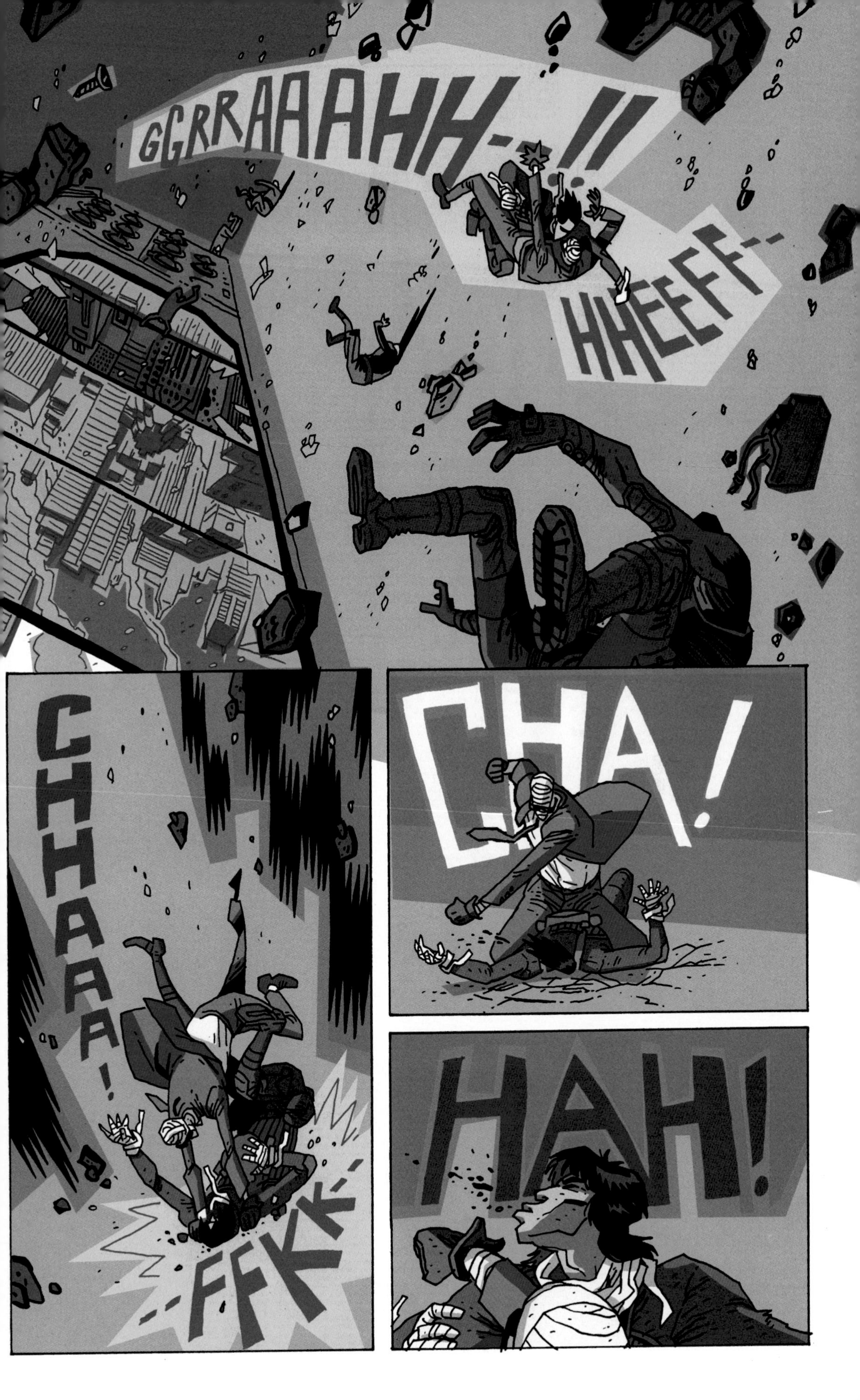
GGRRAAAHH--!!
HHEEFF--
CHHAAAA!
--FFK
CHA!
HAH!

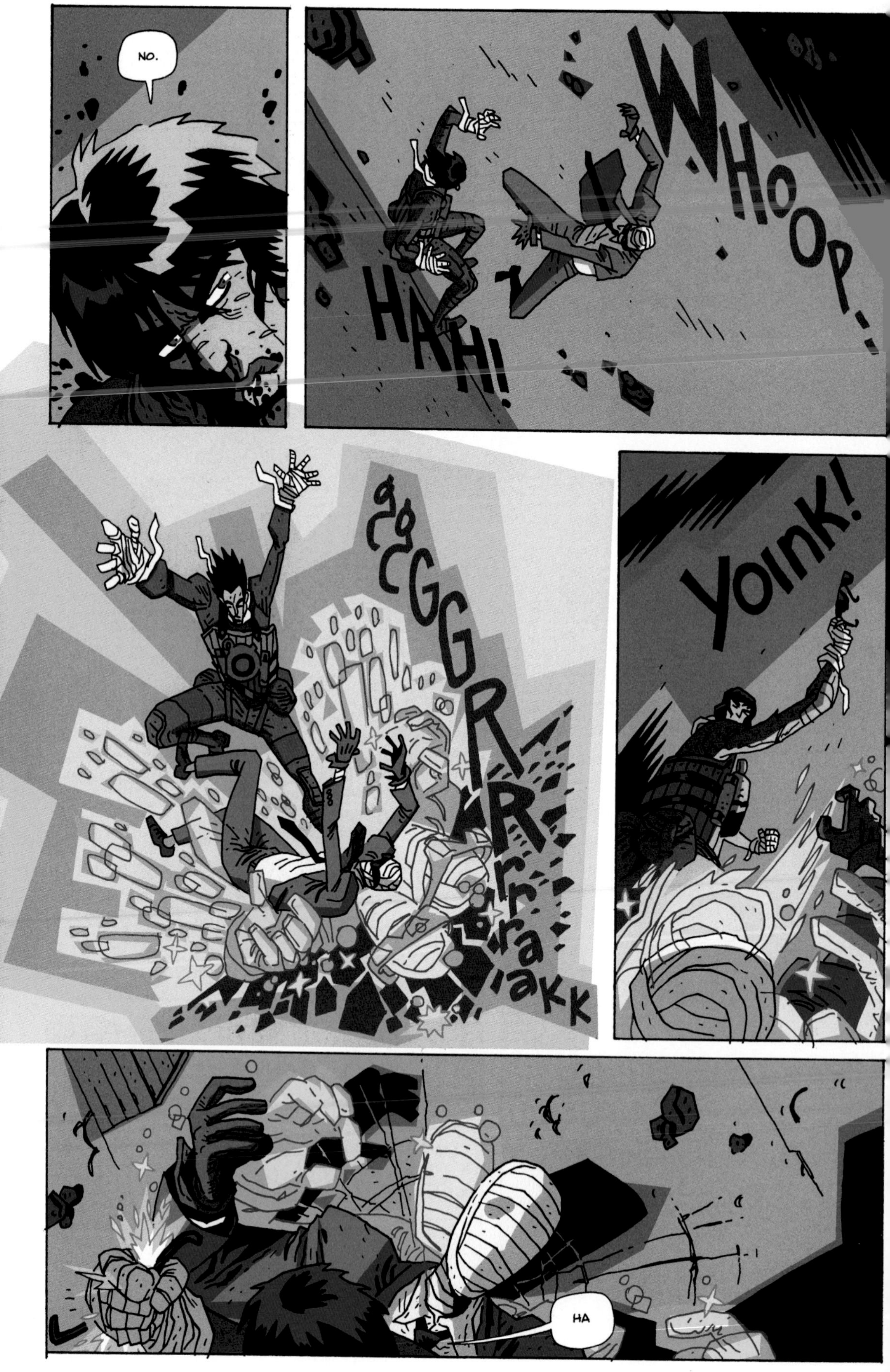
NO.
WHOOP...
HAHH!
ggCGGRRRrrrraakk
YOINK!
HA

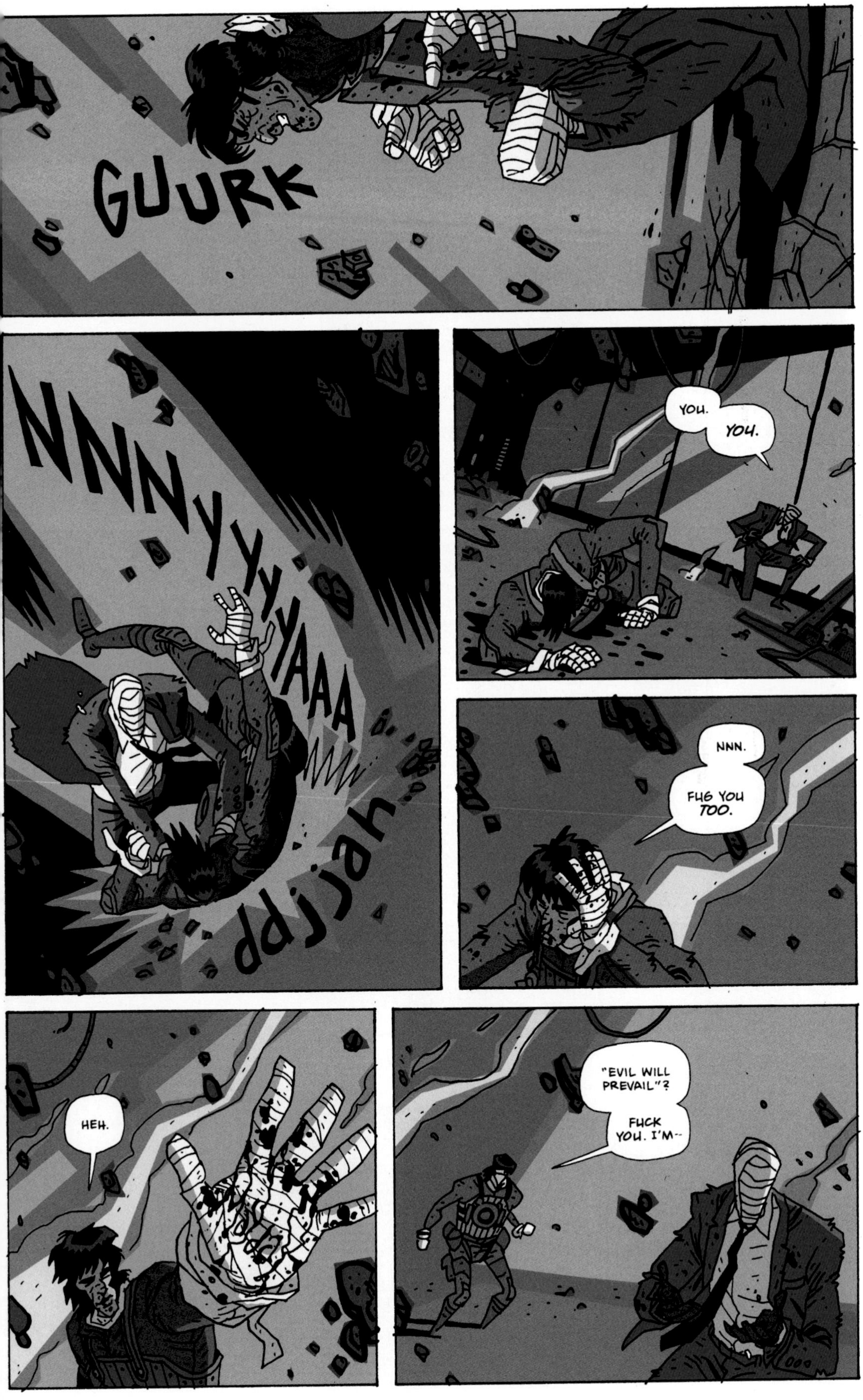
GUURK
NNNyyyYAAA
ddjah
YOU.
YOU.
NNN.
FUG YOU TOO.
HEH.
"EVIL WILL PREVAIL"?
FUCK YOU. I'M--

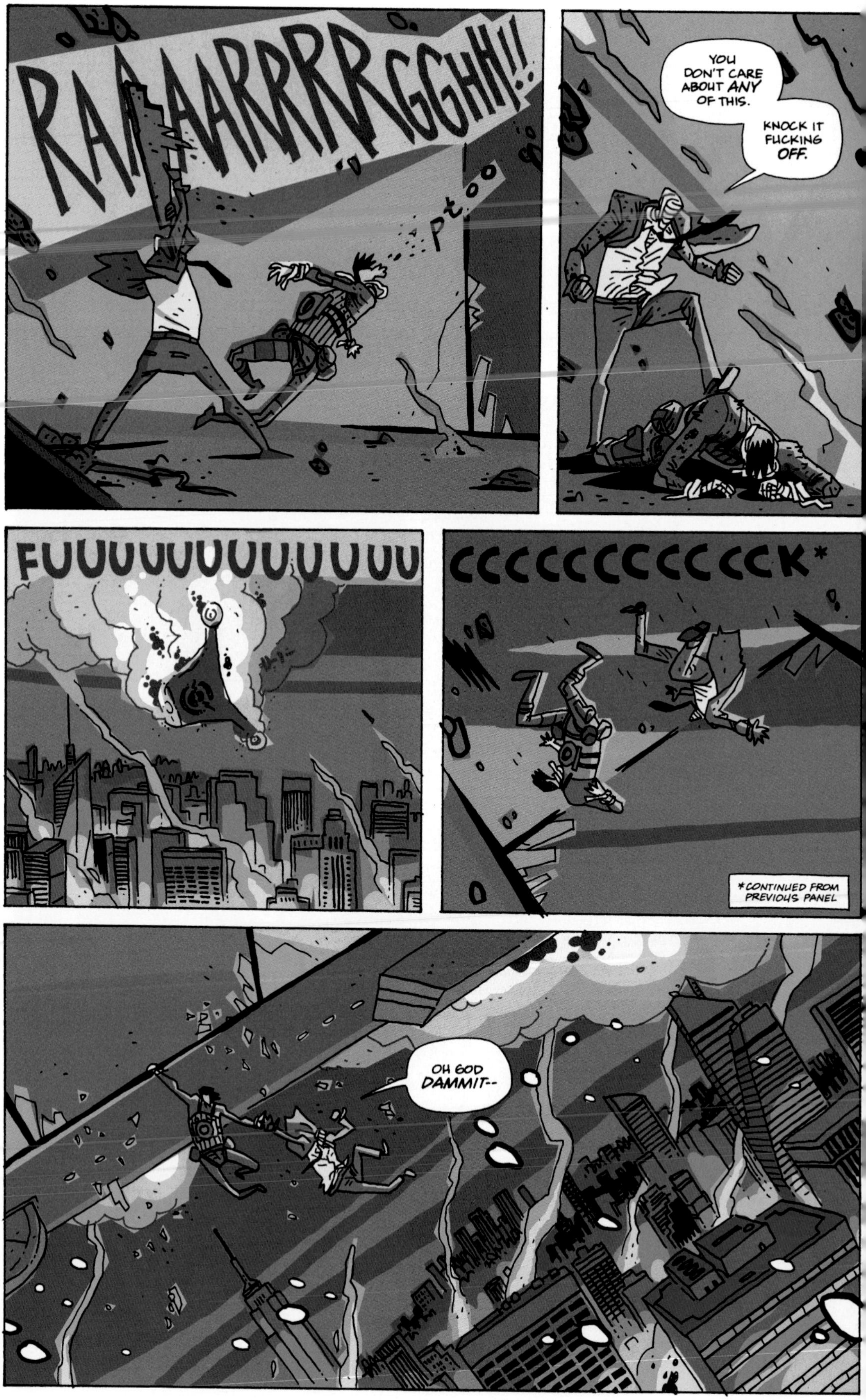
RAAAARRRRRGGHH!!
PTOO
YOU DON'T CARE ABOUT ANY OF THIS.
KNOCK IT FUCKING OFF.
FUUUUUUUUUUUU
CCCCCCCCCCCCK*
*CONTINUED FROM PREVIOUS PANEL
OH GOD DAMMIT--

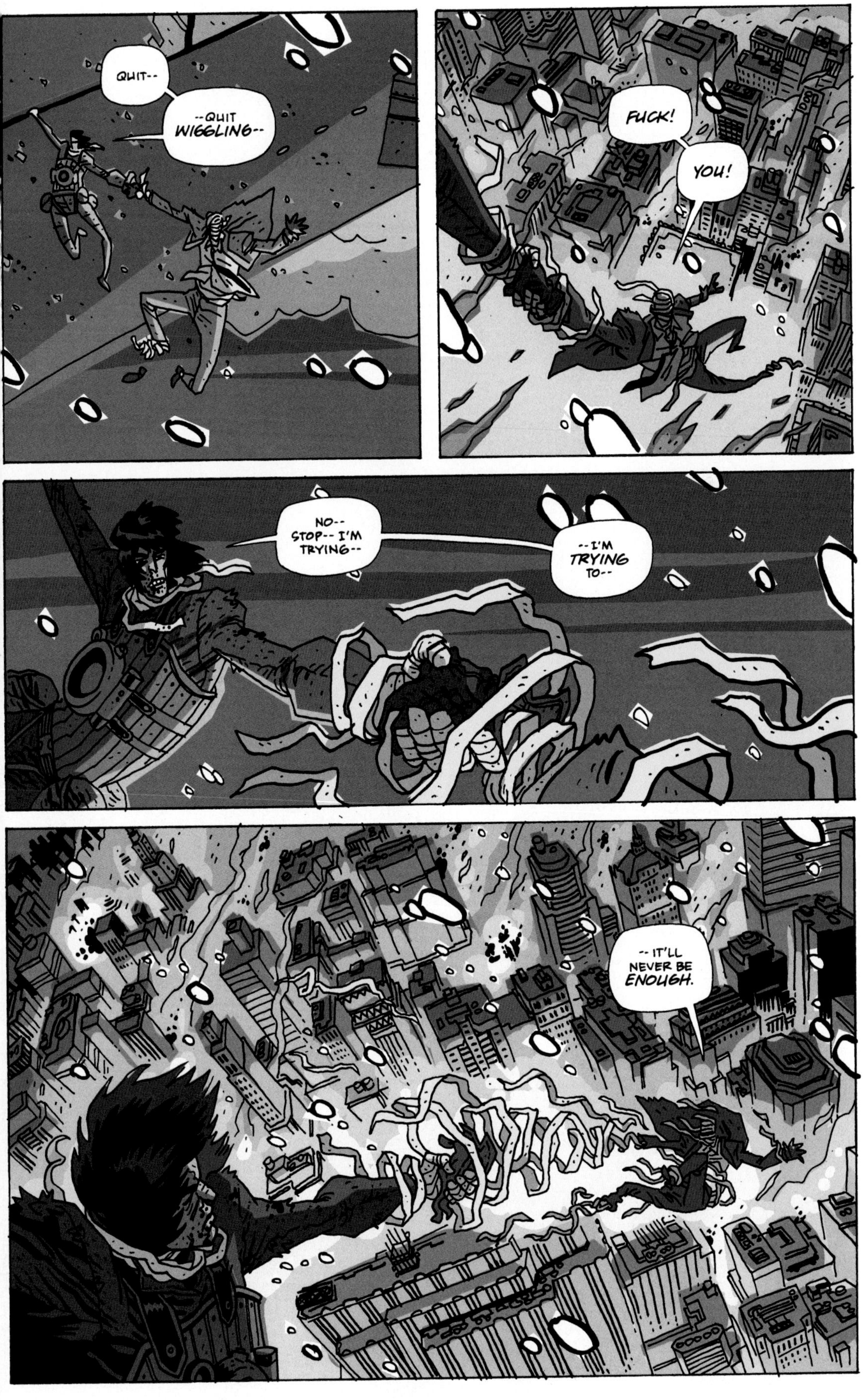
QUIT--
--QUIT WIGGLING--
FUCK!
YOU!
NO-- STOP-- I'M TRYING--
--I'M TRYING TO--
--IT'LL NEVER BE ENOUGH.

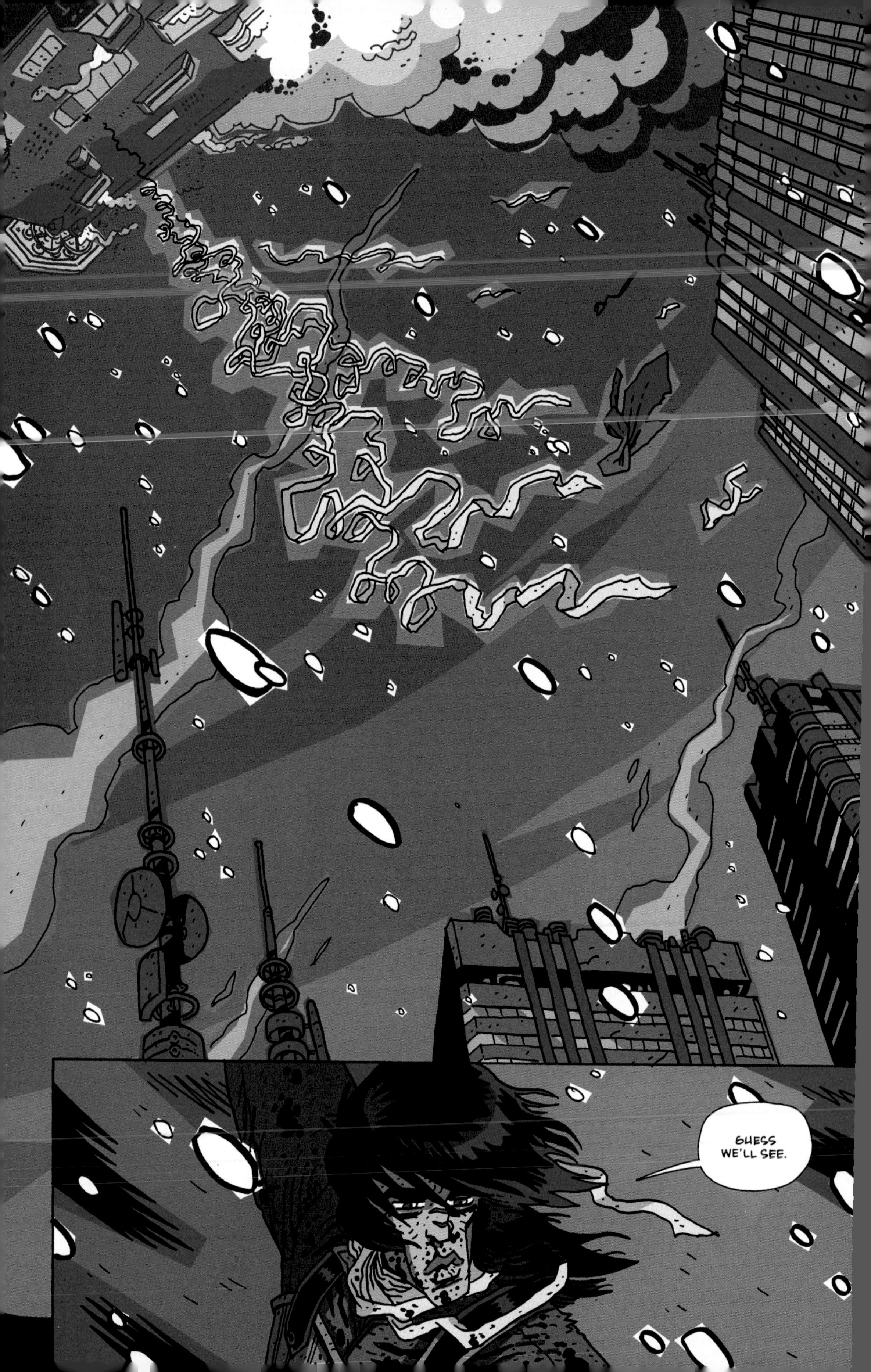
GUESS WE'LL SEE.

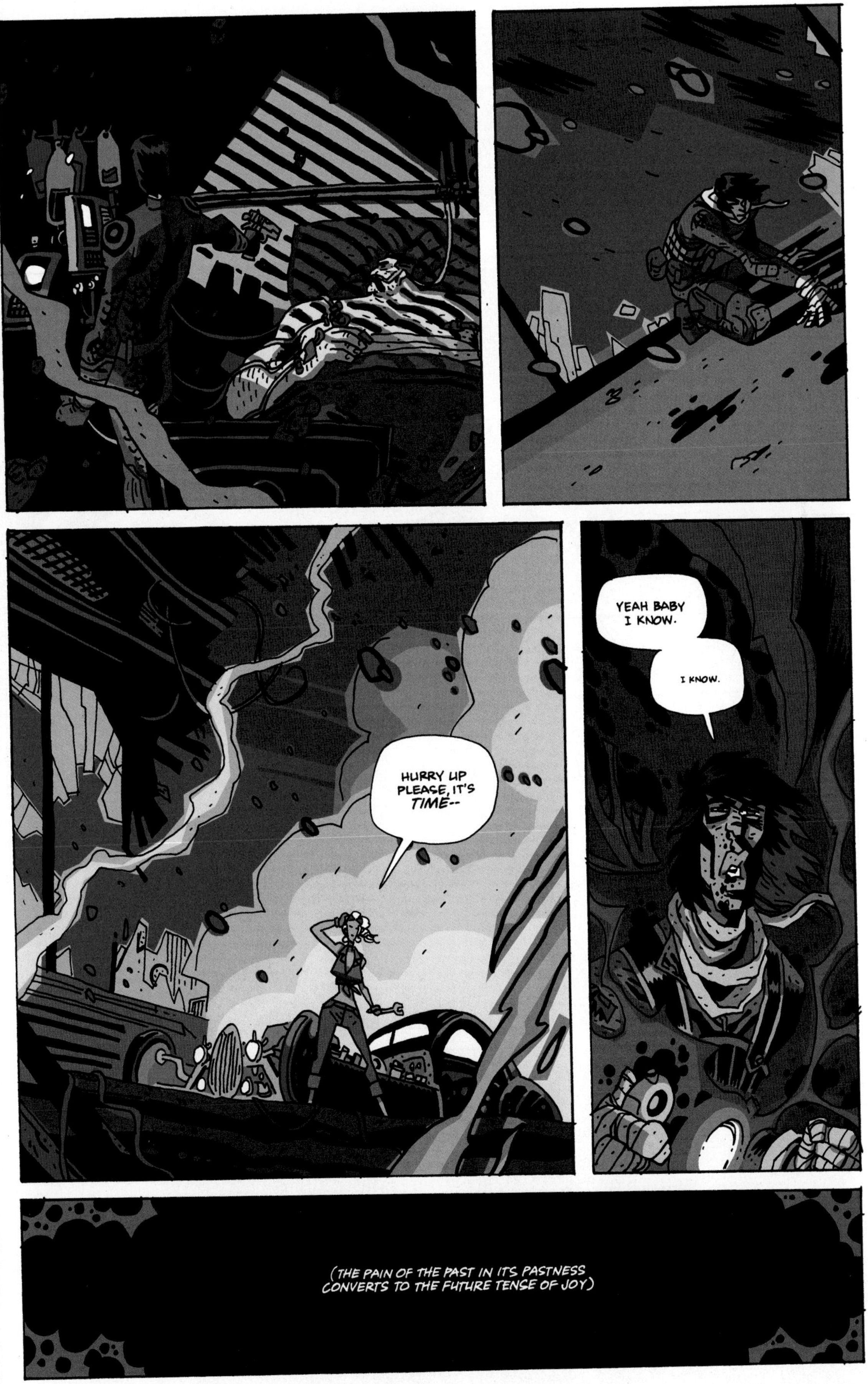

HURRY UP PLEASE, IT'S *TIME*--
YEAH BABY I KNOW.
I KNOW.
(THE PAIN OF THE PAST IN ITS PASTNESS CONVERTS TO THE FUTURE TENSE OF JOY)

12. WE ARE THE DEAD

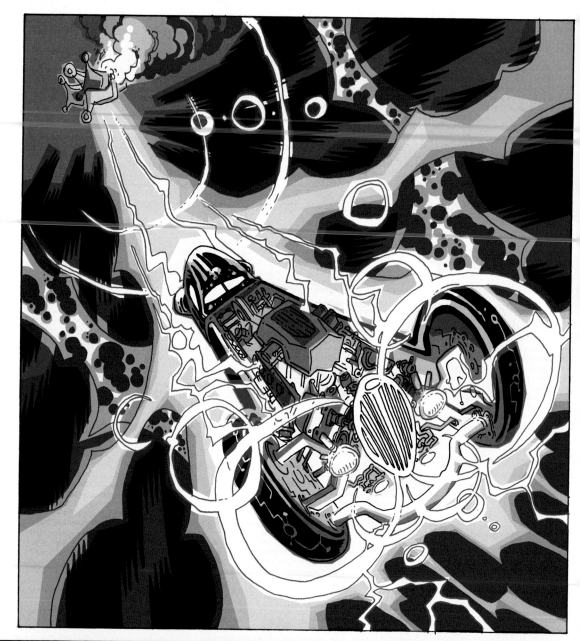

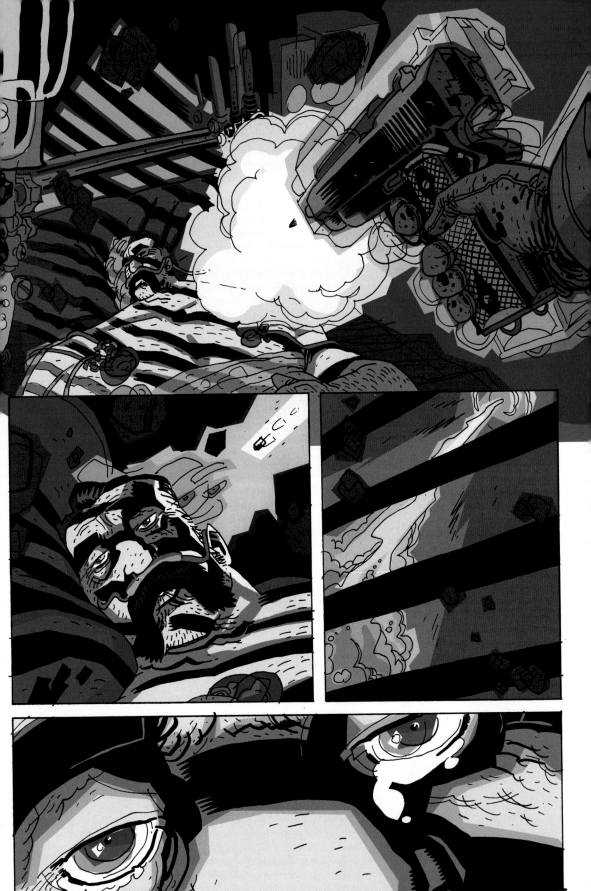

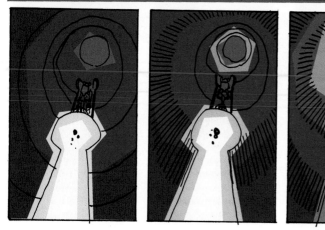

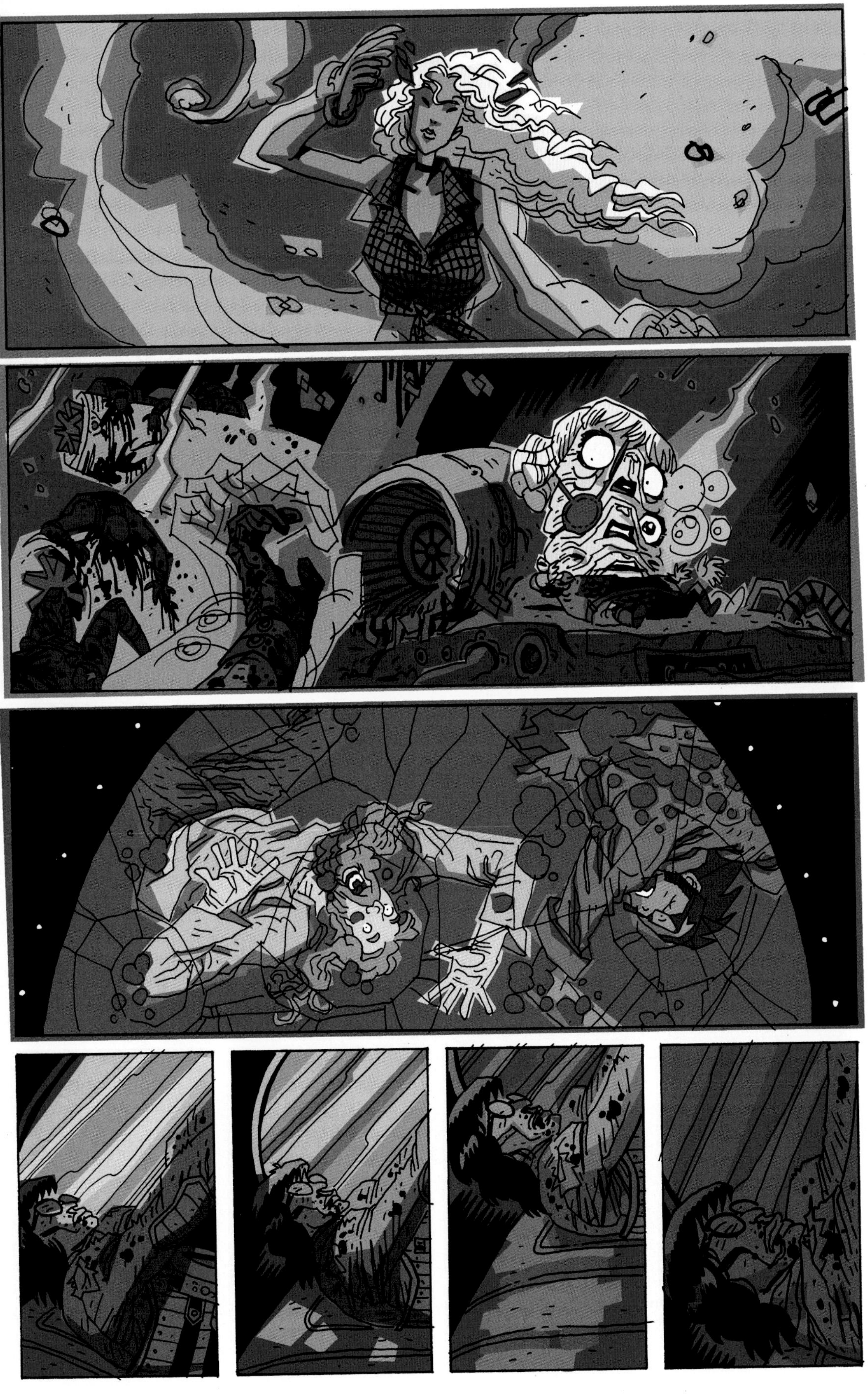

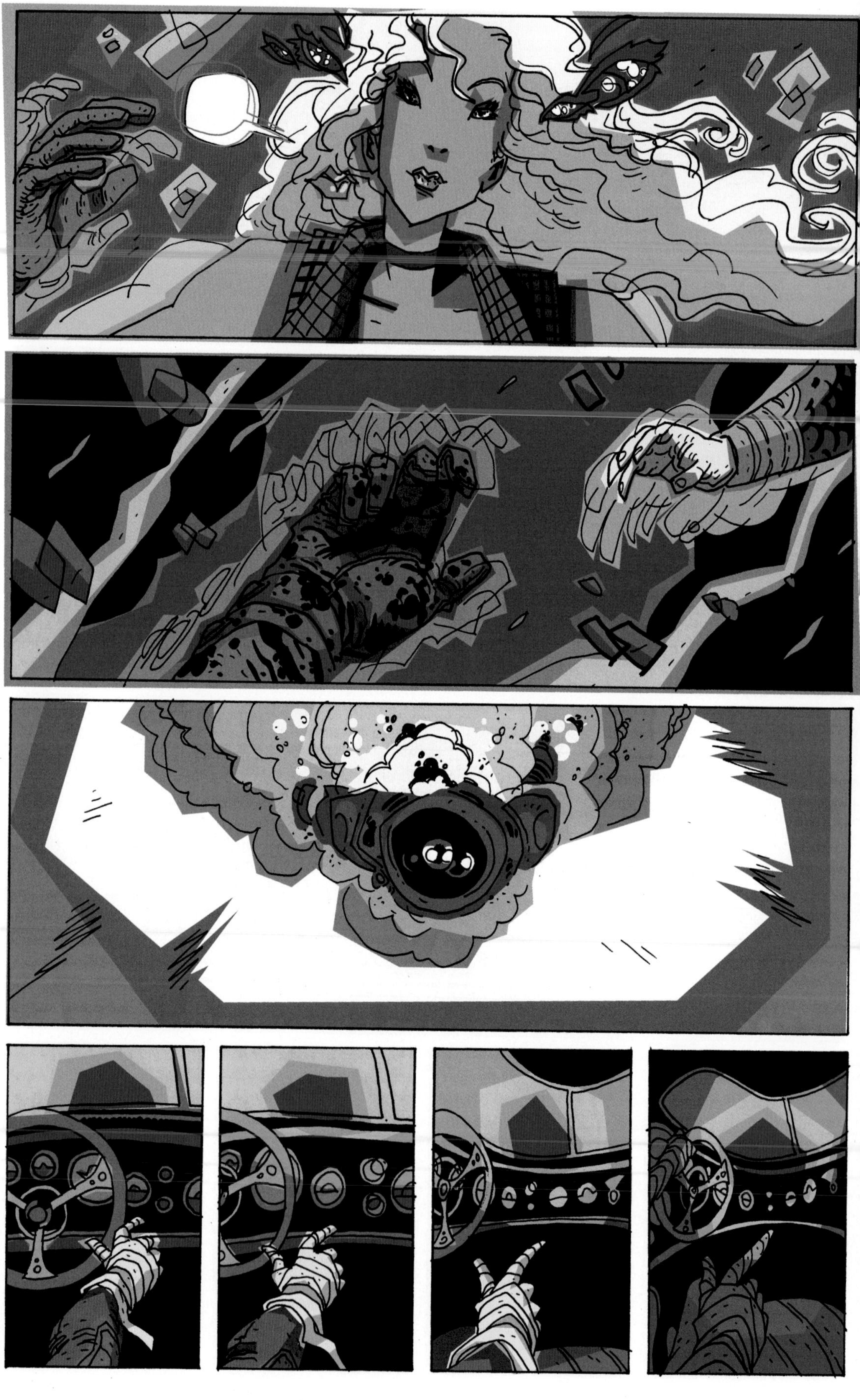

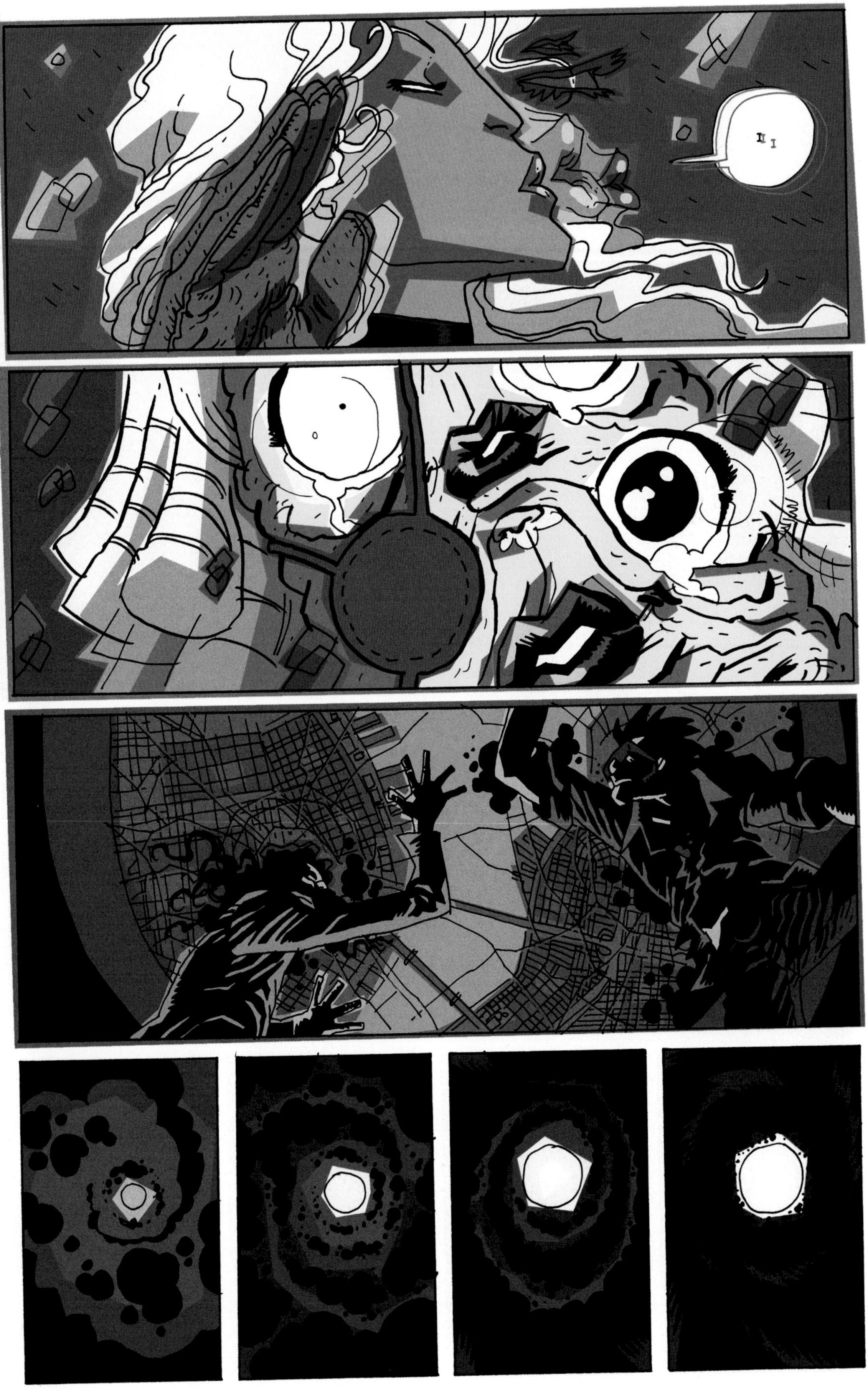
I I I

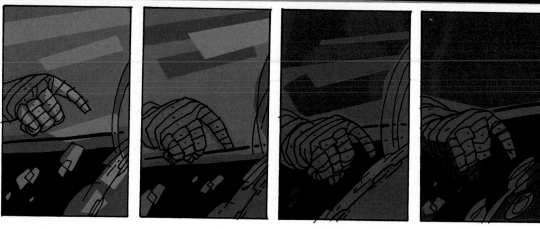

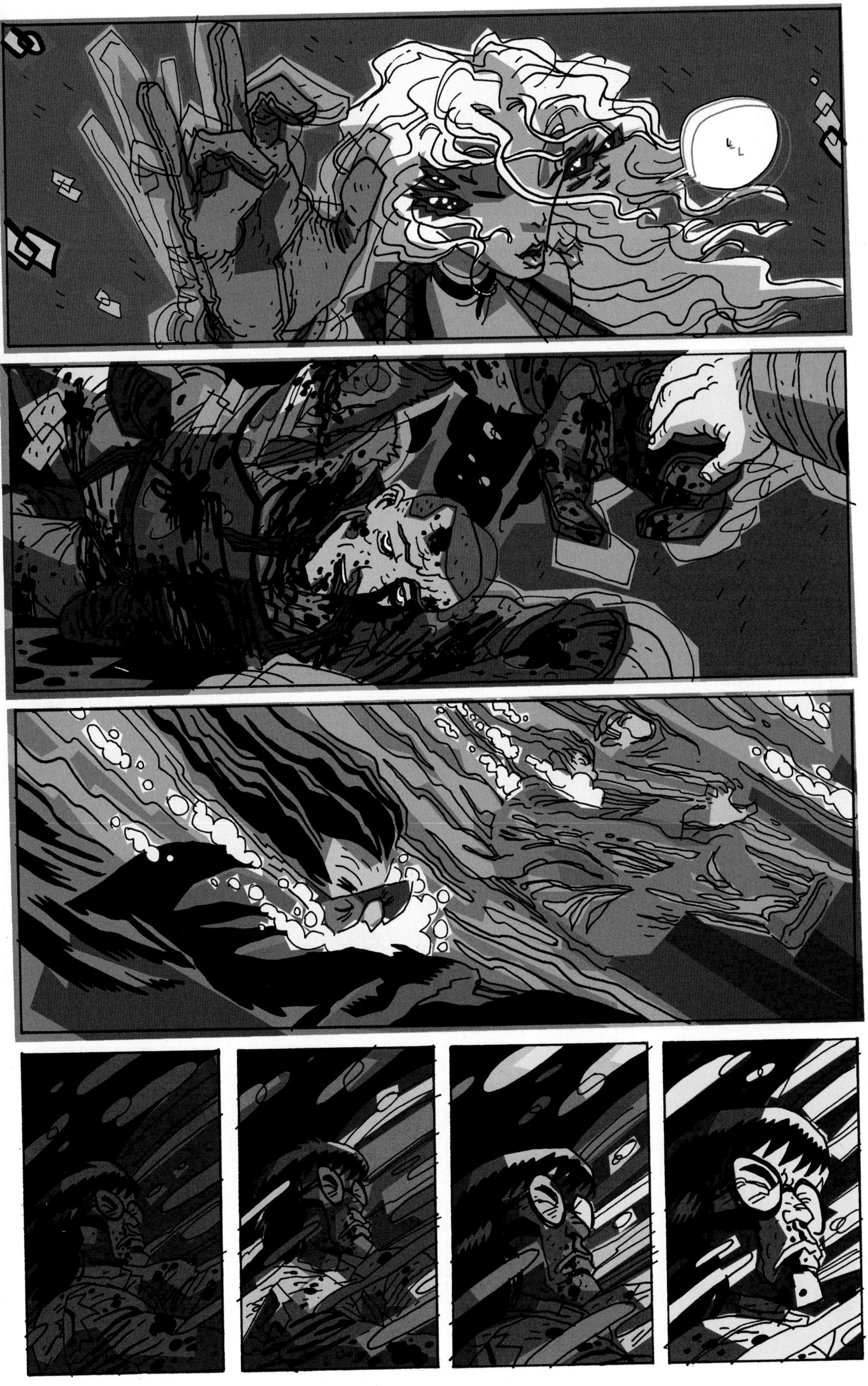

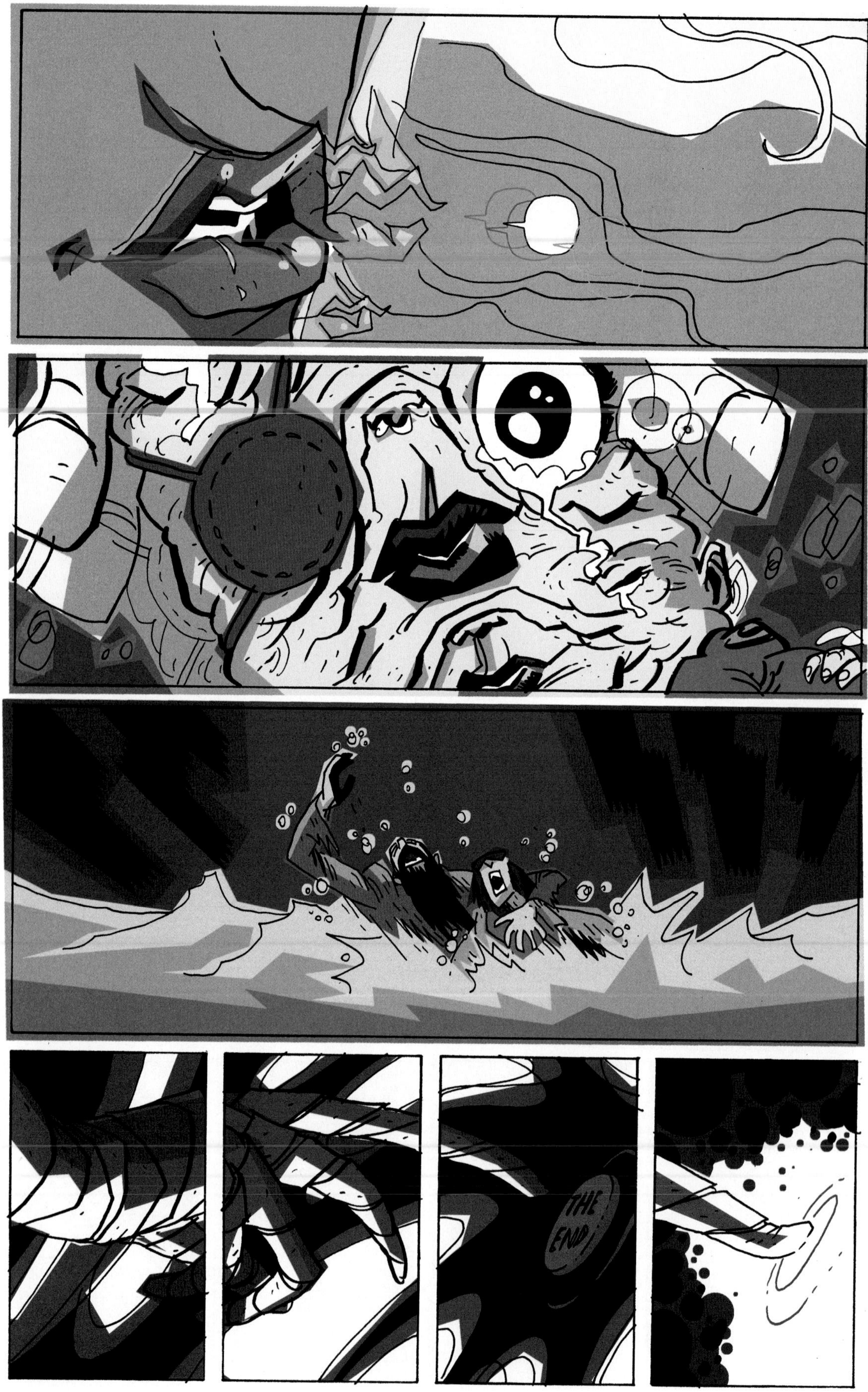
THE END

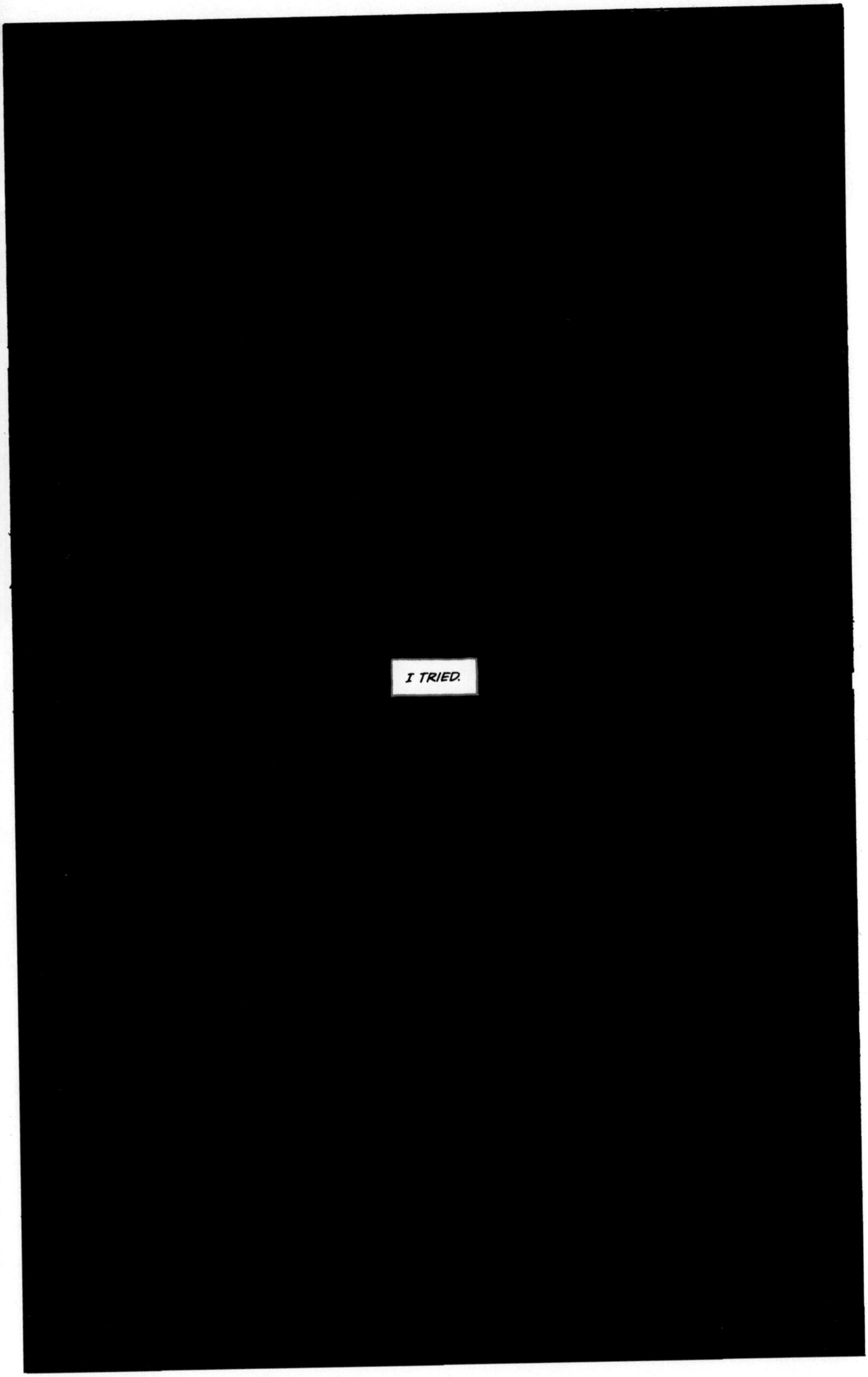
I TRIED.

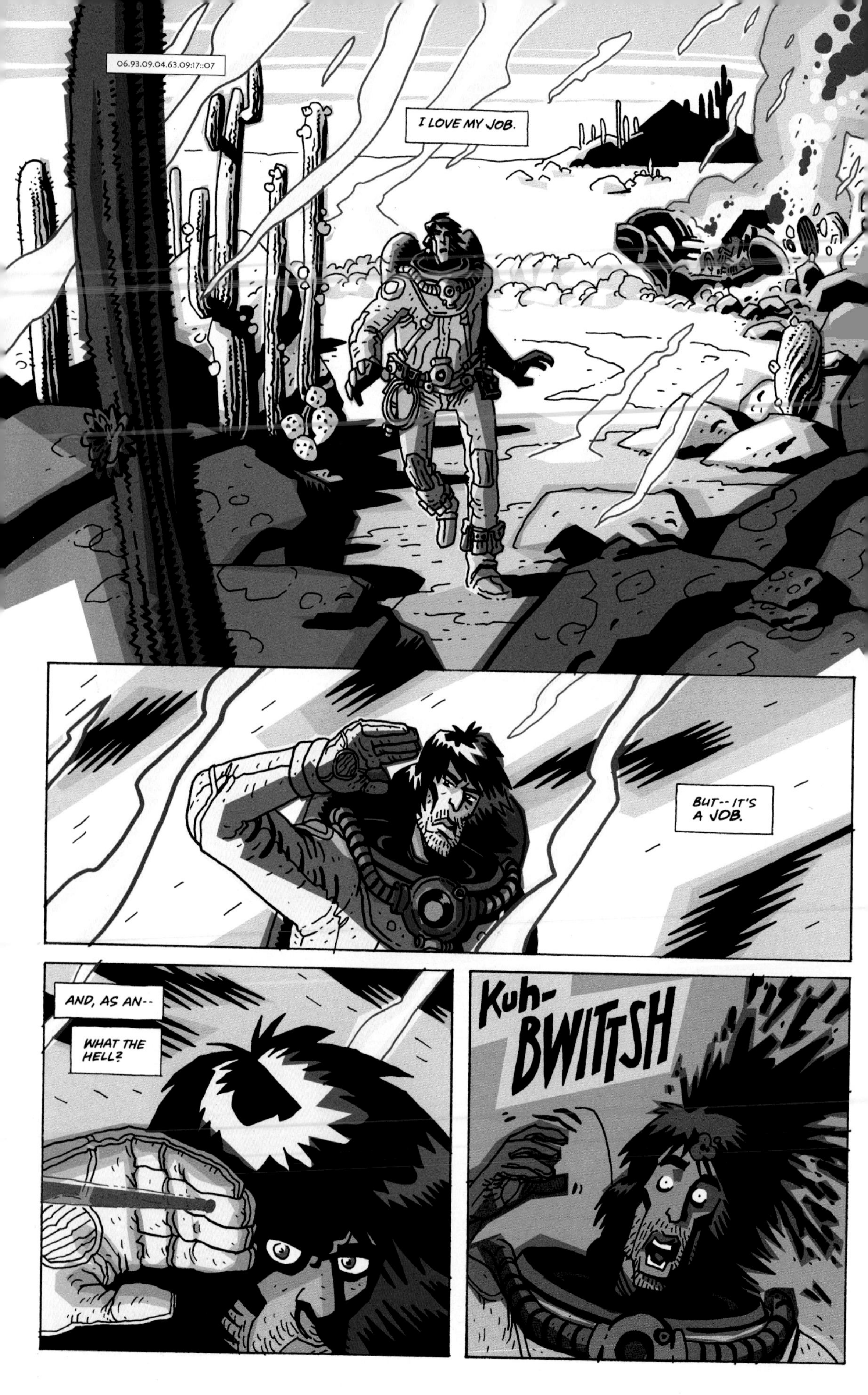
06.93.09.04.63.09:17::07
I LOVE MY JOB.
BUT-- IT'S A JOB.
AND, AS AN--
WHAT THE HELL?
Kuh-BWITTSH

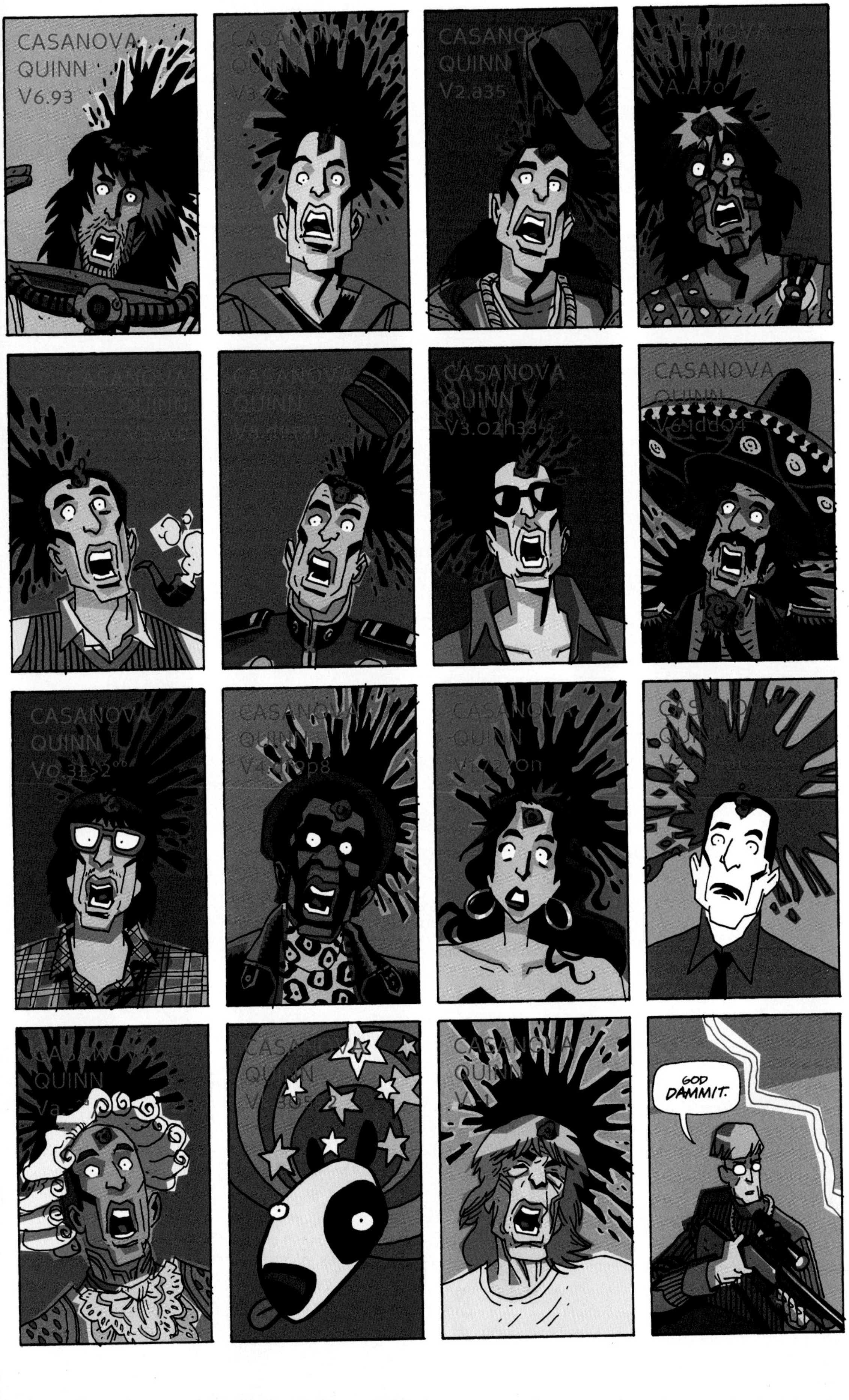
CASANOVA
QUINN
V6.93
CASANOVA
QUINN
CASANOVA
QUINN
V2.a35
CASANOVA
QUINN
CASANOVA
QUINN
V3.02h33
CASANOVA
CASANOVA
QUINN
CASANOVA
QUINN
CASANOVA
QUINN
QUINN
CASANOVA
QUINN
CASANOVA
QUINN
GOD DAMMIT.

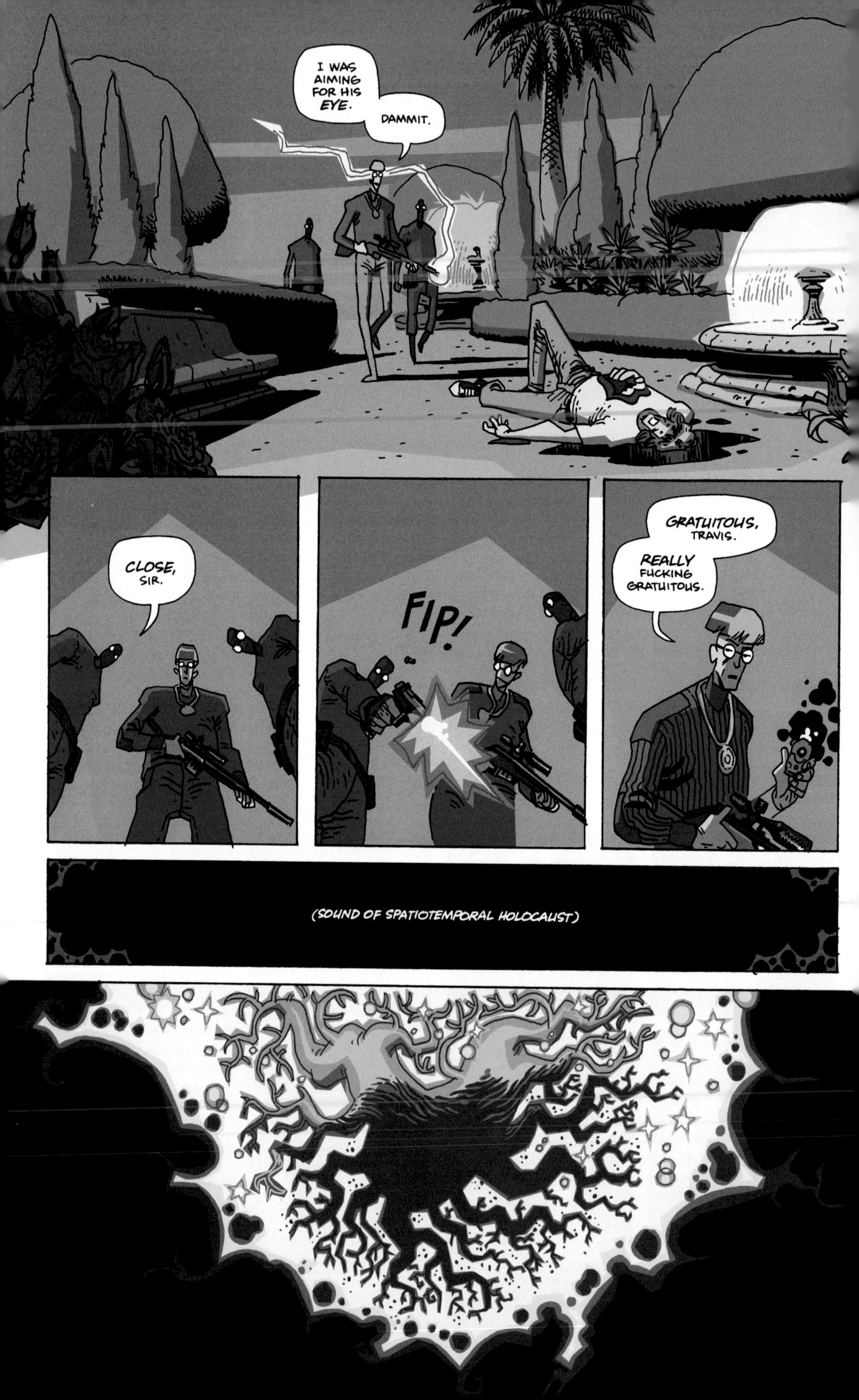
I WAS AIMING FOR HIS EYE.
DAMMIT.
CLOSE, SIR.
FIP!
GRATUITOUS, TRAVIS.
REALLY FUCKING GRATUITOUS.
(SOUND OF SPATIOTEMPORAL HOLOCAUST)

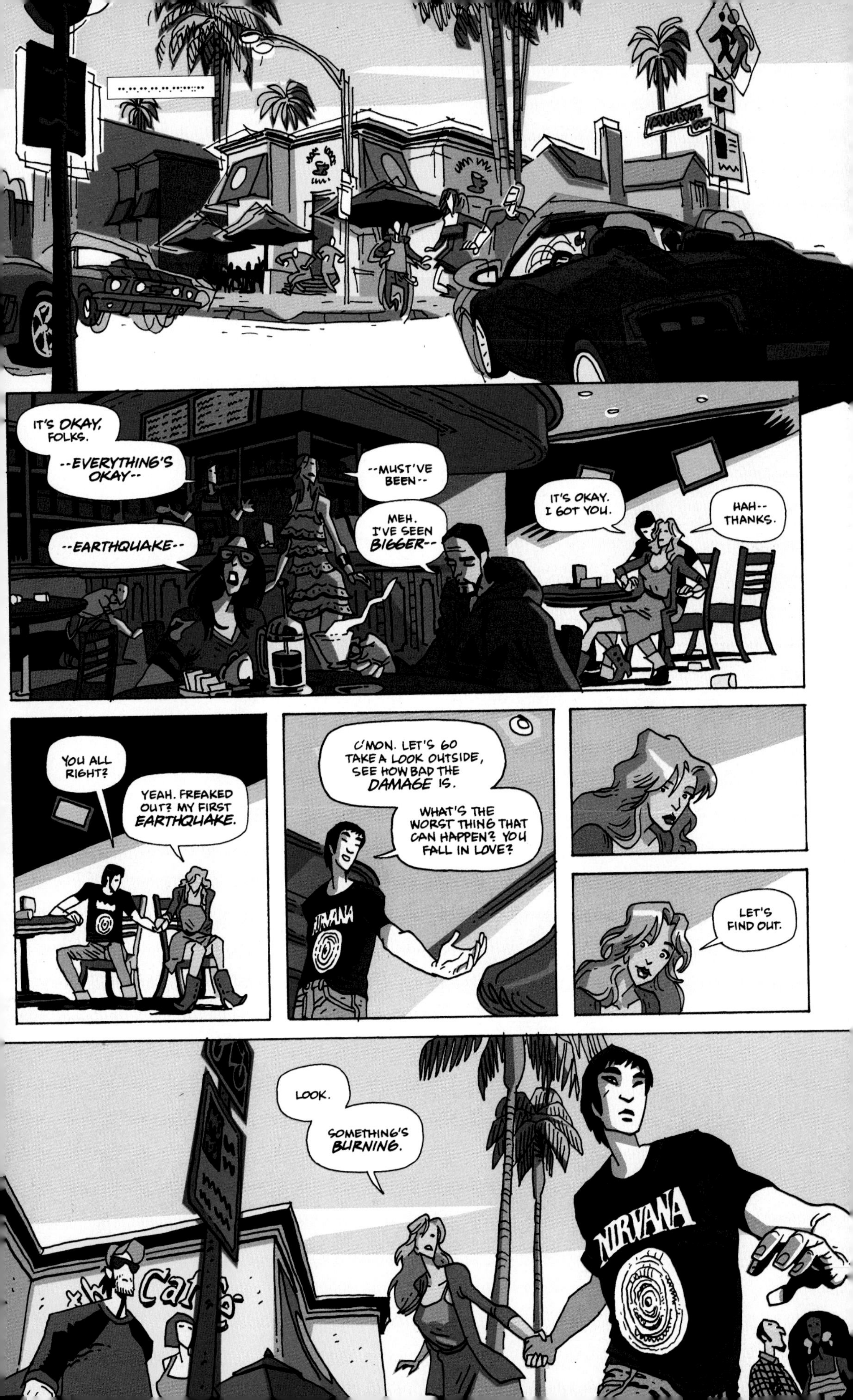
IT'S OKAY, FOLKS.
--EVERYTHING'S OKAY--
--EARTHQUAKE--
--MUST'VE BEEN--
MEH. I'VE SEEN BIGGER--
IT'S OKAY. I GOT YOU.
HAH--THANKS.
YOU ALL RIGHT?
YEAH. FREAKED OUT? MY FIRST EARTHQUAKE.
C'MON. LET'S GO TAKE A LOOK OUTSIDE, SEE HOW BAD THE DAMAGE IS.
WHAT'S THE WORST THING THAT CAN HAPPEN? YOU FALL IN LOVE?
LET'S FIND OUT.
LOOK.
SOMETHING'S BURNING.
NIRVANA

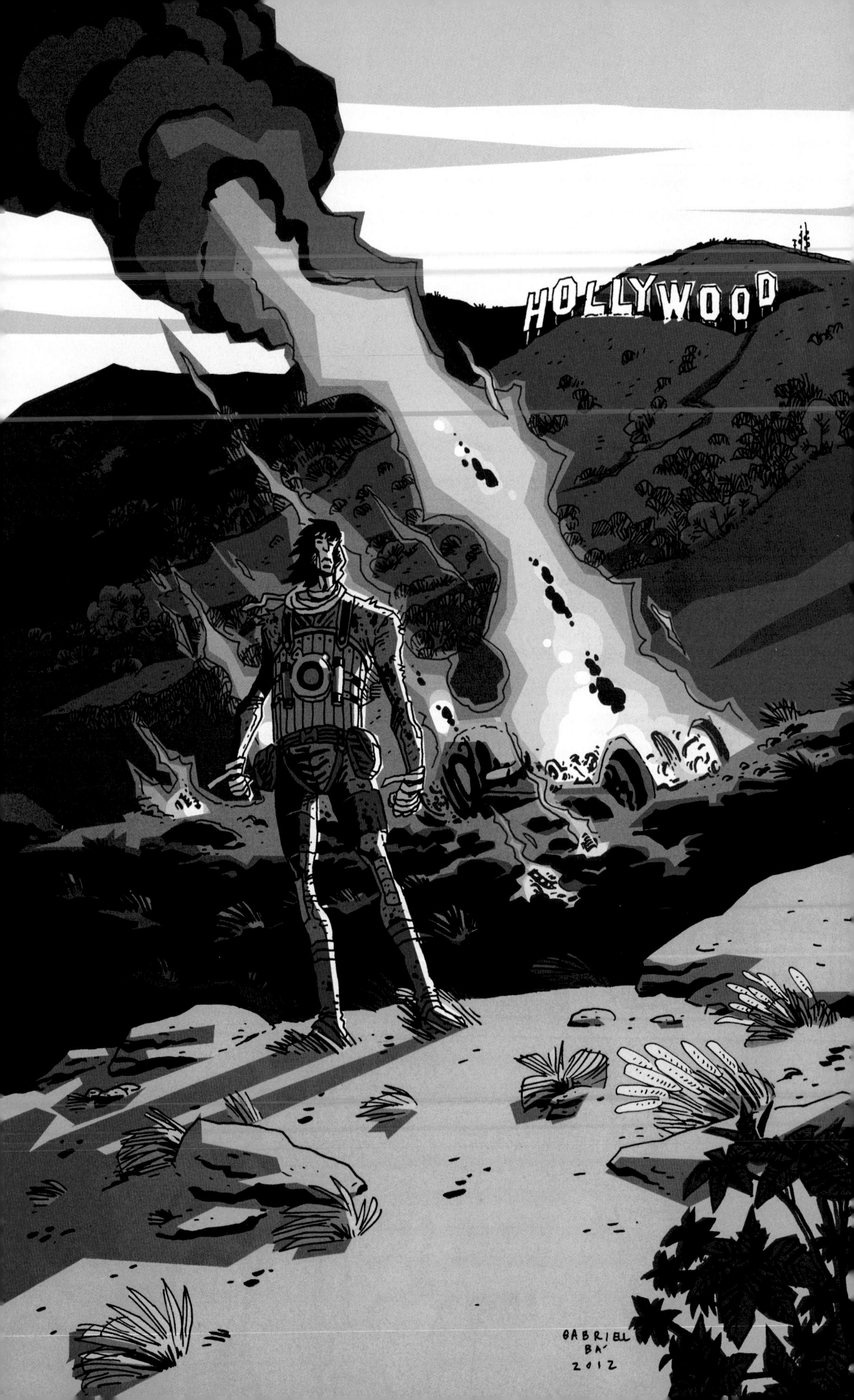
HOLLYWOOD
GABRIEL BÁ 2012

EXTRAS

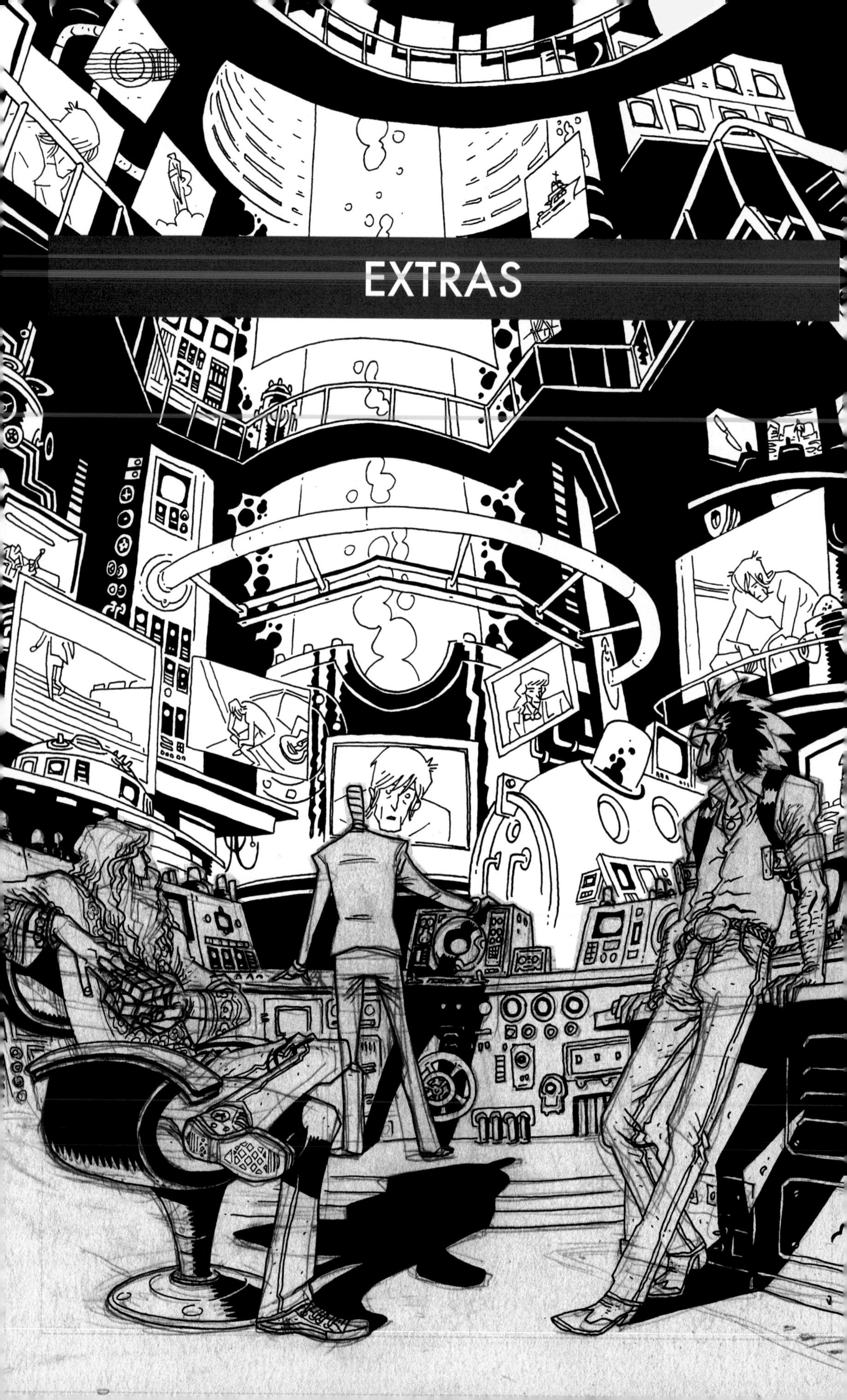

OVERTIME

MATT: So I think by the time Fábio and I finished GULA I felt like he'd taken CASANOVA away from you. In my head when I thought of the book I thought of his brush instead of your pen, almost. Then getting to write the short for him that came after the LUXURIA trade, where he got to not just revisit your characters but your "scenes" even more... I'd forgotten, in a way, what "your" CASANOVA looked like. Then starting with the DIT DIT DIT... short at the end of GULA you came roaring back and thoroughly seized it back. I'm wondering if you had a hard time finding your way back to CASANOVA after the break, and after Fábio's masterful turn behind the wheel.

BÁ: It really was a good choice to put Fábio in charge of the artwork of GULA and he surprised everyone and took over the series. Most of the characters became "his" characters after his interpretation. But Casanova himself was portrayed only on the first and last issues, so I still felt he was my character, the guy I created. I knew his tricks, his moves, his charm. And GULA was a lot more straightforward story-wise than LUXURIA, I think, and when I got the first script for AVARITIA I realized we were back in psycho-crazy land again. What really worried me was the energy I had on the first series and if I could match or surpass that on the new one. The story was clearly more challenging, so I needed to up my game once more, which I didn't expect I would have to do this time. I thought I had CASANOVA all figured out – or that I had YOU figured out – and it would be a walk on the park to go back to the series. I was so wrong.
What about you? It obviously took you more brain-cracking to get back into the series. You really thought it would be easier this time?

MATT: No, no, god no. I don't know what I was thinking. I guess... I mean, I knew the gist, I knew the sweep of the story, but that's almost secondary to something like CASANOVA. I knew, though, that, whatever it was I came up with – by the time it saw publication – it would be a product of "we," of TEAM CASANOVA, that me, and you, and Cris, and Dharb would all have hands on it and whatever I was blowing, you guys, with your varied genius talents, would transform it into

something Greater Than. So I guess... I guess what I'm saying is I had faith I could type "escape pod" and you guys would summon it from the grand unknown cosmic æther and we'd all fly away together. In a way, I think AVARITIA was more underwritten than the other CASANOVA issues – more trust, more faith. All of that somehow became paramount to being able to execute at all.
Did you feel something similar, having Cris and Dharb with us from the start, this time? Do you draw differently for "color," did you know where Dustin would come in? What was it like being more than just you, me, Fábio over your shoulder, and Mário cracking the whip?

BÁ: First of all, I have to say I got really overwhelmed by the amount of stuff that can be told in 32 pages. Every issue looked like a never-ending battle, full of blood, sweat and tears and all that jazz. And I really felt the scripts were beefier – as in a whole lot more stuff written in them – than the first two series. There's a lot in there to digest and end up on the page and that was more work than I expected. I guess you trusted me to understand all you meant, so you said everything you wanted on the scripts. As usual, I was really exhausted by the end of every issue, but completely satisfied by the result. These are my best pages.
About Cris and Dustin, I couldn't really imagine the look of this book without them.
On previous works like UMBRELLA ACADEMY and B.P.R.D., I got used to having my art colored and got a little lazy on the intensive use of black and white and I really wanted to get heavy on the inks on CASANOVA. I have to be honest and say I would still have the story in B&W or monotone because I love that look, so I would never have the guts to color these pages. Cris has no fear of doing that, she's having fun (not easy fun, but hard-working fun) and she totally owns it. We have gone a long way together over all the issues, and she really delivered what I expected and a little more. We still have a very unique-looking book.
And Dustin is the invisible man, in the best sense of the term. The handmade quality of his work is unbelievable and hard to describe and it fits the art so well it'll be hard to go back to digital lettering on my other projects. It seems almost unfair having him lettering our book

instead of just having his stellar career as a cartoonist. We'll be lucky as long as we can hold him with us.

And now there's a hard question: Would you like the CASANOVA team to work on all your books? How different is the work dynamic with your other collaborators? What experiences do you want to transport to the super heroes and what you've learned from writing them that you used on CASANOVA? Or do you think they're two very different types of books that have nothing in common?

MATT: The entire THING was overwhelming. Every issue. This book – this volume especially – was the hardest thing I've ever written, the most work-intensive. I spent a day's worth of work writing just one page, at one point, in the first issue, ten, twelve hours, something like that. It felt like reinventing itself every page-flip.

And yes: I would work with you, Moon, Cris, and Dharb, on anything, everything, everywhere, whenever. It's not just that I'm such a fan, but that... I feel a strange and silent simpatico with all of you. A psychic... whatever goes unsaid I know you'll hear anyway, and understand. I mean, think about it – it wasn't until the VERY END of AVARITIA #4 that you had, I think, EVER written me for clarification and, let's be honest, things were pretty abstract at that point...

The best way I can explain the dynamic is this: when Kelly Sue first saw Cris' colors, she asked me, "Did you know it was going to look that good?" and I said "Yes, but I didn't know how to tell anyone." And I know you knew, too. I knew we were seeing the same thing in our heads when we thought of CASANOVA in color. And then comes Cris and not only delivers that but owns it and makes it her own.

This is the first ongoing series I've done that originated with the creative team – every other comic book I've

done have been work-for-hire segments of a creative relay race. Which I can quite enjoy, both as a reader and a writer, but nothing replaces, as our dear Seychelle says, the "pride of ownership." For all the similarities in collaboration – and I've worked with, for my money, some of the very best – it's not the same as creating a universe from scratch with your friends and then figuring out how it works as you play in it.

What about you? What's it like going from a phenomenon like UMBRELLA ACADEMY or a world-famous universe like HELLBOY'S for B.P.R.D. back to... um... planet weirdo?

BÁ: I consider CASANOVA: LUXURIA as my debut on the North American way of producing comics, to tell a story on a monthly series, and I'd say I had to learn it the hard way. After that, all other projects on that same universe were different and unique on their own way, but I had been well prepared by the first run on CASANOVA, because of its dense storytelling and weirdness of the story.

Being the story on UMBRELLA ACADEMY as bizarre as it was, it was easier to understand and portray in the art than CASANOVA has ever been. And working on B.P.R.D. was the delight of a fan that loves not only Mignola's work, but has grown to love, admire and respect the world he has created. It is the closest I got to a work-for-hire kind of comic and pretty much the only one I would make this exception for.

So I thought that five years of experience with all these other projects, genres and creators would have built a stronger artist and that I would wheel the new CASANOVA pages with a hand on my back. That was very naive of me and I have learned my lesson now. The depths this story can go, the dimensions – literally – it can reach, are really beyond the average comic

book production and I'm glad I'm part of that. It's a comic that it's hard to describe, hard to compare to just one thing instead of a mesh of different realms and forms of cultural production. It's a language-bender and that's what's most difficult about it, it will always be, and why I feel so good with the final result. I love my pages because I have to work so hard on them to do what I think is right for the story. Not a lot of comics are like that.

And the exciting moment of reaching the climax of the story you have told us six years ago, the one we've been waiting so long to reach. I have no idea what comes next and I know we can expect everything to change dramatically. But how much of the original story could you keep this far into the series and how much you adapted once it started getting a life of its own on the pages, with the characters getting faces and voices and all that. It's not just notes on a big bible notebook anymore. How does that help the rest of the story and how does it make it harder and more complex for you to move on?

MATT: My metaphor has always been that... well, I have a couple metaphors. In terms of, I dunno how to put it, the Grand Design – the Grand Design has pretty much remained fixed. In my head, there were these first three books formed a loose kind of trilogy; volume 4 is largely stand-alone; then there's another loose trilogy. With that in mind, the writing has been like taking a road trip without a map but a... y'know, vaguely functional sense of geography. I could leave my house and drive to New York in a few days' time but I have almost no notion of what roads I'd take. But I know it's east, and if I don't pass, like, the Great Lakes or the Mississippi, I've done something wrong. So you knew, six years ago, that Cass was going to end up

holding that bandage with nothing underneath and so did I but I wasn't 100% on how he, or we, would get there. He even says way back in LUXURIA he knows what's under the bandages...

So what I knew-knew about the book was very little but very important. Right? Like – there's 206 bones in the body, right? Pick the top ten. That sort of thing. I never really got lost when I wrote AVARITIA but there were times when I didn't know HOW to get there precisely. The good news was there was enough room so that... well, things like Luther, Luther became more than just a MacGuffin to me and to the story, so we had room to spend time with Luther. And still, Casanova had that date with Xeno's bandage.

Whatever comes next must be more simple and more kind, if for nothing else than I don't have anything else like this IN me right now. Whatever the next new sound is, is out there somewhere. Whatever ghosts and fuel I needed to burn out of me to get to Now are gone and done and burned. Life just needs to be lived.

Here's a question: I've said, for years now, that the dirty secret only me and Gerard Way knew was that you two had no use for the likes of us. The great thing we've NOT spoken of is DAYTRIPPER (which, for folks reading that might not, somehow, know, is your DC/Vertigo series done with Fábio). To say the response to DAYTRIPPER was positive is understating things – where do YOU go now, how do you two follow that up? Do you feel Sophomore Slump pressure? Are you gearing up for your Difficult Second Album?

BÁ: Shit, you're so right. We're really on a tight corner here. Well, what saves Fábio and me is that we have this balance between the types of books we work on that has really helped us go through the years without struggling to have fresh ideas all the time. For as much

as we understand its importance, we were not built for the monthly endless routine, not artistically and even less on the writing side of the deal. We are definitely not "idea machines," and in the end I think it's a good thing because when we have a new idea, it's one we really thought it through and believe in. In the meantime, we have our "more commercial" comics, like UMBRELLA and CASANOVA (and the fact that we only draw these comics makes it a lot easier on us too). These are comics that will never be "more of the same," so they help feed us with excitement for the job while exercising our artistic muscle.

On that same "commercial" zone, we are working with Mike Mignola on a new story, one we're both writing and drawing, which has been proving to be challenging and fulfilling at the same time. So that will keep us busy and we won't be away of the public eye for too long.

That said, what will keep us away from the spotlight for some time is this massive novel from Brazilian literature we are currently adapting into a graphic novel. There has been a lot of book adaptations into comics here in Brazil over the last years, usually the classic ones that fall under public domain – even we did one back in 2007, "The Alienist," by Machado de Assis – but this one we're working on now is a modern classic written by a living author, maybe the most important living Brazilian writer, so the stakes are higher and the game is literally different. I can honestly say it will be our next biggest release, in similar way that the Parker books have been to Darwyn Cooke. We've been working on it for more than a year now and it'll still take us another year to see it all the way to completion.

We have the "second book" shadow over us all the time, but we understood we don't have to hurry.

The world we live in today – with the internet and its instantaneous pacing – really puts a lot of pressure on delivering new stuff right away, all the time, and we don't really work like that. I don't want to make something that is really good NOW. I want something that will endure.

What about you? I know we still have 4 entire series of CASANOVA to cover, but do you have something else you'd like to work on? Do you have one of those great ideas that come up in the middle of this very long project and make you almost wanna stop the presses and start this new project right away? Do you want CASANOVA to be over so you can jump on the next thing?

MATT: Millions. All the time. Constantly. The burners atop my stove feel infinite, all covered with pot after pot of slowly bubbling ideas as CASANOVA does its all-encompassing, all-engulfing, all-consuming thing. The water boils and waits its turn.

BÁ: Being the über-writer of super heroes you have become, you completely master the North American mainstream market of comics, the craft, the way it works, the conventions, the characters, the readers, the format, as well as the wheels that make the machine keep pumping. Because you are part of this big industry of pop culture, your work reaches people all over the world. And now we have contracts closed to publish CASANOVA in Italian, Spanish, French and Portuguese, so this book will break these borders as well. How often do you think about the differences your work can have on different readers, from different countries or cultures? And on the same note, CASANOVA drinks from a much bigger well than the

regular comic and doing so can appeal to a different, more diverse kind of reader. With the great buzz that the super-hero movies have generated, comic creators are really in a big spotlight for a much wider audience. So what I want to know is: Do you think of comics as a bigger thing or are you happy with your role on this picture? Do you want to break this super-hero comics bubble and reach for the stars?

MATT: That is... charming, to say the least. And I don't know that I think too terribly much about my books after they're done and set adrift on the currents of the world – but in terms of capital-C comics, in terms of North American original works produced in English – yes, god yes. My dream for those kinds of Comics is that they engulf the world like the virus in "Outbreak," that they spread internationally through airports, passed from world traveller to world traveller, devouring every inch of open air they can. And the only way that's possible is for as many kinds of stories as there are stars to do the work; I like super-hero comics, I have fun writing them, I enjoy reading them, but this isn't the early day of the printed word. We don't need only the ILIAD and the Holy Bible to serve as the cornerstones of empire anymore. We need variety. That was always the dirty trick of CASANOVA to me: it looked like a "spy comic" (whatever that looks like) but I could tell whatever story I wanted. Ended up that I wanted to tell a story about every story which, y'know, took some time and bandwidth. In theory, though, it was a great plan.
But yes. Moving forward, the stuff that comes from me post-CASANOVA will be as different from CASANOVA as CASANOVA is from any super-hero stuff out there in the world.

I know you guys don't think about this stuff, but to me, that's the most insidiously ingenious thing about DAYTRIPPER – were it a novel there would be no wonder as to its success. Of COURSE it's an international best seller. Its idiom is human experience rather than, you know, one framed by American super heroes or whatever.
I get to do my first European shows this year; I did Brazil and the biggest show in the world last year with you two (and that was before CASANOVA had come out in Brazil)... and it's CASANOVA that's making that all possible, not the super-hero stuff. So, tell me – what's it like, making comics and going around the world, meeting comics readers, reading comics made thousands of miles away from where you come from? You've been everywhere now. What's the world like, through your eyes, for comics?

BÁ: I love comics and the more I travel and see it all over the world, more passionate I become.
What I've learned on my trips is that there is no ONE way to make comics, nor the BETTER way. Super heroes are mainstream in the U.S. and reach the whole world, but Bonelli's empire and characters like TEX, ZAGOR and MARTIN MYSTÉRE are the mainstream in Italy, as well as ASTERIX and TINTIN are still the big sellers on the French market, and every weekly massive MANGA sells more then the best-seller comics on Brazil or anywhere else, for that matter. And that's wonderful! And I believe there's space for everyone, everywhere. Readers and authors alike have plenty to learn if they look out to different comics – or any form of cultural and artistic production – than they're used to. I wouldn't be working on this book if I had not.

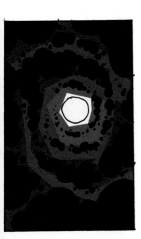

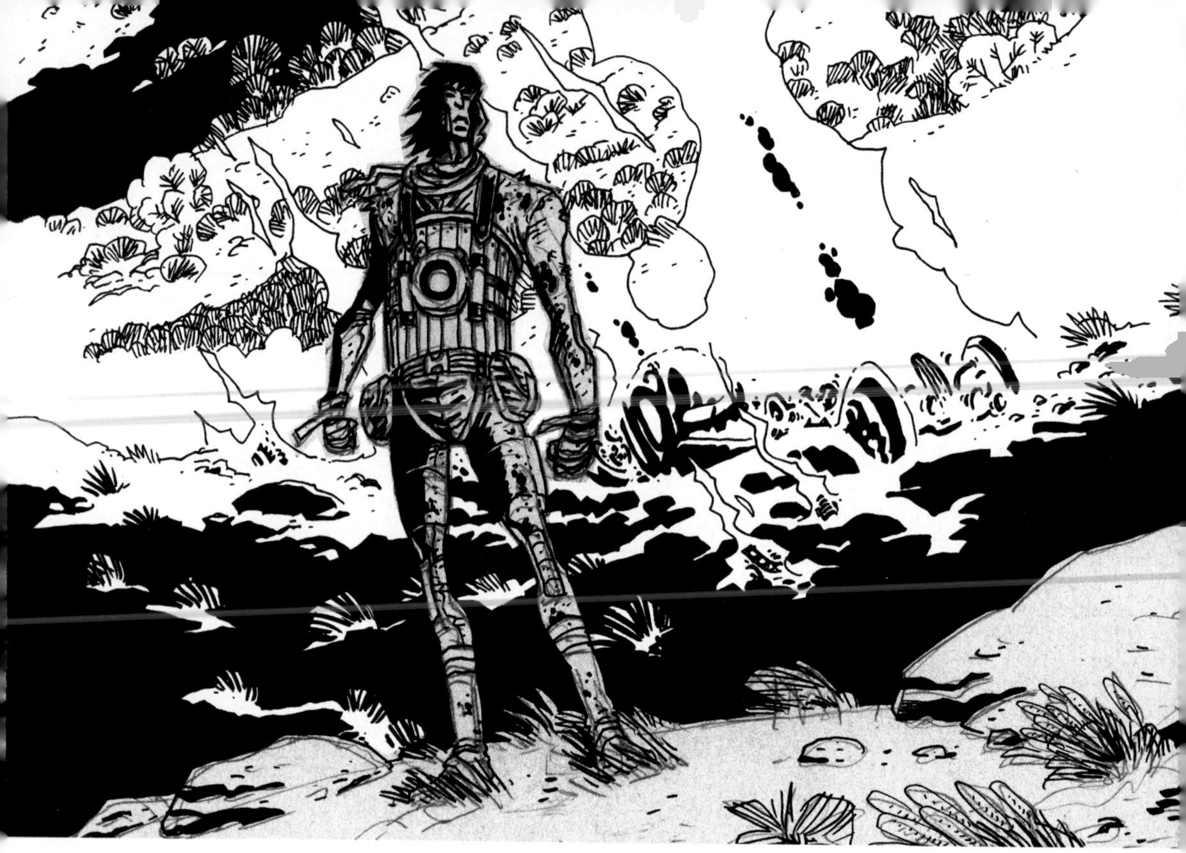

Matt Fraction lives in Portland, Oregon, in the woods, under a canopy of trees, in the rain, with his wife, the writer Kelly Sue DeConnick, and children Henry Leo and Tallulah Louise. He writes, or wrote, THE INVINCIBLE IRON MAN, THE MIGHTY THOR, UNCANNY X-MEN, HAWKEYE, THE DEFENDERS, THE IMMORTAL IRON FIST, and more. And then he got away with writing *this*.

Gabriel Bá lives in Brazil, country of the future. Being from the future, he knows the only way to save the world is through comic books, and he has been saving the world for over fifteen years now. He worked on comics like UMBRELLA ACADEMY, B.P.R.D. and DAYTRIPPER, this last one done with his evil twin, Fábio Moon.

He's won awards for both his indie comics and mainstream projects, and his work has been published in France, Italy, Spain, Greece, Japan and Germany, as well as in the U.S. and Brazil.

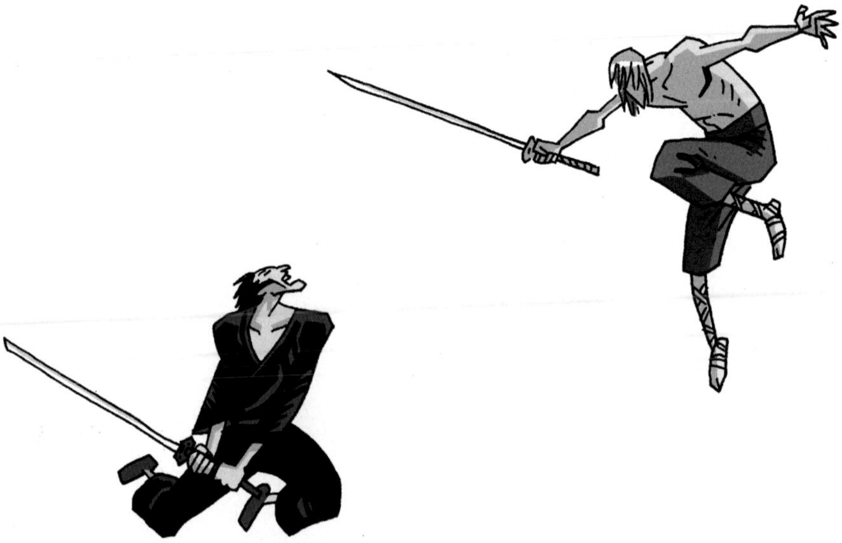
PA-ZOW!